Lecture Notes in Computer Science 1392

Edited by G. Goos, J. Hartmanis and J. van Leeuwen

Springer-Verlag Berlin Heidelberg GmbH

Andreas Barth   Michael Breu   Albert Endres
Arnoud de Kemp (Eds.)

Digital Libraries
in Computer Science:
The MeDoc Approach

 Springer

Series Editors

Gerhard Goos, Karlsruhe University, Germany
Juris Hartmanis, Cornell University, NY, USA
Jan van Leeuwen, Utrecht University, The Netherlands

Volume Editors

Andreas Barth
FIZ Karlsruhe
Postfach 2465, D-76012 Karlsruhe, Germany
E-mail: AB@fiz-karlsruhe.de

Michael Breu
FAST e.V.
Arabellastr. 17, D-81925 München, Germany
E-mail: breu@fast.de

Albert Endres
Universität Stuttgart
Breitwiesenstr. 20/22, D-70565 Stuttgart, Germany
E-mail: endres@informatik.uni-stuttgart.de

Arnoud de Kemp
Springer-Verlag
Tiergartenstr. 17, D-69121 Heidelberg, Germany
E-mail: deKemp@springer.de

Cataloging-in-Publication data applied for

Die Deutsche Bibliothek - CIP-Einheitsaufnahme

Digital libraries in computer science : the MeDoc approach /
Andreas Barth ... (ed.). - Berlin ; Heidelberg ; New York ; Barcelona
; Budapest ; Hong Kong ; London ; Milan ; Paris ; Santa Clara ;
Singapore ; Tokyo : Springer, 1998
  (Lecture notes in computer science ; Vol. 1392)

CR Subject Classification (1991): H.2-6, C.2, E.4-5, I.4.1, I.7, J.1

ISSN 0302-9743
ISBN 978-3-540-64493-4   ISBN 978-3-540-69790-9 (eBook)
DOI 10.1007/978-3-540-69790-9

Typesetting: Camera-ready by author
SPIN 10636926   06/3142 – 5 4 3 2 1 0   Printed on acid-free paper

Preface

Electronic publishing and digital libraries have recently become a major new area of development and research in computer science. The interest is caused on one side by the tremendous growth of all types of publications and the need to provide immediate and selective access, on the other side by advances in computer technology that have brought unprecedented digital storage capacity and network transmisson power to the desktop of every scientist.

Electronic fulltext and multimedia libraries have the potential of changing the entire publication process, particulary in science and related fields. This will affect many scientists in their roles of authors, reviewers, and readers of scientific literature. It will also allow for new types of information to be disseminated at low cost and high speed that cannot be represented on paper. We refer to visualizations, animations, and simulations that in many fields are crucial for explaining and understanding scientific phenomena. The roles of publishers, distributors, and librarians will also undergo changes because different ways will be found to bring information from the producer to the consumer.

Any project addressing this area will be confronted with technical and non-technical problems at the same time. Authors expect advice on how to prepare information that is to be consumed in an electronic environment. Publishers are concerned about user acceptance, asset protection, and accounting. An academic librarian wants to learn how to administer users and the users want to know where to look for relevant information and how to get at it swiftly and quickly. These are just examples of the questions that come to mind.

For computer scientists, the topic of digital libraries has twofold implications. As in all other fields there will be new ways and means for publication and communication. In addition, many questions raised are genuine research topics in computer science. Examples of the latter are the storage and structuring of information, the search and query operations to be applied, and the intelligence behind user interfaces; but also security aspects, accounting methods, and transaction models have to satisfy new requirements.

This volume documents results of a major digital library pilot project, initiated by the German Informatics Society (GI), and involving authors, publishers, librarians, and computer science institutes in Germany. The project MeDoc (abbreviation for Multimedia Electronic Documents) brought together some 30 academic institutions and several industrial partners in Germany and Switzerland in a two-year effort. These institutions participated in the project either as developers or as pilot users. In the first case, the researchers involved generated novel ideas and concepts, then designed and developed prototype software functions to be used and evaluated by themselves and the pilot users. The representatives of the pilot users defined requirements, evaluated existing tools, converted source texts of books to displayable format, and assessed the use of electronic contents at their sites.

The library contents used in the project came from very different sources. Of highest importance were the books and journals provided by some 15 scientific publishers. Other material came from ACM, the IEEE Computer Society, IBM Germany, and several academic institutions contributing hundreds of research reports and other online material. Access was also provided to several existing or newly created reference databases.

The papers in this volume present the technical and non-technical answers arrived at during the MeDoc project. After an overview of the entire project, a detailed discussion follows of the design considerations that went into the MeDoc system. This is a prototype of a distributed digital library facility. Several complementary activities provided important results which are not part of the MeDoc system proper. Valuable experiences where obtained during the conversion of books and journals for the electronic library, experiences that authors and publishers will benefit from. Since the MeDoc digital library is operated in a countrywide trial for several months, first feedback on user behavior was obtained.

At several points in the project, close contacts were made to related efforts in Germany, other European countries and the USA. Two of these projects have submitted material for this volume, outlining the state of the art by showing work being done elsewhere. In a final workshop at Schloß Dagstuhl, the contents of the selected papers for this volume were presented and the writeups subsequently critically reviewed by international experts.

As members of the steering team that led the project, we want to give credit to all participants in the project, be they developers, pilot users, librarians, contributing publishers, or sponsors. The remarkable results achieved are due to a strong technical interest in the matter and to dedicated work carried out in a rather short period of time. We appreciate the excellent cooperation and the explorative spirit of all partners involved. We would also like to acknowledge the indispensable funding received for this effort from the German Federal Ministry of Education, Science, Research, and Technology (BMBF) in Bonn.

Karlsruhe, Munich, Stuttgart, Heidelberg in December 1997

Andreas Barth, Michael Breu, Albert Endres, Arnoud de Kemp

Table of Contents

Part III: Complimentary Activities to the MeDoc System

Part IV: Application of MeDoc Results and User Experiences

Part V: Reports from Related Projects

Author Index

The MeDoc Digital Library Project:
Its Goals and Major Achievements

A. Barth[1], M. Breu[2], A. Brüggemann-Klein[3], A. Endres[4], A. de Kemp[5]

[1]FIZ Karlsruhe
[2]Fast e.V. München
[3]Technische Universität München
[4]Universität Stuttgart
[5]Springer-Verlag Heidelberg

Abstract. Project MeDoc has built the nucleus of a digital library for computer science literature, including multimedia offerings. The library is operated as a network of distributed clients and servers and is available for use by the German academic community. A set of tools has been developed to administer journals and books as copyrighted material and to give users a uniform access to the library itself, as well as to other network-based information sources from the workplace. Processes and services have been introduced to add, store, retrieve documents to or from the library, and to account for use of licensed material. Initial usage patterns and user behaviour have been studied.

1. Introduction

MeDoc (standing for Multimedia Electronic Documents) is a digital library project initiated by a workgroup of the German Informatics society (GI). Its full title is "Development and evaluation of open fulltext information systems for computer science". After a two-year preparation period, the project formally started in September 1995. It is partially funded by the German Federal Ministry of Education, Science, Research and Technology (BMBF) and will be completed by the end of 1997. The project is embedded in a set of related activities coordinated by an initiative of several German professional societies [8].

Many scientists, in particular mathematicians, physicists and chemists have expressed the view that the dramatic advances currently occurring in the information and communication technologies will have a major impact on their work, be it in research or education. Computer scientists have a dual role and responsibility for this transition from analog to digital media. Like other scientists they can take advantage of the new opportunities to make their work more effective. On the other hand, many of the problems associated with electronic publishing and digital libraries are a genuine research area for computer science. The vision leading the German Informatics society (GI) to this project was the desire to give its members first hand experience early and thus generating interest and pressure to address the open issues.

Being a precursor in the application of new media could be of help for other sciences as well.

This paper gives a high-level overview of the project's goals and achievements from the perspective of the project initiators and the project management team. It will concentrate on the deliverables that have been generated and made available for the intended users.

2. Project goals and participants

The project's overall goal is to stimulate the use of electronic media in academic education and in scientific research, as well on the side of authoring and publishing as on the side of referencing and using online information. Its scope is limited to the field of computer science as far as content and users are concerned. The specific goals as given in the original project proposal are
- to offer a „critical mass" of computer science literature as online documents accessible from the workplace of students and scientists
- to evaluate and to develop processes and tools to support the operation of a digital library, and
- to provide an information broker or mediator function to guide users between heterogeneous resources on the Internet.

In addition, we want to understand and to identify the changes required in the scientific publication and information dissemination processes and services as a result of the transition to electronic media.

The project is lead by an alliance of three partners, comprising the GI, the FIZ Karlsruhe (a provider of scientific online information services) and Springer-Verlag (a scientific publisher). In addition to these three leading partners, nine university or research institutes are contributing as research partners, and another 24 universities, technical colleges (Fachhochschulen) and research institutes are participating as pilot users. Tables 1 and 2 list the institutions participating either as research partners or as pilot users.

Freie Universität Berlin	Springer-Verlag Heidelberg
Universität Bonn	FIZ Karlsruhe
Universität Dortmund	Technische Universität München
Fast e.V. München	OFFIS Oldenburg
Fernuniversität Hagen	

Tab. 1 MeDoc research partners

The worksplit among the research partners is based on the particular skills of each group. The project is organized in three working groups
- Information Sources (Technische Universität München, Springer-Verlag)
- Basic Tools and Platforms (Universität Bonn, FIZ Karlsruhe, OFFIS Oldenburg) and

- Information Broker (Freie Universität Berlin, Universität Dortmund, Fernuniversität Hagen)

The representative of the German Informatics society resided with the group of the Technical University of Munich. Project management was assigned to Fast e.V. The pilot users have contributed to the selection of contents and formats and to the definition of system requirements and service criteria. They have evaluated existing and newly developed tools and are providing feedback from a user's perspective. Recently, access to the MeDoc offerings has been opened for additional users from the academic community.

RWTH Aachen	HTWK Leipzig
FH Augsburg	Uni Leipzig
FH Bremen	Uni Magdeburg
TU Chemnitz	Uni Mannheim
IBFI Dagstuhl	FH Regensburg
FH Emden	Uni Rostock
Uni Freiburg	Uni Stuttgart
FH Fulda	FH Ulm
Uni Hamburg	ETH Zürich
Uni Jena	BVIT Bonn
FH Karlsruhe	IBM Heidelberg
Uni Karlsruhe	UBIS Berlin

Tab. 2: MeDoc pilot users

Appendix A gives the names of individuals participating in the project. They can be contacted for information about the local MeDoc installation and arrangements.

It should not come as a surprise to learn that about two months of hard work elapsed until a formal agreement could be reached with all participants with respect to the detailed functional requirements. In the following, only the resulting functions and services are discussed.

3. Document types and library content

The intention is to provide those types of documents that are most valuable for students, lecturers and researchers in an academic environment. Surveys performed among the pilot users showed that highest interest was for computer science journals (both national and international ones), followed by course notes and text books for introductory computer science courses. Research reports and conference proceedings were considered to be of lower priority. A special case were encyclopaedias (general and computer science related). They were considered as ideal candidates for an electronic offering.

In each category, priorities were established for individual topics and works, thus putting us into a position to place specific requests on the copyright owners. To achieve what we considered to be a critical mass we wanted to provide about 50 journals, 100 books and 1000 technical reports. We are planning to make these documents available as electronic fulltexts (with possibly some multimedia extensions) at the desktop of students and scientists.

Since the rights for the books and journals we wanted to offer were owned by commercial publishers we negotiated licence agreements with 14 publishers (see Tab. 3). We obtained the non-exclusive right for electronic storage and display for a total of 80 books and 22 journals.

Publisher	Journals offered	Books	
		Licensed	Offered
Addison-Wesley	-	13	11
Dpunkt	-	7	3
Hanser	-	2	2
Harri Deutsch	-	2	2
Heise	2	-	-
Hüthig	-	2	1
IEEE Computer Society	16	-	-
infix	-	2	2
Oldenbourg	-	10	4
Spektrum	-	5	5
Springer	4	19	18
Teubner	-	7	7
Thomson	-	1	1
Vieweg/Gabler	-	10	4
Total	22	80	60

Tab. 3: Participating Publishers and their Contributions

The difference between books licensed and offered resulted mostly from technical problems (quality of source material, availability of tools for conversion).

This emphasis on fulltext and multimedia offerings resulted from the observation that here more problems would be expected and therefore more progress could be achieved. Bibliographic or reference data would be considered only as far as they provide access to fulltext and multimedia material. A search to be performed at the workspace should supply the desired material electronically, i.e. without delay and without a switch in media.

3.1 Electronic Journals

The first offering we were able to put into place consisted of four journals owned by Springer-Verlag. Two of them were oriented towards members of the German Informatics society (and hence published in German), two of them (J.UCS, VLDB Journal) were addressing an international audience. Whereas J.UCS (Journal of Universal Computer Science) is closely connected with the Hyperwave system [9] for document management and storage, the other three journals could be placed on regular Web servers. The presentation formats also vary. J.UCS relies on HTF (an alternative to HTML) and Postscript; for the others, Postscript and PDF were the formats of choice. This requires the least effort for conversion, but allows (as in the case of PDF) for some fulltext search capability.

For two other publishers the online offering is derived from existing CD-ROM offerings and covers backward issues (up to 1996) only. The information contained on the CD-ROMs is placed online and extended by a remote viewing and search facility. For one journal we offered several alternative layouts in order to obtain user feedback. After having demonstrated the technical feasibility, our work on journals has slowed down somewhat. This was also influenced by the fact that in the meantime several publishers (including Elsevier and Springer) have announced plans to put all their journals online within the next few years.

3.2 Electronic Books

In many fields CD-ROMS are the preferred way to offer material that used to be published as a printed book before. This is particularly true for reference material, such as tax tables, census data and phone numbers. To avoid the usual handling effort associated with CD-ROMs, we wanted to offer electronic books as online products over the network only. To prepare this material soon became one of the most important activities in the entire project.

In the meantime 60 books have been converted from the author's electronic manuscript into a hypertext format suitable for online use. We only considered those books for which the bulk of the conversion work could be done using available text processing tools. Nevertheless, in each instance considerable manual work had to be done. In fact, it turned out that the subject of conversions required considerable attention and resources as will be discussed later.

Among the books converted are some of the best known (German) textbooks on introductory computer science, two standard volumes on algorithms and data structures, and several reference books on UNIX, C++, HTML and Latex. Of particular interest is a 700-page collection of mathematical formulas for geometric and analytical problems. The majority of the books are in German, only conference proceedings are in English.

3.3 Multimedia Supplements

While the books referred to above were conceived as printed products, some have been augmented by the inclusion of animations and video material. In two cases, new products have been developed where the exploitation of electronic media was considered from the outset. One is a course on algorithms and data structures where the explanation of the theory and the invocation of dynamic visualizations is supported by oral comments of the author. The second case is an introduction into image processing and pattern recognition which uses interactive applications to illustrate the concepts taught.

Both products have been developed in close cooperation with a commercial publisher and are being offered outside of MeDoc as well.

3.4 Research Reports

Most university institutes already provide many of their research reports as online documents via their local ftp servers. The intent of the project team was to provide a uniform reference scheme to make all reports known to the entire community. After a meeting with the developers of NCSTRL (Networked Computer Science Technical Report Library) [6] we abandoned the idea of developing a unique solution and decided to join the NCSTRL network. In the meantime 10 NCSTRL servers have been established by project participants. An extension of NCSTRL is under development [1] which covers all types of gray literature, like master theses and course notes.

3.5 Access to reference databases

In addition to the fulltext material described above, access is provided to 16 databases containing bibliographic data relevant to computer science. They can be accessed through the broker function to be described later.

The databases (see Tab. 4) cover different views at and different parts of the computer science literature. Some are very comprehensive and cover the entire field or go even beyond it; others only cover special subfields, like theory, data bases or a particular operating system (e.g. LINUX). Since more and more databases will become available that use a standard interface, like Z 39.50 or free-WAIS-s, this list can be extended easily in the future.

4. Software Tools and Platforms

In order to be able to offer the above material to the intended users a number of software tools had to be developed or adapted. To properly handle the access to and the accounting for licensed material particular accounting and security provisions had to be taken. The basic functionality is provided by an integrated set of tools, referred to as the MeDoc System. A complementary service is provided by a unique subsystem, called Ariadne.

Before the development of new tools started, extensive studies and surveys took place of existing products. New tools were only developed in such cases where existing tools fell considerably short of out requirements.

4.1 The MeDoc System

The MeDoc Systen evolved in several stages. The first set of books and journals were offered via a regular web server. Only those functions available through standard products could be used. The limitations were mainly in the areas of accounting, browsing and user administration. This difference will be discussed in [10].

The final MeDoc System [3] provides two basic functions. One is referred to as the fulltext storage. It provides document management, accounting and security support

Name	Provider	Subject Area
NCSTRL	Cornell University	Research reports in computer science
Achilles	Uni Karlsruhe	Computer science literature
Ley	Uni Trier	Literature on database management
Mayr	TU München	Literature on theoretical computer science
CS Journals	Uni Dortmund	Journals in computer science
HCI Bibliography	Uni Dortmund	Literature on human computer interaction
IR Digest	Uni Dortmund	Literature on information retrieval
IBFI Bibliothek	Dagstuhl	Library catalog of Dagstuhl center
Internet FAQ	FU Berlin	Frequently asked questions on Internet
Internet RFC	FU Berlin	Request for comment on Internet
Linux HOWTO	FU Berlin	Information on LINUX operating system
Books	Bell Labs	IEEE publications
VLB	Börsenverein	Books in print in Germany
VLZ	Börsenverein	Journals in print in Germany
LNCS	Springer-Verlag	Lecture Notes in computer science
Compuscience	FIZ Karlsruhe	Computer science

Tab. 4: Reference Databases

for the licensed material consisting of books and journals. The other basic function provides a consulting facility referred to as the Information Broker. This component provides a uniform interface to multiple information sources, including the MeDoc fulltext storage as a special case. The MeDoc System is implemented as a distributed client-server structure consisting of three types of interacting components (see Fig. 1). As it turned out, this structure is quite similar to that of the UMDL system (University of Michigan Digital Library) [2].

On the user (or client) side of the system a component called user agent extends the functions of a standard Netscape browser to handle user authentication and to administer local data like previously formulated queries or query results. Also the user side of the license administration and accounting will take place here [4]. Normally each participating user location installs one user agent.

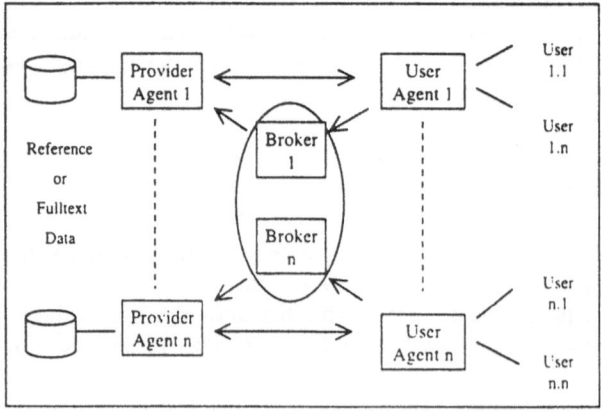

Fig. 1: Structure of the MeDoc System

On the provider (or server) side a component called provider agent adapts the general MeDoc interface to a specific provider interface. These provider interfaces may either be standard interfaces (like Z39.50 or free-WAIS-sf) or are unique for a particular provider. Special providers that are supported are NCSTRL, Ariadne and the MeDoc fulltext storage.

The information broker (which is part of the server functionality) obtains and utilizes descriptive information on a number of providers. If a user starts a query without specifying a provider the broker will advise the user as to which provider is most qualified to satisfy the query. In a second step the user may then direct his query to (some of) the recommended providers. Although the design provides for multiple brokers, currently only a single broker is provided in the system.

Most newly developed functions have been implemented in Java, complemented with parts in C, SQL and HTML. The basic functionality is provided by off-the-shelf products like Netscape and Hyperwave. Document management and indexing services are provided by a commercial text management system (Fulcrum). The current implementation requires a UNIX platform (Solaris 2.5).

4.2 Ariadne

The name Ariadne [7] is used to designate a set of software functions developed to provide a unique information service. Its core is a database containing references to network-based information sources (i.e. sources accessible by URL). These sources are classified, based on the CR Classification scheme. In addition the sources have been validated as to their relevance for the computer science community. Periodically checks are performed to test reachability and to determine whether any updates have occurred. Based on this, an alert message can be produced. The Ariadne database currently contains about 4.000 references.

5. Processes and Services

One of the prime goals of the MeDoc project was to learn more about changes required in the entire scientific publication process as a result of the introduction of new technologies. In addition, the tools and contents developed should be used to try to establish a self-supporting service structure lasting beyond the project period.

5.1 Writing for electronic media

Through a number of investigations and user surveys we developed a concept for what we consider the „ideal electronic book". It is intended and specifically designed for the reading of short passages on the screen, the navigation along hypertext links and for fulltext searches. An electronic book is a tree structure of segments. Each segment is a hypertext node. Screen layouts and fonts are chosen to view an entire segment at a time. Tables of content and indices are clickable entries to the individual segments. Fulltext searches encompass single books or multiple books within the MeDoc library.

Converting a source text into a format suitable for display and use at a PC or workstation is a straight forward process only if the new mode of use has been anticipated. This starts with the selection of a target presentation format (prime candidates are HTML and PDF) and a source format that allows an automatic conversion from the one to the other. Whether a third format (e.g. SGML) is advisable for long term storage is an additional consideration. After these more formal hurdles are taken, the question arises how the internal structure of the document should be optimized to facilitate non-sequential use. This modularization will form the basis for the hyperlink structure to be applied. Finally, any addition of electronic value-adds (animations, visualisations) needs to be considered.

The experiences made during the conversions done so far have been collected and will be documented. Additional information will be gained from the feedback provided by pilot users in the ongoing evaluation phase.

5.2 Populating and operating the electronic library

If librarians have a workload problem filing and cataloguing new acquisitions today, this problem will not go away. To the contrary, if information is to be provided that allows navigation in an electronic book below the level of the entire book (which is desirable) additional descriptive information needs to be generated. For the books entered into the MeDoc library, this resulted again in quite significant workload problems. Some adhoc tools that were developed, could only partially automate this process. The same problem arises for journals as well.

For the operation of the MeDoc library five different sites are involved. They have been chosen based on their capability to guarantee a certain level of service. They all use the identical tools but offer different parts of the library content.

5.3 Administration of licenses and users

MeDoc is one of the few projects for which the handling of licensed material is a central issue [5]. After the appropriate business models were agreed upon, simple and reliable mechanisms for the administration of the licenses and the accounting of use had to be implemented.

In MeDoc, individual users or institutions can acquire licenses to use individual products. How the institution that acquires licenses for multiple users does its administration is not predetermined. To reduce the workload for the institution, users are allowed to register themselves as long as the number of licenses acquired by the institution is not exhausted. The next step that was implemented are so-called floating licenses. In this case, only the number of currently active licenses is controlled.

Before acquiring a licence the user can browse through a sample of the book. The sample typically contains the title page, the table of the contents, the index and the first chapter of the book. The digital book itself contains the complete document and a full text search mechanism.

5.4 Accounting and usage statistics

So far the basic accounting principle is that of prepaid licenses. This is not only easier to handle by the system, it also gives the institution a simple way to plan their expenses. For the librarian, this is similar to the purchase of the books. From a contractual point of view, we are allowed to charge for individual pages. We discourage this mode of use, however, because of the billing problems associated with it. Currently billing is done by sending out paper invoices from one central site.

What is desirable are usage based accounting schemes and the charging for individual papers (or small units of information). This, of course, puts higher demands on the accounting facilities. It is the mode that is really appropriate for the new medium, as it allows to obtain valid usage data. We are looking at electronic cash options in a follow-on project.

Currently usage data are collected through questionnaires or through the analysis of network statistics. From November 1996 to October 1997 there were about 3200 visits to one of the licensed books or journals. In the same period the samples were visited more than 6000 times.

6. Summary and Outlook

Project MeDoc has accomplished most of the goals that had been set up at its inception. We were able to offer enough material to get scientists and students interested to look at it, at least at some locations. Also the number of publishers and authors involved is significant.

The surveys we did of existing tools only reflect that particular point in time. New products pop up constantly in this dynamic market. Most of the tools developed are of a prototype nature, meaning that they do not satisfy all usability and performance aspects yet. Also some of the converted contents could be improved, as would be expected. The administration and accounting facilities as implemented will have to be extended in order to simplify the work in this area.

It is intended that the services established so far will be continued beyond the actual project period. As a long range goal they should be self-supporting. Some of the experiences gained in the electronic publication process have already been communicated to people outside of the project. Documentation is being provided to cover all development and usage experiences. Individual tools that have been developed can be freely used by any interested party. We hope that other projects can be started that will build on the basis that has been provided.

Acknowledgement. A project of this magnitude benefits from the work and contributions of many individuals. As shown in Appendix A, some 70 people were directly involved. It is our strong desire to recognize the work of all groups that have participated. As representatives of them we like to thank those collegues that contributed to the initial project proposals. These are H. J. Appelrath, G. Cyranek, D. Fellner, N. Fuhr, R. Götze, H. Helbig, H. Schweppe and C. D. Ziegler. We also thank all authors of this volume. They contributed their time to document their respective part of the project and to pass along the experience they gained.

References

1. Adler, S., et al.: Grey Literature and Multiple Collections in NCSTRL. In this volume.
2. Atkins, D. E., Birmingham, W. P., et al.: Toward Inquiry-Based Education Through Interacting Software Agents. IEEE Computer, May 1996, pp. 69-76
3. Boles, D., et al.: The MeDoc System – A Distributed Digital Library Facility. In this volume.
4. Breu, M., Brüggemann-Klein, A., Haber, C., Weber, R.: The MeDoc Distributed Electronic Library - Accounting and Security Aspects. *In*: Proc. of the ICCC/IFIP Conference. University of Kent, Canterbury, April 1997
5. Breu,.M., Weber, R.: Charging for a Digital Library – The Business and the Cost Models of the MeDoc Digital Library In: Research and Advanced Technology for Digital Libraries, LNCS 1234, Heidelberg Springer 1997, pp. 375 – 386
6. Davis, J. R., Lagoze, C.: Dienst: An Architecture for Distributed Document Libraries. CACM 38,4 (1995) p.47
7. Dreger, M., et al.: Ariadne – An Interactive Navigation and Search System for Computer Science Information
8. Endres, A.: Digital Library and Electronic Publishing Activities of German Professional Societies. *In*: Proc. IEEE Forum on Research and Technology Advances in Digital Libraries (ADL '97). May 7-9, 1997. Washington DC pp. 63-68
9. Maurer, H. (Ed).: Hyper-G/now Hyperwave – The Next Generation Web Solution. Addison-Wesley, Harlow, England, 1996
10. Meyer, J., Appelrath, H-J., Design and Implementation of the MeDoc Fulltext Server. In this volume

Appendix A

MeDoc Project Participants

A. Research partners

H. Schweppe, M. Dreger, S. Lohrum (FU Berlin)
D. Fellner, A. Kusserow (Uni Bonn)
N. Fuhr, K. Grossjohann (Uni Dortmund)
M. Breu (Fast e.V.)
H. Helbig, D. Menke (Fernuni Hagen)
A. de Kemp, U. Schwab (Springer-Verlag)
A. Barth, M. Schwantner, C-D. Ziegler (FIZ Karlsruhe)
A. Brueggemann-Klein, A. Endres, C. Haber, R. Weber, (TU Muenchen)
H-J. Appelrath, R. Götze , D. Boles, J. Meyer, G. Moeller, M. Schlattmann (OFFIS Oldenburg)

B. Pilot partners

M. Jarke, B. von Buol (RWTH Aachen)
L. Kern-Bausch, C. Papenfuß (FH Augsburg)
A. Spillner, W. Tegethoff, J. Cornehls (HS Bremen)
U. Hübner, A. Müller (TU Chemnitz)
R. Wilhelm, P. Meyer (IBFI Dagstuhl)
U. Schmidtmann, J. Musters, (FHO Emden)
Th. Ottmann, M. Will (Uni Freiburg)
W. Ehrenberger, H. Hollenbach (FH Fulda)
W. Lamersdorf, S. Adler, H. Spahn (Uni Hamburg)
G. Weißenburger (Uni Jena)
K. Gremminger, St. Kastinger (FH Karlsruhe)
P. H. Schmitt, S. Claußen (Uni Karlsruhe)
K. Bastian, U. Zimmer (HTWK Leipzig)
E. Rahm, D. Sosna (Uni Leipzig)
G. Saake, M. Hollatz (Uni Magdeburg)
W. Effelsberg, R. Lienhart (Uni Mannheim)
H. Kopp, H. Feyrer (FH Regensburg)
K. Hantzschmann, H. Meyer (Uni Rostock)
K. Rothermel, U. Berger (Uni Stuttgart)
F. Pieper, S. Böttcher (FH Ulm)
C. A. Zehnder, E. Rothauser (ETH Zürich)
A. Bojanowski (BVIT e.V. Bonn)
M. Salmony (IBM WZ Heidelberg)
M. Eimermacher (UBIS Berlin)

The MeDoc System – A Digital Publication and Reference Service for Computer Science

D. Boles[1], M. Dreger[2], K. Großjohann[3], C. Haber[4], A. Kusserow[5], S. Lohrum[2],
D. Menke[6], J. Meyer[1], G. Möller[1], R. Weber[4]

[1] OFFIS Oldenburg, Escherweg 2, D-26121 Oldenburg,
{boles, meyer, moeller}@offis.uni-oldenburg.de
[2] FU Berlin, Institut für Informatik, Takustr. 9, D-14195 Berlin,
{dreger, lohrum}@inf.fu-berlin.de
[3] Lehrstuhl für Informatik VI, Universität Dortmund, D-44221 Dortmund,
grossjohann@ls6.informatik.uni-dortmund.de
[4] TU München, Arcisstr. 21, D-80290 München,
{haber, weberr}@informatik.tu-muenchen.de
[5] Universität Bonn, Institut für Informatik III, Römerstr. 164, D-53117 Bonn,
kusserow@cs.uni-bonn.de
[6] FernUniversität Hagen, Praktische Informatik VII, D-58084 Hagen,
dirk.menke@fernuni-hagen.de

Abstract. The object of the MeDoc project is the conception of a full
text based publication and reference service, its prototypical implementation and evaluation. The service shall enhance information exchange and
supply researchers with literature more easily. Therefore we developed an
Internet based system that allows for searching, browsing, delivering and
storing documents and supports searching in heterogeneous, distributed
databases. Part of the documents offered via the MeDoc system are billable. This article gives an overview of the functionality and architecture
of the MeDoc system.

1   Introduction

MeDoc (Multimedia electronic Documents)[1] is a German digital library project
that brings together 14 German and international publishing houses on the producer side and 24 universities and industrial user institutions on the user side
[1]. The project is led by a consortium consisting of the German Society of Computer Professionals (GI); the FIZ Karlsruhe, a data base provider for technical
and scientific information; and the scientific publishing house Springer.

The aim of this research and development project is to initiate the MeDoc
Service: a distributed digital computer science library that makes available a
critical amount of literature on the desktop of computer scientists, students
and practitioners all over Germany [2,4,10]. MeDoc aims at making about 50
books and 22 journals accessible via Internet by the end of 1997. These books

---

[1] The Project MeDoc is sponsored by the German Ministry for Education, Science,
Research and Technology (no. 08 C 7829 6)

are available with their billable full text and free samples. They are mostly electronic editions of paper versions. But multimedia supplements of paper books and full text searching facilities are also provided that could not be published by traditional means. The project understands itself not as a pure research project but intends to collect hands-on experience now to start up a professional service after August 1997.

Goals within the MeDoc project were

- stimulation of the transition from print to digital media with books and journals to enable scientists to access scientific information from their desktop via open networks,
- development of effective delivery and citation services for dissemination and retrieval of scientific information, and
- improvement of the usability of digital information.

To reach those goals a prototype of the MeDoc System has been developed. This distributed information service allows storage, presentation, query and retrieval of scientific information in full text over the Internet. For now the MeDoc System specializes in providing computer science specific information, but the software itself can be used for any kind of information.

This article presents a synopsis of the MeDoc System. Its overall architecture is described. Further details about individual components of the MeDoc System can be found in the respective separate papers [3,5,6,9,7,8,11,12].

2   General Design Principles of the MeDoc System

When analyzing the publication process three principal role models can be discerned. A *producer* entitles a *provider* to offer information to a *user*. Producers of information are, for example, authors, publishers and lecturers. Users can be scientists or students. The MeDoc System serves as an information provider and therefore as a mediator between producers and users. The MeDoc System stores scientific information in form of citations as well as in full text. It supports users in searching distributed citation and full text data bases for information and in managing the information retrieved.

Main aspects in the design of the MeDoc System were:

- development of a server for storage, administration and billable usage of digital documents in full text,
- navigation in the document base, browsing full text documents and ordering of documents from the full text servers,
- development of an information brokering system for searching in distributed, heterogeneous information sources on the Internet,
- development of a unified query language for the information brokering system,
- extensibility of the information brokering system with respect to the integration of further data bases,

- development of a unified user friendly interface for the full text server and the information brokering system,
- development and integration of different cost and accounting models for usage of documents in the MeDoc full text servers, and
- securing transmission of sensitive information.

3   Concept and Architecture of the MeDoc System

The MeDoc System acts as a mediator between information producers and information users. Providers offer information in form of citations or as full text documents. Because of their ubiquity, the MeDoc System can be accessed using standard Web browsers.

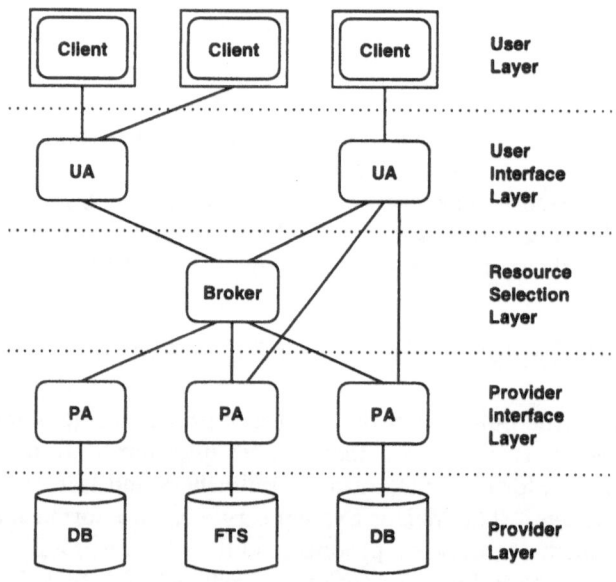

Fig. 1. Architecture of the MeDoc System

The functionality required is located at different layers within the MeDoc System:

- The *User Interface Layer* offers the interface for the user to the MeDoc System;
- main task of the *Provider Interface Layer* is to encapsulate heterogeneous provider systems so that the User Interface Layer can access each provider homogeneously;
- for mediation between users and potential suitable providers for a given query the *Broker Layer* offers specialized services. It stores *meta data* about provider systems.

In the actual implementation of the MeDoc System these layers are represented by different software components. The components of the User Interface Layer are *User Agents* (UA), those of the Provider Interface Layer are *Provider Agents* (PA), and the Broker Layer is realized by *Brokers*. These components form a distributed communicating system. The communication follows a unified protocol, the *MeDoc protocol* [6]. The queries are formulated with respect to a common global schema, the *MeDoc Schema* [7].

User Agents are usually responsible for a fixed group of users, for example a department, and can be installed locally if required [3]. Their special tasks are

- administration of users and user groups,
- offering query forms,
- accepting and executing queries,
- distribution of queries to other components,
- collection of results from other components,
- storage and administration of results, and
- visualization of results to the user.

For each provider system a Provider Agent is installed [9,7]. Provider Agents encapsulate special details of their provider system. A Provider Agent has the following tasks:

- Registration at and transfer of meta data to the Broker
- accepting queries from the User Agent,
- the transformation of queries and delivery to the provider system,
- accepting results from the provider system, and
- the transformation of results into the MeDoc Schema and delivery to the User Agent.

Brokers hold meta data about provider systems and their contents [5]. If a user does not know which provider systems are available or when searching for certain specialized providers in connection with a given query the user can contact a Broker via a User Agent. The Broker determines suitable provider systems based on stored meta data and returns those providers to the User Agent. Brokers can be replicated but all Brokers are identical with respect to functionality as well as content.

The MeDoc project developed a special provider system, the *MeDoc Full Text Server* (FTS), which to date has been installed in Germany five times [11]. The MeDoc Full Text Servers store and offer their own selected computer science literature in full text. With the help of the User Agent the user can not only search document bases of Full Text Servers but also order documents, navigate within the document base and browse individual documents. The MeDoc Full Text Servers usually charge for documents, but so-called "samples" may be free of charge [12]. In the following we will use the term *non-free* to refer to those documents that are not free of charge. They can be subject to subscription and license agreements or individual pay per usage pricing. The following cost and accounting models have been developed so far: The *floating license model* offers a predefined number of users out of a large group access to a document for a certain timespan. This license model is well known from commercial databases and software but has been adapted slightly for the usage on the Web. In *usage based cost models* each access to a document is billed separately. The transfer of non-free documents is encrypted to offer protection against snooping or modification [8].

4 Usage of the MeDoc System

The MeDoc System offers the following functionality to its users:

- registration,
- login,
- queries,
- navigation in the document base,
- browsing full text documents, and
- ordering documents.

To make use of the MeDoc System the user must register with the User Agent first. For users who only want to access the free information registration via a Web form is sufficient, but users who want to use non-free information must register with the administrator of the User Agent.

Users log in to the system by entering their login (usually their email address) and a password into a form. If the login is valid a session key is assigned that entitles the user to use the MeDoc System for a certain timespan. After expiry of the session key the user must log in again.

A query can be sent to selected Provider Agents via the User Agent. The results are returned to the User Agent which then merges and presents them to the user. Alternatively the query may be sent to a Broker. The Broker determines suitable provider systems and returns their addresses to the User Agent. The user can modify the proposed provider list and send the query to the selected Provider Agents.

A mechanism to explore, i. e. to navigate the documents stored in the MeDoc System is provided as well [3,11]. We distinguish between *implicit navigation* and *explicit navigation*. Implicit navigation means that the user starts with a list of document references. In each of the document references shown, some fields are marked as clickable. Clicking such a field means issuing a query for similar documents; for example, clicking on the author name means searching for documents by the same author. Implicit navigation is possible within one provider as well as across several providers, the latter being implemented as a query to the broker. Explicit navigation does not start from a given document reference. Rather, the user is presented a list of all providers that support explicit navigation. After choosing one of them, the user is presented the top level of the navigation hierarchy, usually the set of attributes (fields) that can be used for navigation. After choosing one of the possibilities, the subsequent level of the navigation hierarchy is presented. For example, for author names the highest level might be a list of letters, then a list of author names that start with that given letter. When a leaf of the hierarchy of navigation criteria hierarchy is reached, choosing a value produces a list of document references. At present explicit navigation is only supported by the MeDoc Full Text Servers.

One way of accessing the actual documents in Full Text Servers is browsing full text documents [11]. The full text documents are not stored locally in the User Agent, but browsing takes place in the Full Text Server itself. The User Agent serves only as a mediator and offers the entry point for browsing to the user. This access is especially suitable in context of license models.

Another way of accessing documents is offered by document order and delivery [11]. After placement of an order the document is delivered by the MeDoc Full Text Server to the User Agent and stored locally in the User Agent on behalf of the user. This mode of access is suitable primarily for usage based cost models.

5 Implementation

For the implementation of the MeDoc System modern programming methods, languages and standards were taken into account:

- implementation was done completely in the object oriented programming language Java,
- the user interface was realized via HTML; we did not use JavaScript and Java-Applets because of known security problems,
- the Broker mechanism was derived from the Open Distributed Processing Trading Function, an ISO standard,
- communication between the components is based on an extension of the HTTP protocol, and
- transfer of information with costs is secured via the SSL (Secure Socket Layer) protocol (SSLeay, i. e. full key length, no export restrictions).

No special clients were developed for access to the MeDoc System. Instead of this common Web browsers may be used. As far as possible existing systems and libraries were used:

- The class library of the Java development kit (JDK 1.0.2, later JDK 1.1),
- Postgres95 as a public domain relational database in the User Agent, the Broker and the MeDoc Full Text Server,
- HyperWave in the User Agent for administration of delivered full text documents, and
- the commercial full text database system Fulcrum for implementation of the MeDoc Full Text Server.

6 Evaluation and Outlook

With the present MeDoc System a working system was designed and implemented that offers computer science literature in digital form and supports scientists and students in the area of computer science in searching for scientific information. Nevertheless, the MeDoc System can easily be used almost unmodified in further fields of interest. Only the contents have to be adapted and new types of external databases must be encapsulated by new Provider Agents.

Some improvements might be necessary for increased user acceptance. Besides natural shortcomings of the prototypical implementation with respect to efficiency, a number of additional functions might be desirable:

- inclusion of further documents and document bases:
  - integration of further documents into the MeDoc Full Text Server, and
  - addition of further databases to the information brokering system.
- functional extension of the MeDoc System:
  - support of interest groups,
  - user profiles for active information supply,
  - annotations,
  - support for reviewing processes, and
  - further cost and accounting models and electronic payment facilities.

Currently, the MeDoc System primarily supports information users and providers. Possible further extensions might include support for producers who require assistance at the production of digital documents.

References

1. A. Barth et al. The MeDoc Digital Library Project: Its Goals and Major Achievements, in this volume.
2. D. Boles, M. Dreger, and K. Großjohann. MeDoc Information Broker - Harnessing the Information in Literature and Full Text Databases. In *Contribution to the NIR-Workshop of the SIGIR Conference*. ETH Zürich, September 1996.
3. D. Boles et al. Conception of the User Agent – the User Interface of the MeDoc System, in this volume.
4. A. Brüggemann-Klein. MeDoc Pflichtenheft. Technischer Bericht, TU München, June 1996.
5. M. Dreger et al. Provider Selection—Design and Implementation of the Broker, in this volume.
6. M. Dreger, S. Lohrum, and P. Müller. The MeDoc Communication Protocol, in this volume.
7. K. Großjohann and D. Menke. Query Transformation for Heterogeneous Provider Systems in MeDoc, in this volume.
8. C. Haber and A. Brüggemann-Klein. The MeDoc Library - Security Aspects, in this volume.
9. H. Helbig, D. Menke, and C. Gnörlich. Access to local and distributed data bases, in this volume.
10. MeDoc. Home Page. Available online at `http://medoc.informatik.tu--muenchen.de`, 1997.
11. J Meyer and H.-J. Appelrath. Design and Implementation of the MeDoc Fulltext System, in this volume.
12. R. Weber and A. Endres. Cost Models and Accounting in MeDoc, in this volume.

Design and Implementation of the MeDoc Fulltext System

J. Meyer and H.-J. Appelrath

OFFIS, Escherweg 2, D-26121 Oldenburg
{meyer|appelrath}@offis.uni-oldenburg.de

Abstract. The MeDoc Fulltext System is a distributed storage and access system for documents of any format and any structure. Documents stored in the system can be searched for bibliographic attributes or in fulltext. Retrieved documents can be browsed with standard web browsers. Due to accounting issues, access may be restricted to an arbitrary part of the document. To ease the retrieval of documents, it is possible to navigate by formal criteria within the document set. The Fulltext System is an integral part of the MeDoc system, extremely extensible and flexible. Compared with a possible web server based solution, it is more complex but better capable of handling large amounts of heterogeneous data.

1 Overview

The MeDoc Fulltext System (FTS) - a storage and access system for documents of any format and any structure - enables users to comfortably access copyrighted material offered as part of the MeDoc service. Therefore the FTS must provide methods for users to identify documents of interest. After the documents are identified, the users may access the fulltext of a document for browsing and reading.

The FTS provides two different method to find documents of interest. The first is a database search either by bibliographic attributes or in the fulltext (the FTS understands the MeDoc query language). The second is to navigate in the pool of documents stored in the FTS. This navigation provides an easy and intuitive point-and-click interface to the document pool.

Browsing the documents fulfills two conflicting requirements: On the one hand the fulltext is usually not free, which means that access to it is restricted to authorized users. On the other hand, browsing needs to be fast and easy for users. It is most important that documents can be accessed through the MeDoc System as if it were a normal web server. The hyperlinks in the documents and all other features, like multimedia components or PDF documents, work as expected.

The system makes it possible to define document parts, such as articles in proceedings, that may be licensed and accessed separately. Particularly, it is also possible to define an arbitrary part of the document as a sample that may freely be read by anyone.

The FTS has to cope with different document formats and structures - the documents stored currently vary in structure from one single PDF file to more than 20.000 HTML, image and movie files. Since other formats may presently be included or current formats enhanced, the FTS does not parse and interpret the contents of files. Instead, files are regarded as *black boxes* (with unknown contents).

2 Requirements and Design Decisions

Before the implementation of the Fulltext System was begun, a set of functional as well as non-functional requirements were identified. The most basic assumption was that reading documents would not generally be free. Various accounting models were developed [7] and integrated into the FTS and it had to honor possible access restrictions of the fulltext documents imposed by them.

The functional requirements of the FTS:

Searching. The contents must be searchable by bibliographic attributes and in fulltext.

Browsing. The documents will be accessed with an ordinary WWW client. Access must be restricted according to the accounting requirements.

Navigation. It must be possible to navigate throught the contents and easily identify documents of interest.

Format Independency The FTS must be able to handle any document that can currently be published in the Web.

Security. The access must be secured against abuse, since accessing the documents may cost money,

In addition to functional requirements there were various non-functional prerequisites and design decisions that had to be fulfilled. It was decided to integrate the Fulltext System into MeDoc's Information Brokering System (IBS) [2]. Moreover, it should be distributed, i.e. several instances of the system should be able to cooperate and thus form *one* online library. Finally, the system should use Postgres95 as a relational database and Fulcrum as a fulltext database.

3 Implementation

3.1 Document Model

In order to fulfill the previous requirements, it is necessary to store information along with the documents themselves. A document model (fig. 1) was developed to do this.

The document model is based on the concept of a *literary item* as a deliverable unit, i.e. a document or a document part that may be separately accessed by users. It:

- defines types of literary items;

- describes the logical structure of individual literary items;
- describes relations between different types of literary items;
- defines bibliographic attributes for the various types of literary items and
- describes the connection between a (logical) literary item and the (physical) files that make up the document's text.

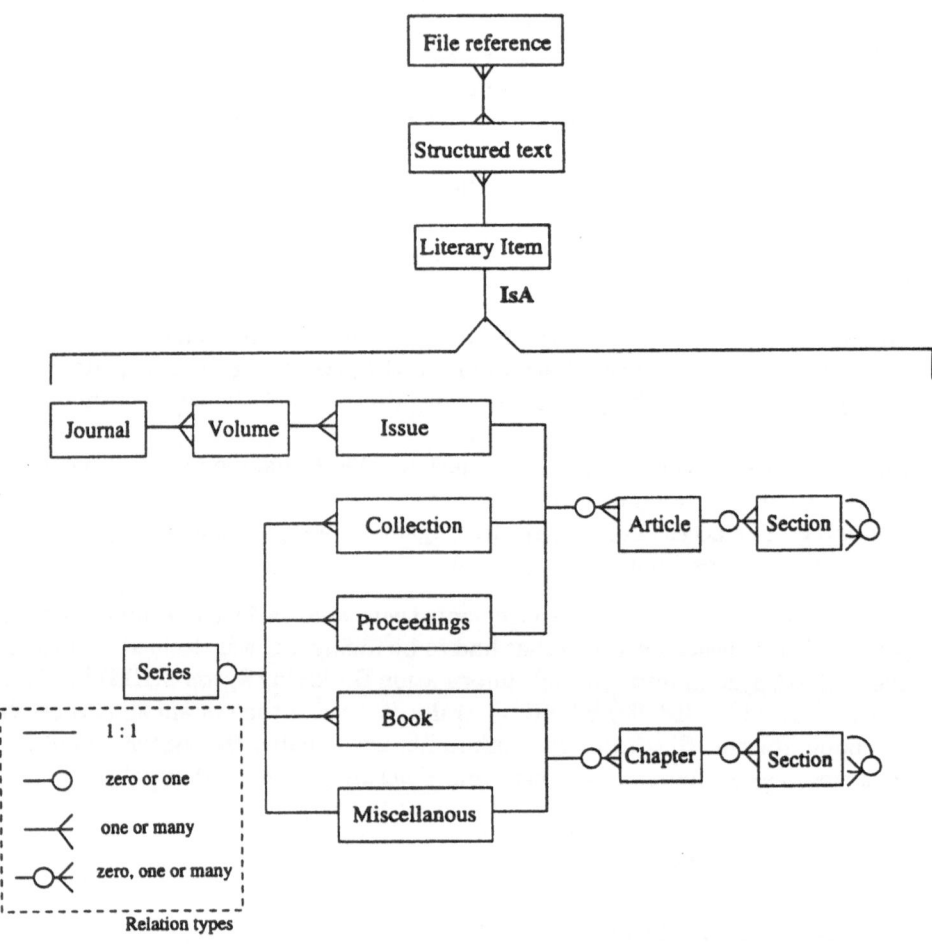

Fig. 1. MeDoc FTS Document Model

The document model assumes that a document consists of an arbitrary set of files. Since the files may be of any format, for example SGML, HTML, PDF, GIF or MPEG, it was decided that the content of the files should not at all be parsed, analyzed or modified. A lot of work would be needed to continuously support new formats and versions. Instead, the files should be regarded as black boxes that are stored in a database or the file system. The only exception to the rule is the fulltext database used to enable a fulltext search on text files. This system, of course, must be able to parse the file's contents to create a fulltext index. A tool was chosen that fulfills this requirement.

This assumption has a severe consequence: there is no *general* possibility to extract bibliographic data like author, title or keywords from the document files. It might be possible in highly structured formats like SGML, but would generate very much work and result in questionable quality if it were possible at all in non-structured formats like PDF. Thus it was decided that bibliographic data should always be supplied separately. Currently, a simple, proprietary script-language is used to describe a document's bibliographic data and also the relation between the document and its physical files. If the documents are highly homogeneous, as is the case with a journal which consists ultimately of hundreds of articles, it is possible to implement tools that automatically generate these scripts from the document files. In general, however, the scripts containing the bibliographic data are generated manually.

The relation between the types of literary items is based on the hierarchies of documents: Books and miscellaneous documents may belong to a series and consist of chapters which may further consist of sections forming sub-chapters and so on. Collections and proceedings may also belong to a series but consist of articles which may further consist of sections. Journals are divided into volumes, which are further divided into issues which in turn are divided into articles which are finally divided into arbitrary sections.

Every literary item may be linked to an arbitrary set of physical files. There may be more than one set of files linked to a single literary item. One set of files might form a sample of a book that can be freely read while another may make up the entire fulltext of the book. The first set may be, but not necessarily, a subset of the second.

Structured texts may differ in three parameters:

Format. There may be one set of files in HTML format that comprises the text of the literary item and another set that contains the same text in PDF format.

Usage. One set of files may be optimized for printing for example by inclusion of high-resolution images. Another set of files may be optimized for on-screen-display. There may also be files that cannot be printed, such as specially prepared PDF files.

Content. One set of files may comprise the entire fulltext of the document. Another set may hold only a sample. The latter is usually a subset of the first, but this need not always be the case. Another set may define an abstract or a table of contents.

Particularly the last parameter, the content of structured text, is a very powerful instrument. It allows to define tables-of-contents of journals, samples of books, abstracts of articles etc. Access may later be limited by structured texts. For example, a user may be given access to the abstracts of every journal, thus implementing a kind of abstract service.

3.2 General Architecture

The MeDoc FTS is an integral part of the entire MeDoc System (as described in [2]), and was realized by implementing a basic Provider Agent (PA) [5] and extending it to handle navigation, user authentication and document browsing. The PAFTS may only be accessed through the User Agent, as there is no separate user interface. Therefore, the extensions of the FTS over a standard PA require a counterpart in the UA as well.

The Provider Agent for the Fulltext System (PAFTS) is a standard Provider Agent that understands and handles all PA messages and supplies the Broker with metadata. The MeDoc FTS is seamlessly integrated into the MeDoc Information Brokering System in this way.

A detailed view of the PAFTS' architecture, its interaction with the User Agent and the user's web browser is given in figure 2.

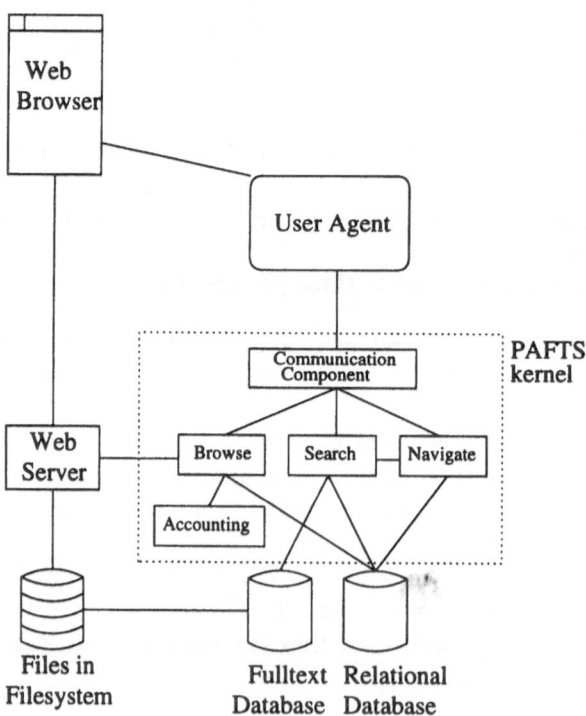

Fig. 2. Detailed architecture of the PAFTS

The most important components of the FTS are a relational and a fulltext database, a web server and the kernel itself.

The two databases are used in parallel to store literary items according to the document model. Since the documents in the FTS should be fulltext searcheable, the fulltext database is necessary in order to index the document's text files and textual bibliographic attributes such as titles and keywords. The relational database stores structured information such as relations between literary items and connections between literary items and physical files. It also stores other kinds of structured data such as accounting and licence information and user data. It it also possible to use just one database system that supports fulltext indexing, but at the time the design decisions were made, no such product was available.

The web server is needed to enable access to documents through standard web browsers. It is enhanced by a specific plug-in that controls access limitations according to the relevant accounting and licencing model. It contacts the kernel to inquire the validity of a particular access.

The kernel of the PAFTS uses the standard MeDoc Communication Component [3] to handle communication with the Broker and the User Agent. It accesses the accounting component [7] to manage access rights, licencing and accounting. Users' requests to search, browse and navigate are handled by approriate components. It should be noted that search requests are the only actions that make it necessary to access the fulltext database. Moreover, the text files themselves are only accessed via the web server. Most of the information on documents, particularly the document model is stored in the relational database.

3.3 Searching

The FTS should be searchable by the Brokering System. Thus it is required that the FTS be able to handle queries in the MeDoc query language. Several additions have been made to the language to enable fulltext searching and support other special FTS features, but these extensions do not mean elementary changes to the language.

The MeDoc query language, as explained in [4], is based on a prefix syntax allowing weighted boolean queries. A typical query looks like this: (AND (CONTAINS author 'meyer') (CONTAINS keywords 'medoc'))

The basic query handling is done in the same way as in other PAs and is also described in [4]. The query is translated into SQL statements for the relational and the fulltext databases and the results transformed back into MeDoc format.

Translating the query into SQL is non-trivial, particularly since the data spans across two different databases, one relational and one fulltext. Thus it is in general necessary to translate *one* MeDoc-query into *several* SQL queries. The resulting sets of individual SQL queries have to be manually combined into one set, thereby taking care of calculating the correct weights. The latter is further complicated by the fact that the fulltext database is file based whereas the MeDoc language is document based. Thus, given the weight of a file, a matching weight for the document has to be calculated. This should be performed efficiently, since it must be done for every literary item in a result set. Moreover it must be done based only on the weights of the files without inside knowledge about the inverted index. Therefore, a fairly straightforward solution was chosen based on the average weights of the document's files.

3.4   Browsing

Browsing in the PAFTS means accessing the text files of a literary item. As described in section 3.1, the files themselves are stored in the filesystem. Therefore, to enable browsing, it suffices to make the files accessible through a web server.

Browsing starts with a query result that is sent back from the PAFTS to the User Agent as a result of a query or navigation. This result carries information on which structured texts are available for each literary item. The User Agent allows users to select one structured text to browse. The actual visualization of the files of the selected structured text is a two-step process: first the PAFTS generates a special *Browse-URL*, then the user contacts the PAFTS' web server with this Browse-URL. This process is outlined in figure 3.

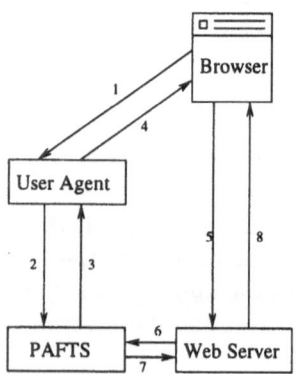

Fig. 3. Processes while browsing

The generation of the Browse-URL works as follows: the User Agent contacts the PAFTS with information about the requested document, structured text and the user, as indicated by step (2) in figure 3. The PAFTS checks if the user is authorized to access the requested document and also requests a password from the User Agent to check the user's authenticity. If all checks are passed, the PAFTS generates a *Session* containing information about the accessed document and structured text plus user data. Session data is persistently stored in the database and given a unique key. This key is part of the so-called *Browse-URL*, a URL sent to the user (3) to access the document via the web server. A typical

Browse-URL has the form: `http://medoc.offis.uni-oldenburg.de:8081/-105633114/Books/gulbins/index.htm`. The rather cryptic number 105633114 in the URL is the coded session key.

In the second step, the user contacts the PAFTS' web server using this Browse-URL (5). The web server, a standard Apache web server [1], is enhanced by a special plug-in. This plug-in carves the session key out of the Browse-URL and contacts the PAFTS kernel with the session key and the requested file (6). The PAFTS accesses the session information with the help of the session key. Then it checks if access to the requested file is permitted and the result is transferred back to the plug-in (7). If accessing is allowed, the plug-in allows the web-server to handle the request (8). If not, it presents an error message to the user.

This mechanism interferes very little with normal request handling. Particularly, since the session key is added to the *beginning* of the URL, relative links resolve correctly in the browser without any additional preparation. Moreover, there is no need to manipulate the original files. The actual http request handling is done by the web server itself; the plugin only allows or rejects access to files in the very early state of request handling. Therefore advanced web features such as byte-serving PDF documents depend only on the web server, not on the PAFTS.

One important special feature has been implemented in the plugin. If a user accesses a file without supplying a session key, the PAFTS still checks if the file is free. This makes it possible to access free samples without having to request a Browse-URL. Particularly, it is possible to simply generate a list of all samples in the MeDoc system.

3.5 Navigation

Navigation in MeDoc is an interactive, intuitive and iterative way to select literary items based on fixed criteria. In the Web, the terms *browsing* and *navigation* are often used interchangeably. In the context of MeDoc, however, there is a strict, technology based distinction between the two: *browsing* means viewing the document's contents, i.e. the text files that make up the document itself; *navigation* means selecting and viewing the document's bibliographic references. It must complement the search mechanisms and offer a web-like way to select document references based on simple point-and-click mechanisms.

A navigation is handled in two steps. In the first step, the criterion for selecting documents is chosen. This may be an author's name, a keyword, a classification or some other attribute. In the second step, the documents matching this criterion, i.e. the documents written by a given author, having a given keyword or matching a given classification, are retrieved.

There are two ways to get a navigation criterion: The user can *implicitly* define a criterion by selecting an attribute of a given reference or *explicitly* choose a criterion in an interactive process.

Implicit navigation starts with a document reference that was previously found by either search or navigation. For instance selecting an author's name defines a criterion, "Select all documents that have the same author as this doucment." In the same way, implicit navigation by keywords, classification, publisher and other bibliographic attributes can be implemented.

The navigation up and down the document hierarchy according to the document model is a special case. Given a document reference, selecting a *dowm* button is interpreted as "Select all documents whose super-document is this one." Accordingly, selecting an *up* button means "Select the super-document of this one." A frequent usage is to move from a journal via a volume and an issue to an article.

Implicit navigation is a feature of the user interface. Selecting a document's attribute can be translated into a plain query. For example, choosing the author "meyer" translates into the query (CONTAINS author 'meyer'), which can be handled by the PAFTS. Since the query is a standard MeDoc query, implicit navigation also works with any other PA.

With *explicit* navigation, the user explicitly browses the possible navigation criteria to select a criterion. It may be viewed as moving through a hierarchy of criteria, as displayed in figure 4. The leaves of the tree are the actual criteria, e.g. the author names or the keywords. Inner nodes usually represent only intermediate interaction steps, but may also represent criteria. This is particularly valid for the CR-classification, where the user may for instance either choose classification C.3 or may further specify classification C.3.2.

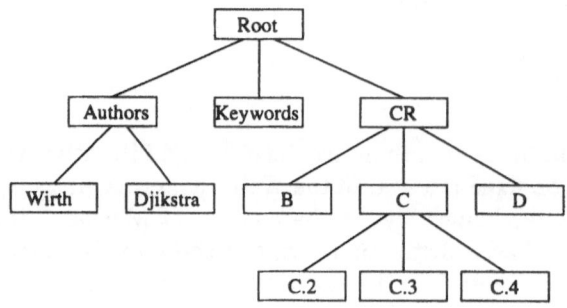

Fig. 4. Extract of Attribute Hierarchy used in FTS

There is one important difference between the various possible navigation criteria. Some of them are *static*; they don't depend on the contents of the database. The CR-classification is an example. It is defined in advance and publicly known. Other criteria however are dynamic; their values depend on the contents of the database. For instance the list of authors cannot be generated unless the database contents are known.

Due to the possibly dynamic attribute values, explicit navigation cannot be realized in the User Agent alone. Instead, it is handled by the User Agent and the PAFTS together. The User Agent asks the PAFTS about possible criteria and presents them to the user. The user's selection is then sent to the PAFTS where either matching documents are selected or new criteria generated and passed back to the User Agent.

Once a criterion has been selected, either by implicit or by explicit navigation, the documents matching the given criterion are retrieved from the database. The criterion is converted into a query and answered by the PAFTS.

With implicit navigation, as was already described, the User Agent can convert the selection into a query. With explicit navigation, however, only the PAFTS knows which criteria are defined and can generate and handle the appropriate query. The latter is done by simply "redirecting" the navigation to a query. There is no special handling of queries originating from explicit navigation.

4 Experiences with the Fulltext System

4.1 Known Problems

The Fulltext System has been operating for about half a year. It contains about 50 different books and 5 journals with different formats, structures and licence requirements and is regularly accessed by users of various institutions. It is virtually inevitable that problems appear that were initially invisible, underestimated or not remedied due to a lack of time.

The strict separation between the user interface and the distributed databases adds to the extensibility and scalability of the system. It has, however, strong effects on the user interface. The influence of response times on the quality of the user interface was underestimated. Also, the distribution of the Fulltext Systems is not properly hidden from the user. The search results are not merged among the Fulltext Systems which results in an overall result set that looks poor. The user still has to cope with several databases with identical functionality instead of just one distributed database.

The document model is quite complex, complicating administration. Currently, there are only simple tools to support these tasks. In general, the FTS is designed from the point of view of users. There were time constraints and administrative requirements could not properly be handled. Over time, some technical and organisational improvements were implemented and are currently in use. It would be worthwhile to have a general understanding of creation, publication and administration of electronic literature.

The relational database used is one of the key components of the FTS. The chosen system Postgres95 is quite inappropriate. Performance is low, data sometimes corrupted, standard features of advanced RDMBS' like protection of referential integrity not supported. Thus performance as well as the reliability of the FTS would be considerably improved by using a high-quality database system.

4.2 Appropriateness of Concept

The MeDoc Fulltext System is fairly complex. It is questionable if the general concept of a distributed system of agents is adequate to solve the problem; the organizational overhead may not be worthwhile. To resolve this, the Fulltext System is compared to the straightforward solution of using a standard web server to offer the fulltext contents. Such a solution was implemented and used as an interim solution to publish MeDoc contents before the Fulltext System was available[6]. The following comparison will emphasize this MeDoc web server, but should be looked at as a general comparison of a pure web solution with the Fulltext System.

The MeDoc web server provides the following functionality:

- Search for bibliographic attributes;
- Search for specific a author, editor or publisher;
- Browse documents, authors/editors, publishers, keywords, classification;
- Free access to sample for everyone;
- Access to fulltext in several formats, password-protected by normal web access rights.

Most of the functionality of the FTS was implemented in the web server as well. The various browsing options mentioned above match the explicit navigation in the FTS. Implicit navigation is implemented in the same way as in the FTS; in a document reference a click on an attribute selects all documents that match the given attribute. The search, however, is limited to bibliographic attributes. There is no general fulltext search available.

The main technical differences between the web server's approach and the FTS are:

Integration into IBS. The web server is not integrated into the MeDoc Information Brokering System (IBS). Therefore the documents available in the web server are not searchable by the IBS. Integrating the server would require a major effort.

Distribution. The FTS is a distributed system. There are more than one PAFTS running and it is possible to search all of them simultaneously. This eases the load on individual machines. Due to time constraints, the distribution is not yet entirely hidden from the user. Therefore the user still has to cope with more than one database, which is particularly difficult during the presentation of search results and during navigation. This could however be solved in the future. The web server, in contrast, is a local system, and all documents reside on one machine. Users can conveniently navigate through all of them at once. However, this imposes heavy loads on the machines particularly regarding hard disk space.

Access Control. The web server controlls access per directory. Therefore, to offer free access to samples, data is duplicated into different, freely accessible directories. The FTS, in contrast, has much smarter access control. Users must login only once into the User Agent and then access is granted to all documents available to them. Any portion of a document can be declared as a sample or another structured text with different access rights.

Slimness. The web server is certainly a slim solution - fast and implemented without much effort. The FTS, however, is a heavy-weight solution - integrated into a complex distributed system with additional communication requirements between components. which have rather sluggish response times.

To sum up, the web solution holds the edge when it comes to comfort and performance. Fast navigational access to documents being the main advantage compared to the FTS. However, it is doubtful that the resource requirements and the adminstrative overhead for access control will be acceptable when it handles a large set of documents. In contrast, the FTS has been designed for handling large amounts of data, but as long as there is only a small number of documents, this advantage hardly takes effect. Also, the fact that the distribution of the PAFTSes is still visible to the user must be considered a major disadvantage of the FTS. To its advantage, the FTS is extensible, though currently there are no concrete plans to actually realize extensions.

4.3 MeDoc versus Publisher's Efforts

A considerable number of publishers of scientific material are entering the market of electronic publishing by offering a significant part of their paper publications online. Although these efforts have much in common with the MeDoc approach, there are a few significant differences that make a direct comparison misleading.

The main difference between MeDoc and the publishers' efforts lies in the types of documents handled. MeDoc publishes documents from several sources and must therefore be able to handle documents of any structure and format, while publishers only publish their own material and can thus rely on a specific structure and format. This allows a higher degree of control over appearance of documents and enables supporting technical features such as navigation within the document set. The IEEE/CS effort is a good example, where the fulltext of articles is stored in SGML format in a database and converted on-the-fly into HTML. During the process of conversion, default headers and navigational aids are added to the HTML code, resulting in a common look-and-feel and additional links in the displayed documents

MeDoc publishes many books and only a few journals, while publishers strive for the exact opposite putting a strong emphasis on the publication of journals. This results in a different, usually much simpler view on the data and thus an easier document model and possibly simpler administration.

The licence and accounting models of publishers are mostly based on the classic subscription model. MeDoc has much more sophisticated models with more and complex features. There are, for example, concrete plans to include pay-per-view concepts and electronic payment methods. This, of course, means an increase in administrative overhead.

Access control in MeDoc is based on a user and group concept that enables very complex relations. Although licences are assigned to institutions, it is possible to define local groups within the institution that have dissimilar access rights. With current publishers' initiatives such complex relations cannot be modeled.

In general, the MeDoc approach is more flexible than the solutions currently offered by publishers. This flexibility means a rather complex system.

5 Summary

The MeDoc FTS is capable of handling the requirements of publishing books and journals on the web. It provides the basic functionality that is necessary to find and read documents of interest. Moreover, it provides a powerful method of defining and supervising access rights for arbitrary parts of documents. Documents in the FTS can be found using the MeDoc Information Brokering System.

The system currently in use is a good proof of concepts. It is, however, not without problems. The great flexibility, on the one hand causes increased complexity on the other. By now, other, simpler solutions may have been developed that fulfill the same functionality. Yet, once the requirements of users or publishers increase and the number of documents to be published in the Fulltext System increases beyond a critical mass, the advantages of the FTS become extremely significant.

References

1. The Apache HTTP Server Project. Online `http://www.apache.org`, 1997.
2. Boles D. and others . The MeDoc System – A Digital Publication and Reference Service for Computer Science. in this volume.
3. Dreger M., Lohrum S., and Müller P. The MeDoc Communication Protocol. in this volume.
4. Großjohann K. and Menke D. Query Transformation for Heterogeneous Provider Systems in MeDoc. in this volume.
5. Helbig H., Menke D., and Gnörlich C. Access to local and distributed data bases. in this volume.
6. MeDoc . MeDoc - The Electronic Computer Science Library. Available online at `http://medoc.informatik.tu-muenchen.de`, 1997.
7. Weber R. and Endres A. Cost Models and Accounting in MeDoc. in this volume.

Conception of the User Agent –
The User Interface of the MeDoc-System

D. Boles[1], A. Kusserow[2], G. Möller[1],
H.-J. Appelrath[1], D. Fellner[2]

[1] OFFIS Oldenburg, Escherweg 2, D-26121 Oldenburg,
{appelrath,boles,moeller}@offis.uni-oldenburg.de
[2] Institut für Informatik III, Universität Bonn, Römerstr. 164, D-53117 Bonn,
{fellner,kusserow}@cs.uni-bonn.de

Abstract. Main objectives of the MeDoc project are specifying, developing, and evaluating full text based information and publication services for computer science literature. To achieve this goal, the MeDoc system has been developed. It provides a consistent user interface for searching and navigating in distributed and heterogeneous databases.

The architecture of the MeDoc system consists of the following components: *MeDoc User Agents* provide the user interface to the MeDoc system, *MeDoc Provider Agents* encapsulate the underlying database systems of the providers, and *MeDoc Brokers* mediate the information between users and providers. *MeDoc Full Text Servers* are special providers, which store and manage computer science literature in full text.

Basically, MeDoc User Agents are augmented World Wide Web servers. The user logs in to the system with a common WWW client and sends his requests via the WWW-protocol (HTTP). The MeDoc User Agent accepts user requests, forwards them to Brokers or Provider Agents addressed, and presents the results to the user. This paper describes the development and implementation of the MeDoc User Agent.

1 Motivation

MeDoc User Agents form the interface to the MeDoc system [2] by offering a single point of access for distributed searching in heterogeneous citation and full text databases. Users formulating queries do not have to know the query language of a special provider; instead, they just formulate the query in the MeDoc query language [6], address the query to the Broker or Provider Agents, and get the results. In this context the Broker is a special provider that does not send a list of document references, but a list of Provider Agents recommended for that query.

The internal communication in the MeDoc system uses a *MeDoc Protocol* [5] based on HTTP. The MeDoc User Agent transforms user requests into the MeDoc Protocol and the results of a query back into the format presented to the user. The design of the MeDoc User Agent allows for different clients to access the MeDoc system, e.g. email clients or WWW browsers.

Conceptionally, each institution installs its own MeDoc User Agent. This way the administrator of each MeDoc User Agent may grant or deny access to billable services (viewing a document) to special users or user groups and thus no central MeDoc registration is needed.

2 Requirements for the MeDoc User Agent

The MeDoc User Agent was designed according to the user requirements specified in [3]. As the MeDoc User Agent is the first component users get into contact with, its user friendliness and functionality are vital for the acceptance of the MeDoc system. All functionality provided by the MeDoc system has to be accessible through the MeDoc User Agent.

To be accepted by the users the MeDoc system requires a modern, convenient, and efficient user interface, its use must be intuitive and a help system has to be integrated.

Flexibility in the design is necessary to permit changes complying to special user desires. Furthermore, the system needs to be extendable to add further functionality. Since MeDoc User Agents are to be installed at various institutions third-party modules (e.g. WWW-server or DBS) have to be exchangeable. Object-oriented methods were used to design the MeDoc User Agent according to the requirements described.

Installing a MeDoc User Agent has to be straightforward as it has to be installed at various institutions. System administration must be possible at minimum overhead.

3 Functionality of the MeDoc User Agent

The MeDoc system can be divided into two parts. The *Information Brokering System (IBS)* [4, 7, 1] supports searching in distributed and heterogeneous databases, the *MeDoc Full Text Server (FTS)* [9] stores and manages full-content computer science literature, i.e. full-text documents with multimedia content.

It allows the user to navigate the document base and browse or order documents. To browse documents, each user needs a licence. The MeDoc User Agent administrator can allow or deny the use of licences according to the user or the groups the user belongs to.

The MeDoc User Agent offers IBS functionality as well as FTS functionality through one interface.

3.1 General Functionality

User Management. The user management module stores user data like user id's, passwords, email addresses, user names, and so on in a relational database system. This data is inserted with the registration. The user id in combination with the password is checked whenever a user enters the system. A session is initiated and a session id is assigned to it. This session id is checked each time a user interacts with the system. After a fixed period of time the session id becomes invalid and the user has to log on to the system again.

User Group Management. Each MeDoc User Agent corresponds to a so called *Global Group* according to the institution where the MeDoc User Agent is installed. Additionally, the MeDoc User Agent administrator can define *Local Groups* to divide users into different groups. Each user is a member of the global group of the hosting MeDoc User Agent and can be a member of several local groups. With these groups the access to the MeDoc Full Text Servers can be managed. The administrator allows and denies individual rights to special local groups for accessing full text documents.

Broker and Provider Agent Management. The Broker and Provider Agent management module manages all addresses of Brokers and Provider Agents known to the MeDoc system. The data is requested by the MeDoc User Agent from a default Broker as part of the MeDoc User Agent startup and is refreshed at a specified time interval.

3.2 Functionality of the Information Brokering System (IBS)

The IBS functionality supports retrieval in distributed and heterogeneous databases. A Broker recommends Provider Agents offering the most relevant document references for a special query. Thereafter, the user may forward the query to one or all of the recommended Provider Agents. Of course, a user can send query requests directly to one or several Provider Agents.

In the MeDoc system searching is based on asynchronous communication [5] to allow users continuing their work while waiting for results. On the other hand, browsing (3.3) affords synchronous communication to present the results to the user immediately.

Communication with Brokers and Provider Agents. Query requests have to be sent to Brokers as well as to Provider Agents and the results obtained have to be handled.

Retrieval. The MeDoc User Agent presents a form for entering new queries or modifying existing queries. Those queries are sent to a Broker or several Provider Agents, respectively. As described before, the results are obtained asynchronously. Therefore, a user may get the actual status of a query at any time, i.e. the results already received, information about providers that cannot be reached, and so on.

A request to a Broker results in a list of Provider Agents offering the most relevant document references according to the query. The user may then choose the Provider Agents the query is sent to. Alternatively, a query request can be sent to Provider Agents directly.

Query and Result Management. Since retrieval is based on asynchronous communication, queries and query results must be stored to be accessible any time.

Implicit Navigation. The *Implicit Navigation* is a special kind of a query. By choosing a certain attribute value in a document reference, a query is created based on the attribute and its value. This query is sent to the Provider Agent that sent the original document reference. Using the Implicit Navigation a user can ask for all document references which fulfill a special condition, e.g. all references containing the author "Smith". This mechanism is not limited to a single Provider Agent. It can be extended to send Implicit Navigation requests to a Broker or several Provider Agents.

3.3 Functionality of the Full Text Server (FTS)

The FTS is a layer providing access to the MeDoc Full Text Databases. As the FTS is contacted via the MeDoc protocol and supports IBS functionality, it can be seen as a Provider Agent offering additional functionality [9].

Communication with MeDoc Full Text Servers. The MeDoc User Agent sends requests to full text servers for accessing documents and receives the results. There are two ways to access documents: *Browsing* documents and document *delivery*.

Access and Licence Management. Since access to full text documents may invoke costs it must be controlled. Users who want to view documents have to obtain licences and accept the MeDoc user agreement. The licence management module [10] closely cooperates with the user and user group management modules.

Browsing Documents. If the user asks to browse a document, a *Browse URL* is sent to the MeDoc User Agent, provided that the user has a licence to access the document. In fact, a Browse URL is the URL of the MeDoc Full Text Server containing a special session key. Without a valid session key, the document cannot not be viewed. After a specified time the session key becomes invalid so that later requests with the same URL will be refused. The MeDoc User Agent is not involved in the browsing itself; at this point the user directly communicates with the MeDoc Full Text Server.

Document Delivery. Besides browsing a document, the user can request to get it delivered as a whole. The document will be stored within the MeDoc User Agent, and the user can access the document locally. The process of document delivery is asynchronous because the data transfered to the MeDoc User Agent might be quite large and the transfer may take too long for interactive handling. Thus, the user does not have to wait until the complete document has been delivered, but can proceed doing other tasks in the meantime.

Order and Document Management. Since document delivery is an asynchronous process, the document orders as well as the documents delivered must be stored locally. This functionality is provided by the order and document management modules of the MeDoc User Agent.

Explicit Navigation. Using explicit navigation a user requests a list of attributes from a full text server. By choosing an attribute the user refines the field of interest until he gets a list of attribute values. After choosing an attribute value the user gets a list of document references that correspond to the attribute and its value. A good example for using this mechanism is the explicit navigation within the ACM classification scheme. From the top level users may navigate e.g. to *software*, from there on to *software engineering*, and so on, until they reach a list of documents. The same process is possible by choosing an attribut that is not hierarchically structured like *author*, listing all *authors beginning with "S"* and all *references by author "Smith"*. Since use of the explicit navigation shall be intuitive and the choice of attributes depends on previous actions this process is based on synchronous communication.

Up/Down Navigation. A special case of Implicit Navigation is the *Up/Down Navigation* to get parents or children of a document node according to the MeDoc document model [9]. This kind of navigation uses the same mechanisms as the implicit navigation described in (3.2). The only difference is that there is no explicit attribute and attribute value. A query asking for parents or children of the document referenced is created and sent to the corresponding Provider Agent. Since the Up/Down Navigation is based on the document model of the MeDoc Full Text Servers this functionality is only offered by their Provider Agents.

4 Architecture of the MeDoc User Agent

The implementation of the MeDoc service aimed at using existing software tools as far as possible. Since users prefer access to the MeDoc system via WWW browsers, an HTTP daemon is needed. Structured data like user data, query data, and result data is stored in a relational database system. Furthermore, a full text database or document management system is used to store documents delivered by the MeDoc Full Text Servers.

Communication between these components is structured as follows: the **MeDoc User Agent Kernel** is responsible for the internal communication. The interaction with the HTTP daemon is implemented through CGI (Common Gateway Interface) scripts. This module is called **Connector**. The Connector accepts user requests and presents the results obtained from the kernel. Alternative kinds of connectors may be implemented to support other user clients than WWW browsers. In fact this possibility has been verified as the first prototype of the MeDoc system had a WWW, an email, and a Java interface.

Access to the relational and the full text databases is realized through management modules which build the **Database Interfaces**. There is a special module for each kind of data, e.g. for the user data and the query data.

The **Communication Component** realizes the communication between the MeDoc User Agents and the Brokers and Provider Agents. The Communication Component is only responsible for the correct transmission of the information from one component to the other. It forwards requests from the MeDoc User Agent Kernel to Brokers and Provider Agents. The results received from them later are given back to the kernel.

The following figure illustrates the architecture of the MeDoc User Agent.

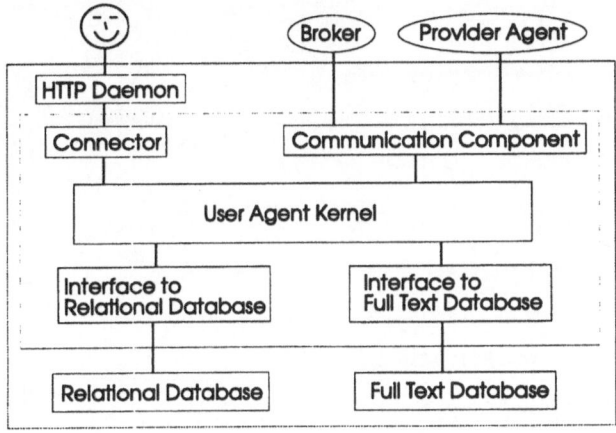

5   Design of the User Interface

The users and the MeDoc User Agent communicate via WWW browsers. To provide a modern, convenient, efficient and intuitive user interface, HTML code with frames is used. The use of JavaScript and Java applets was dismissed in an opinion poll with the MeDoc pilot users [8]. Therefore, it is not possible to inform the users about alterations in the query status, e.g. if the MeDoc User Agent has received retrieval results. For users less reluctant to use Java or JavaScript an HTML-based user interface including Java and JavaScript is planned.

The user interface is divided into two parts. The left part contains the menu with the main functions of the MeDoc system. This part of the user interface is available at any time.

The right frame shows data dynamically generated as a result of the chosen function. This frame follows the metaphor of "folders with tabs, where each query is represented by a folder and each folder contains the statement, the provider list, and the results belonging to the query.

The following figure demonstrates the user interface of the MeDoc system.

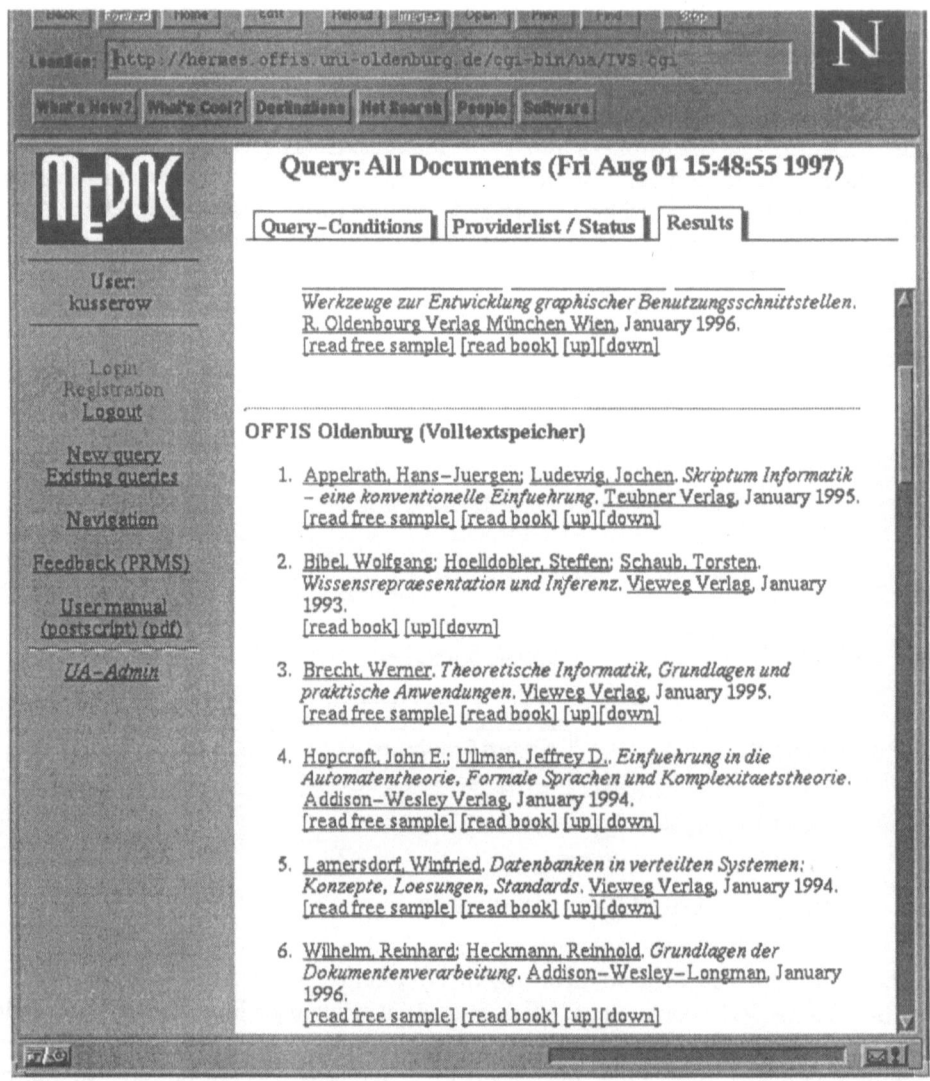

6   The MeDoc User Agent at Work

This section describes the flow of control for each function of the MeDoc User Agent. In the following figures rectangles represent information provided by the MeDoc User Agent presented to the user. Arrows between rectangles represent actions changing the status of the MeDoc User Agent.

6.1 Main Menu

The following figure describes the entry point to the MeDoc system and the main menu of the user interface of the MeDoc system. As mentioned in section 5 the main menu is available any time after login or registration of a new user.

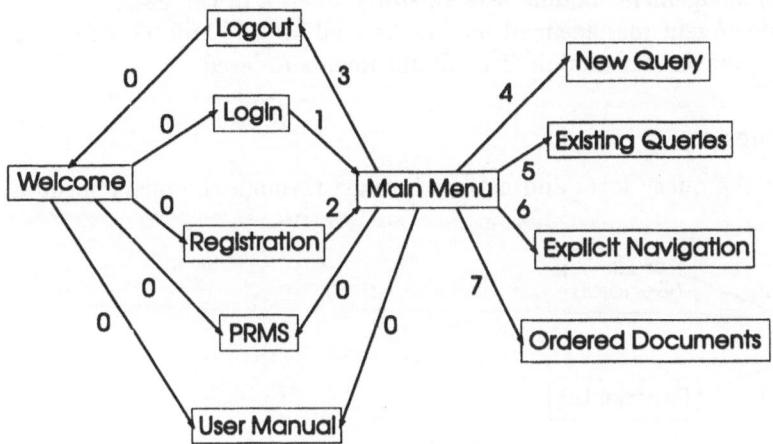

Welcome: This is the entry point to the MeDoc System.

Login: Registered users can enter the MeDoc system with their user id and password. Anonymous users are restricted to services free of charge.

Registration: Users can register themselves by entering personal data.

PRMS: The *Problem Report Management System* (PRMS) allows users to contact the MeDoc system administrator, especially if some problems occur.

User Manual: A user manual is available in various formats.

Logout: Log out of the system (not mandatory).

Main Menu: After login or registration all functions of the MeDoc system are available.

New Query: See (6.2).

Existing Queries: See (6.3).

Explicit Navigation: See (6.4).

Ordered Documents: See (6.5).

0: The user follows a link without any action performed by the MeDoc User Agent.

1: After login the user management module checks the user id in combination with the password. If the login succeeds a session id for further access to the MeDoc User Agent is created and all user related data from the last session that is not needed anymore is removed. Otherwise, access to the MeDoc User Agent is refused.

2: The user management module stores the information about the user. The user enters the system and is assigned a session id.

3: The MeDoc User Agent removes all user related data that is not needed any longer[3].

4: The MeDoc User Agent provides the query form to the user. This form contains a list of all Provider Agents known to the MeDoc system, built by the Provider Agent management module.

5: The query management module lists all stored queries of the user.

6: The Provider Agent management module lists all MeDoc Full Text Servers.

7: The order management module lists all documents ordered.

6.2 New Query

In this section the query form and actions invoked through the query form are described.

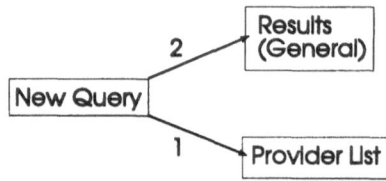

New Query: The MeDoc User Agent presents a form for creating a new query, based on the MeDoc query language [6]. The query can be sent to the Broker or to selected Provider Agents, e.g. to all known MeDoc Full Text Servers.

Results (General): See (6.6).

Provider List: See (6.6).

1: Before the query is sent to the Broker the query management module registers the query and transforms it into the MeDoc protocol. Thereafter, the user is given back control over the MeDoc User Agent. The result received from the Broker is a list of Provider Agents recommended for that query. This list is stored by the result management module in cooperation with the query management module.

2: If the query is sent to several Provider Agents, the query management module registers the query and transforms it into the MeDoc protocol. Since this action also is asynchronous, the user gets back the control. Each Provider Agent sends back a list of document references that the result management module stores in cooperation with the query management module.

6.3 Existing Queries

Queries need to be stored because of the asynchronous communication within the MeDoc system. A user must be able to view stored queries. Moreover the user may want to resend a query, to forward it to another Provider Agent, and so on.

---

[3] Since it cannot be guaranteed that the user logs out of the system, the same clean up procedure is performed after login of a user.

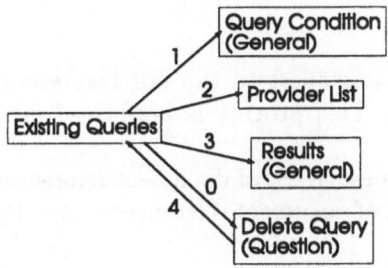

Existing Queries: The user gets an overview about all queries stored.
Query Condition (General): See (6.6).
Provider List: See (6.6).
Results (General): See (6.6).
Delete Query (Question): See (6.6).

0: The user follows a link without any action performed by the MeDoc User Agent.
1: The query management module displays the query chosen in the query form.
2: The list of Provider Agents that has been delivered by a Broker or the list of selected Provider Agents to which the query has been sent is provided by the result management module.
3: A list of all document references received from the Provider Agents is presented to the user.
4: After confirmation, all data related to this query, the query itself and the results delivered by Broker and Provider Agents are removed from the MeDoc User Agent.

6.4 Explicit Navigation

The Explicit Navigation is an intuitive way to access the MeDoc Full Text Servers. A user can navigate the bibliographic data of a full text server and can subsequently obtain a list of document references according to the navigation path.

Explicit Navigation: A list of MeDoc Full Text Servers offering explicit navigation is provided.
Attribute List: The list of attributes of an actual level gives the user the possibility to refine the navigation through the bibliographic data. By choosing an attribute or attribute value the user can move up or down the hierarchy until he reaches a list of document references.

Results (Explicit Navigation): See (6.6).

1: The MeDoc User Agent sends a navigation request to the full text server and visualizes the attribute list received. This process is performed synchronously.
2: Choosing a value at the lowermost level requests a list of document references from the MeDoc Full Text Servers. The list of document references is directly presented to the user.

6.5   Ordered Documents

Ordered Documents: The list of all documents ordered by the user is provided.
Document Components: See (6.8).

1: The order management module provides all available components of the document including, information concerning access restrictions sent by the Provider Agent.

6.6   Query Management

The query management enables the user to formulate, edit, and resend queries, as well as to view results.

Having sent a query form, the user is presented a menue offering the functions Query Condition, Provider List, and Results. Implicit Navigation allows the user to choose the functions Query Condition and Results. This is presented in the following figure.

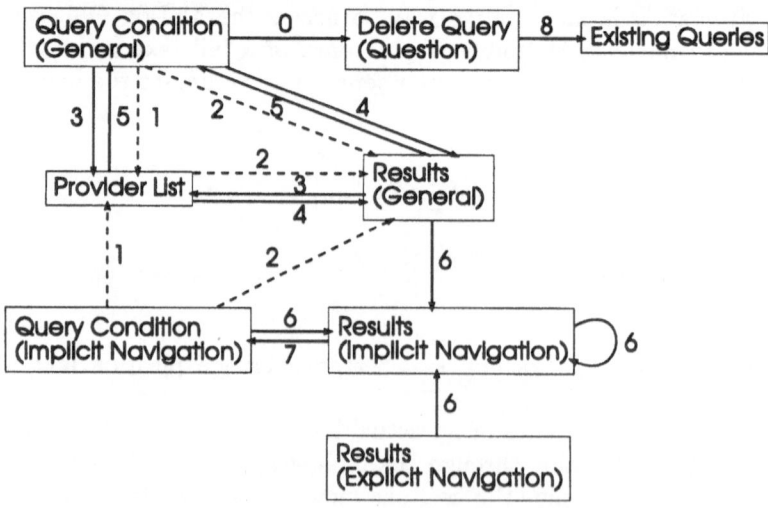

Query Condition (General): A query form with the query condition is presented. The user can alter the query condition and send it to the Broker or Provider Agents. There is no need to change the query, it may just be resent or forwarded to other recipients, thereby deleting the original query.

Provider List: A list of Provider Agents recommended by the Broker is displayed, Provider Agents the query was sent to are marked. If the query was sent directly to a selected list of Provider Agents these are displayed instead of the Broker results.

Results (General): All document references received so far are presented to the user. The user can initiate further actions from this point like Implicit Navigation or viewing the documents (6.7).

Results (Implicit Navigation): Results that have been obtained by an implicit navigation request. In contrast to the document references received as a reply to a query, the navigation results refer to exactly one provider. Therefore, showing the provider list is not possible. Results of an implicit navigation are not stored. Of course, a user can initiate another implicit navigation.

Query Condition (Implicit Navigation): This is a query form, showing the query condition based on the navigation request with a single attribute and its value. The difference to the general query condition is that no resend or deletion of the query is possible since the query has not been stored.

Results (Explicit Navigation): As with the results menu after an implicit navigation these results has been received by a single Provider Agent and are not stored. The difference between these two lists of results is that after an explicit navigation it is not possible to call the query condition.

Delete Query (Question): The user is asked if he really wants to delete the query.

Existing Queries: See (6.3).

0: The user follows a link without any action performed by the MeDoc User Agent.

1: See (6.2) [1].

2: See (6.2) [2].

3: See (6.3) [2].

4: See (6.3) [3].

5: See (6.3) [1].

6: A user has entered an implicit navigation request by choosing an attribute and a value. The MeDoc User Agent generates a query condition with these data and sends it to the corresponding Provider Agent. The Provider Agent evaluates the query and sends back the results to the MeDoc User Agent. These results are then presented to the user.

7: The user is shown the query condition constructed by the implicit navigation within the query form.

8: See (6.3) [4].

6.7 Document Access

The IBS and the FTS parts of the MeDoc User Agent provide two different kinds of access to documents. In the IBS part document references usually contain a link to the document given by a URL. Access to documents via the FTS part is more complex. The user must have a licence [4] to access the whole document.

The options for viewing a document are the same regardless the document-type.

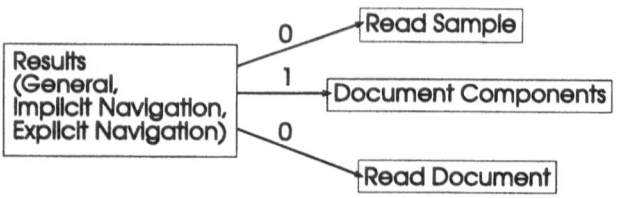

Results (General, Implicit Navigation, Explicit Navigation): See (6.6).
Read Document: A new browser window opens, containing the document requested[5].
Read sample: A part of the document is presented in a new browser window[5].
Document Components: See (6.8).

0: The user follows a link without any action performed by the MeDoc User Agent.
1: See (6.5) [1].

6.8 Document Components

There are several components of documents available according to the document model of the MeDoc Full Text Server [9] like abstract, sample, glossary, index, table of contents and full text. All these components may be available in different formats like HTML or PDF. According to the user agreement there may even be different ways to use the document, e.g. read it, print it, and so on. The user has to select between these alternatives.

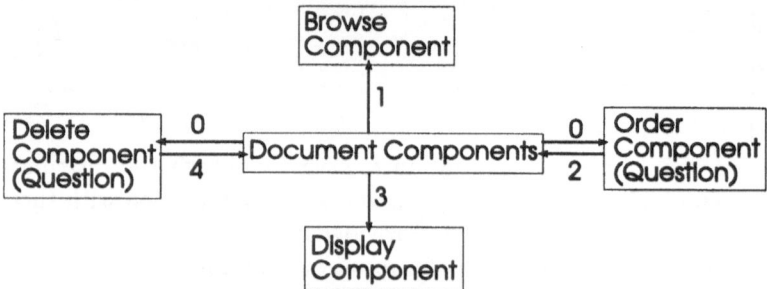

Document Components: All components of a document available are presented to the user, including information concerning access restrictions. The user can initiate browsing or order components of the documents (if he has a licence) as well as display or delete components delivered earlier.

---

[4] A sample part of the document is available for all users in most cases.
[5] The user has left the MeDoc system in the new window.

Browse Component: The component ordered is displayed in a new browser window[5].

Order Component (Question): The user has to confirm the order of a component because this order can cause costs.

Display Component: The component is displayed. In contrast to browsing a component this functionality is provided by the MeDoc User Agent since the document is stored in the MeDoc User Agent.

Delete Component (Question): The user is asked to confirm the deletion of the component.

0: The user follows a link without any action performed by the MeDoc User Agent.

1: A browse request is sent to the MeDoc Full Text Server that delivered the document reference. Subsequently, the full text server asks for the user password to check if the access is permitted. If access is permitted the full text server immediately sends a "Browse URL" that is redirected to the user client. The user gets a new window containing the document. The access and licence management module takes part in this process.

2: If a user has confirmed the order of a document component an order request is sent to the corresponding MeDoc Full Text Server, and the order management module registers this order. As with the browsing functionality the full text server asks for the server password to check the permission before sending the complete document component. The user directly gets control over the MeDoc User Agent because this process is performed asynchronously. If the user passed the access permission check the full text server sends the document component. The component can consist of several files which are stored locally by the document management module. The access and licence management modules of the MeDoc User Agent are involved in this process.

3: After a component has been delivered and stored locally the user is able to view the component. Therefore, the document management module of the MeDoc User Agent selects the document component in order to display it.

4: If a user wants to delete a document component all data related to the order of the component including the component itself is deleted by the order and document management modules. Otherwise, no action is performed by the MeDoc User Agent.

7   Conclusion

Currently the MeDoc User Agent can be regarded as a working prototype that makes available the basic functionality of the MeDoc system. To increase the acceptance by the users the MeDoc User Agent should be extended with additional functionality. For example the integration of user profiles could guarantee users an active delivery of new information according to their interests. Also, an upgrading of the MeDoc User Agent to a workbench for working groups would be desireable. Users should be facilitated in distributing retrieved information to other users. Annotations are a possible supplement to this feature.

The document delivery described in (3.3) was only supported in the first prototype of the McDoc system. It is still implemented in the MeDoc User Agent but currently not supported by the MeDoc Full Text Servers since the experiences have shown that browsing documents is prefered by the users. Nevertheless, document delivery should be re-integrated since this is a suggestive functionality.

Even with its limited functionality the MeDoc User Agent became a complex server system that supports multi-user access and which must perform a large number of database actions. The MeDoc User Agent consists of about 100.000 lines of Java code and is based on Java threads to allow multi-user access and communication with other components of the MeDoc system at the same time.

References

1. D. Boles, M. Dreger, and K. Großjohann: MeDoc Information Broker - Harnessing the Information in Literature and Full Text Databases. In *Contribution to the NIR-Workshop of the SIGIR Conference.* ETH Zürich, September 1996.
2. D. Boles et al.: The MeDoc System – A Digital Publication and Reference Service for Computer Science. In *Digital Libraries in Computer Science: The MeDoc Approach*, Lecture Notes on Computer Science. Springer Verlag, Heidelberg, 1997.
3. A. Brüggemann-Klein: MeDoc Pflichtenheft. Technischer Bericht, TU München, June 1996.
4. M. Dreger et al.: Provider Selection—Design and Implementation of the Broker. In *Digital Libraries in Computer Science: The MeDoc Approach*, Lecture Notes on Computer Science. Springer Verlag, Heidelberg, 1997.
5. M. Dreger, S. Lohrum, and P. Müller: The MeDoc Communication Protocol. In *Digital Libraries in Computer Science: The MeDoc Approach*, Lecture Notes on Computer Science. Springer Verlag, Heidelberg, 1997.
6. K. Großjohann and D. Menke: Query Transformation for Heterogeneous Provider Systems in MeDoc. In *Digital Libraries in Computer Science: The MeDoc Approach*, Lecture Notes on Computer Science. Springer Verlag, Heidelberg, 1997.
7. H. Helbig, D. Menke, and C. Gnörlich: Access to local and distributed data bases. In *Digital Libraries in Computer Science: The MeDoc Approach*, Lecture Notes on Computer Science. Springer Verlag, Heidelberg, 1997.
8. A. Kusserow: Ergebnis der Nutzerbefragung zur zukünftigen Gestaltung der Benutzeroberfläche des MeDoc-Dienstes, January 1997. http://www.graphics.uni-bonn.de/medoc2/papers/nutzerbefragung.ps.
9. J Meyer and H.-J. Appelrath: Design and Implementation of the MeDoc Fulltext System. In *Digital Libraries in Computer Science: The MeDoc Approach*, Lecture Notes on Computer Science. Springer Verlag, Heidelberg, 1997.
10. R. Weber and A. Endres: Cost Models and Accounting in MeDoc. In *Digital Libraries in Computer Science: The MeDoc Approach*, Lecture Notes on Computer Science. Springer Verlag, Heidelberg, 1997.

Access to Bibliographic Data Bases
– The Provider Agents in MeDoc

D. Menke and C. Gnörlich and H. Helbig

e-mail:
carsten.gnoerlich@fernuni-hagen.de
hermann.helbig@fernuni-hagen.de
menke@vhs-ge.mmedia-ge.de

FernUniversität Hagen, LG Praktische Informatik VII/Künstliche Intelligenz, 58084 Hagen

Abstract. The realization of a user-friendly access to local and distributed information resources is broadly acknowledged as a growing need with regard to the globalization of our informational world. In this context, three methods for developing interfaces to information providers are discussed which support the end-user in finding the information matching his requirements. The central part of this paper deals with the approach followed in the general framework of the MeDoc project. It is realized in the form of so-called provider agents (PA) developed on the base of an object-oriented design method. Each PA is assigned to a special information provider and translates the form-oriented user query in formal language expressions of the Internet interface supported by the provider (which is generally unknown to the user of MeDoc). One important feature of the provider agents is their division into a general reusable part (the PA framework) and a special (provider-specific) part.
The MeDoc approach is complemented by two other methods providing the user with a natural language interface (NLI) to dedicated bibliographic data bases (one representing a library of AI literature and the other containing the bibliographic information of all university libraries of the Land North-Rhine Westphalia). The corresponding NLIs are based on a functional approach and a logic-oriented approach, respectively. It is argued that there is only a comparatively small step left to close the gap between formal meaning representations of natural language sentences and the query languages used by the PAs in the MeDoc project. The long-term goal of our work is the combination of the techniques developed for the natural language interfaces to local data bases and the methods for realizing the access of end-users to information providers in the Internet.

1 Introduction

It is generally acknowledged that there is a growing need for technical support in a world of globally distributed information resources. Even if the information providers were in principle able to answer the queries of the end-user, the latter either doesn't know the appropriate provider or he isn't able to address the provider properly, because this step possibly requires the knowledge of a complicated formal language interface (as is the case with the interface Z39.50 to libraries accessible via Internet, see [12]). In this paper we report on three contributions to bridge the gap between the end-user and different information providers, though - according to the topic of this volume - the main emphasis is laid on the work done in connection with MeDoc.
On the one hand, we developed two natural language interfaces for dedicated local bibliographic data bases (see sect. 2) giving the user the full advantage of the expressiveness of his native language (in this case German). On the other hand, we developed within the general framework of the project MeDoc[3] so-called provider agents screening the user from

the peculiarities of the information resources. The approach followed in the project MeDoc currently permits only form-oriented queries.

For a better understanding of the discussion in sect. 3, the general structure of the information mediating system of MeDoc and the position of the provider agents in this system are shown in fig. 1. The terminus "provider agent" denotes the module which controls the communication between the MeDoc components and the external information resources (in short: the providers).

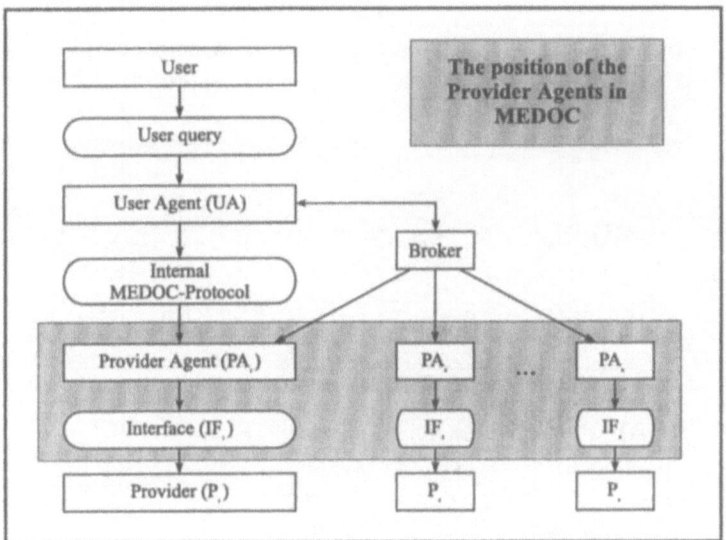

Fig. 1. The embedding of the provider agents into the MeDoc information mediating system

The user communicates directly only with a user agent (UA) which translates his query into the internal MeDoc protocol. He can decide whether he needs the help of a broker to find a suitable information provider or not. In the first case, the broker sends the user one or more proposals where to direct the query to. Otherwise, the user has to select a special provider himself and to direct the already translated query to the corresponding provider agent which prepares the query for transmission to this provider.

In the following section, we give a short impression of the interfaces developed at the University of Hagen and the information resources connected to them.

2   Three approaches for realizing the access to information resources

To meet the user requirements and to study the different methodologies we developed and implemented four interfaces, two of them within the project MeDoc (cf. fig. 2).

The first interface NLI-AIDOS is connected with the document retrieval system AIDOS supporting the semiautomatic generation of dictionaries and the inclusion of thesauri and decimal classifications into the search. The system AIDOS is used as a local bibliographic

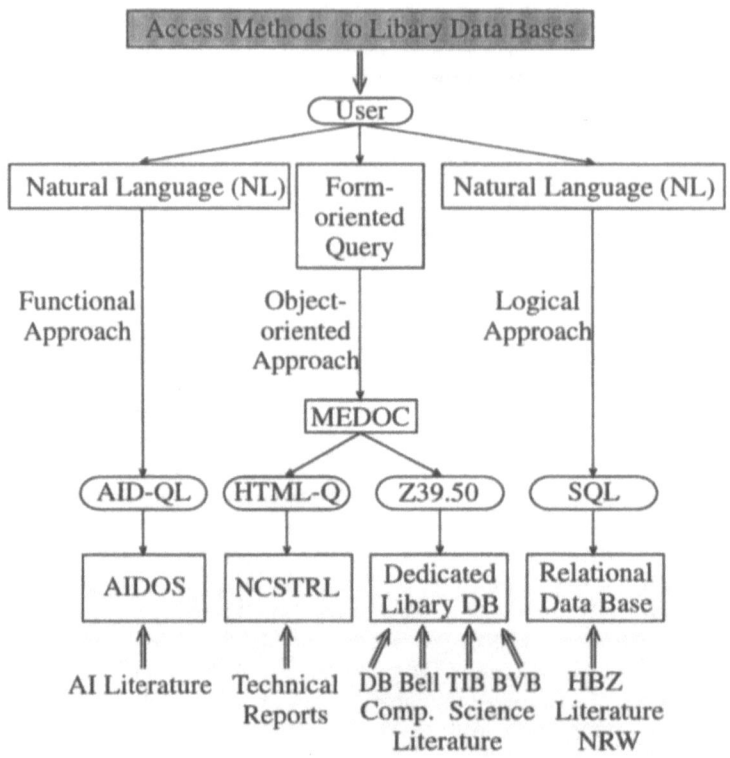

Fig. 2. Different access methods to practically relevant information resources

system at the chair of Artificial Intelligence (AI) at the University of Hagen. It is used to store and manage bibliographic data in the field of AI. Its natural language interface (abbreviated: NLI) translates natural language queries of the user into the AIDOS query language AID-QL allowing for a quite natural dialog including references between different questions or between questions and foregoing answers. The NLI-AIDOS is based on a word-class oriented functional analysis [8] and is characterized by a functional approach of design and implementation. This interface is described elsewhere in greater detail (see [7], [6] p. 358-369) and is therefore not dealt with in this paper.

The second group of two interfaces uses the technology of provider agents realized with an object-oriented method in the algorithmic framework of MeDoc[4]. By means of these provider agents we are able to reach libraries all over the world[1] which provide the international standardized interface Z39.50 (see [12]) as well as dedicated full-text data bases, as for instance the technical report server NCSTRL [13]. The latter can be accessed by an HTML-oriented query language HTML-Q. The Z39.50 interface which in the long run will possibly be the most important of these interfaces is described in sect. 3.4. Last not least, we developed a

---

[1] among these are: DB - Deutsche Bibliothek (German Central Library), Frankfurt; Bell - Library of Congress, Washington; TIB - Technische Informations-Bibliothek (Technical Library), Hannover; BVB - Bayrischer Bibliotheksverbund (Association of Bavarian Libraries), Munich.

natural language interface on the base of logic-oriented methods for relational data bases using SQL as its retrieval language. By means of this NLI, the user has access to the collection of bibliographic data of all university libraries in the Land North-Rhine Westphalia (Germany) which are maintained by the Hochschulbibliothekszentrum (HBZ[2]) in Cologne. Combining this interface, which is described in sect. 4, with the Z39.50 interface permits the user to access information providers supporting international standardized query languages.

3   Interfaces to reference data bases in the Internet – Provider agents in the MeDoc information mediating system

3.1   Design criteria

The provider agents whose role in MeDoc has already been explained in sect. 1 were developed according to three basic design considerations:

Reusing instead of rewriting: The provider agent should be largely built on top of already existing tools and data base access mechanisms. This decision helps to reduce the costs and guarantees the import of expertise already won in other projects.

Stratification of the provider agent: The number of available information providers is expected to grow rapidly, so the PA has to be separated into a general, reusable core system and a small provider-specific layer. In this way, the effort of integrating new providers by supplying additional provider agents to the system can be minimized.

Correspondence of design and programming methods: To support the above goals from the first design stages down to the programming language and implementation level a methodology has to be chosen which provides some kind of inheritance mechanism. This criterion almost automatically leads to an object-oriented approach which has also been backed by the insight that many functionalities of provider agents can be generalized and inherited by special PA's in concrete applications.

3.2   The general tasks and the structure of a provider agent

The concept of a provider agent is used in the MeDoc system to allow for a uniform treatment of the heterogeneous information providers in the Internet. Generally, a provider agent (PA) has the task to mediate the information exchange between the information provider and the MeDoc system screening in this way the user and the user agent from the peculiarities of a special information provider (cf. fig. 1). The most important subtask in this connection is the transformation of the user query represented in the internal MeDoc protocol and delivered by the user agent into the protocol of the target data base. After receiving the results from the provider (i.e. the bibliographic information the user has asked for), the PA translates this information back from bibliographic standard formats like USMARC, UNIMARC [10] or MAB [2] into the internal MeDoc protocol. Since many of the tasks in this process are similar for different provider agents, a general framework (the so-called PA-skeleton) has been developed which covers the functionalities common to all provider agents. This framework has to be complemented with specific components for a special PA to complete its implementation. According to the above mentioned design criteria an object-oriented approach has been chosen as an implementation paradigm for the PA (cf. fig. 4), which is explained later on.

---

[2] Center for University Libraries of the state NRW, Germany

The general workings of a PA can be characterized as follows: Receiving an incoming message and examining its content, the PA has to decide which task to perform, i. e. depending on the content of the message each time another chain of processes (message exchanges) is initiated in the object hierarchy representing the PA. The PA receives messages from different external participants in the communication process and sends its own messages back to them. The most important communication partners of the PA are the user agents and the broker within the MeDoc system on the one hand and the external information providers on the other hand. Thus, the PA is the interface and mediator between these two sides.

To explain the functionalities of the provider agent, its three main tasks will be discussed in more detail:

1. Reception of a preprocessed query from a user agent and translation of this query into a special target protocol. If the provider agent receives a document query from a user agent, it performs the following actions:
   - the query is translated
   - it is compared with the queries in the cache. If the query is already contained in the cache, because it has been asked before, the answer can be taken from the cache.
   - otherwise, the query is transmitted to the provider
   - the PA waits for the answer from the provider
   - finally, the PA translates the answer received from the provider into the internal MeDoc protocol in order to guarantee its further processing by the user agent.
2. Registration of a provider with the broker. The provider agent sends a registration message to the broker executing the following steps:
   - the provider agent collects the meta data from the provider,
   - the data are transformed according to the internal MeDoc protocol,
   - finally, they are conveyed to the broker.
   The transformation of the meta data includes the processing and modification of these data [3] and the partitioning of the meta data into blocks of manageable size which can be easily transported to the broker.
3. Cancellation of the registration with the broker. The provider agent unregisters with a broker by sending a special message to the broker.

After finishing its task, the PA returns a message to the component that asked for the service. Some tasks are performed automatically. For instance, there is no need to send a request to the provider agent to register or to unregister with a broker. If an error occurs during the work, the partner must be informed about it. In this case, a convenient message explaining the reason of the failure is created and sent back.

To explain *how* the provider agent performs these tasks, it is helpful to have a short look at the components which the provider agent consists of (see fig. 3):

The communication component

This component supports the communication between the parts of the MeDoc service, i.e. the communication between the provider agent and the user agent as well as the communication between the provider agent and the broker. The communication is carried out according to internally defined rules.

The initialization component

To set the starting parameters for the provider agent correctly, an initialization file has to

---

[3] Two examples are the stemming of entries which are marked as "Keywords" and the correct ordering of surnames and first names of the authors, if necessary.

PA Sceleton (general part)	• Communication • Initialization • Message queue • Query cache • Transformation framework • Broker registration • Status log

PA (provider specific part)	• Communication with the provider
	• Query Treatment
	   1. Translation of the query for the provider
	   2. Transformation of the results (return formats)
	• Meta data acquisition

Fig. 3. The components of the provider agent

be read. The data in this file is used as actual values of the specified parameters. Missing values in the file are set to default values listed in the general class *Initialize Values*.

The message queue

The incoming messages are saved in a queue. A special thread takes the messages out of the queue and starts the correct chain of processes according to the contents of the message (document query, registration with a broker or a new start of the provider agent).

The query cache

The cache records the last N queries and the corresponding answers from the provider in order to save time at a later request. If a user agent sends the same query twice, it can be answered without starting a new communication with the provider. The size N of the cache is one of the parameters of the initialization file mentioned before. The use of the cache can also be activated or inactivated by setting special parameters.

The transformation framework

The queries for documents have to be translated from the internal MeDoc protocol into the protocol required by the provider. Correspondingly, the answers from the provider must again be translated into the internal protocol. Several classes were implemented to achieve this task, some of them belong to the PA-skeleton, some of them to the part specific for a special provider.

The broker registration

The provider agent regularly registers with the broker when a certain amount of time has elapsed. The purpose of this registration is to send the broker the transformed meta data it has received from the provider. A special daemon waits for a certain time interval specified in the initialization file and starts the new registration after expiration of this time. If desired, this registration can be forced also by a special command.

The status log

Every communication with the provider agent is recorded. The status vector informs at every stage of the processing about the successful end of a task or of an error, if one happens to occur.

Communication with the provider

This component realizes the external communication between the provider agent, which is

57

part of the MeDoc system, and the external providers. The modus of this communication is determined by the protocol stipulated by the corresponding provider (as an example, it can take place according to the rules of the Z39.50 protocol).

Query treatment

Every incoming query is matched against the information stored in the cache. If the query had been processed earlier and belongs to the N last queries, it can be answered on the base of the information stored in the cache. Otherwise, the query will be transformed and sent to the provider. The answer of the provider is sent back to the requesting component after the necessary transformation.

Meta data acquisition

The meta data (information about the contents of the provider data base) is requested from the provider by the PA. When this meta data arrives, the PA stores it for further processing and sends it to the broker after the completion of special transformations.

3.3 The object-oriented realization of provider agents

The clear distinction between general parts of the PA, the so-called PA-skeleton, and provider-specific parts in the PA shown in fig. 3 can be very elegantly expressed by means of an object-oriented approach. Fig. 4 mirrors this division in the hierarchy of object classes representing the PA. The goal had been to anchor as many classes as possible in the general framework. These are the abstract classes characterized by non-shadowed ellipses in fig. 4. A new provider agent is implemented by extending the general classes and adding special classes to the general framework (shadowed fields in fig. 4). For example, the class *StartPA* extends the class *ProviderAgent* and *Initialize* extends the abstract class *InitializeValues* from the general framework package. The most important classes are explained in table 1.

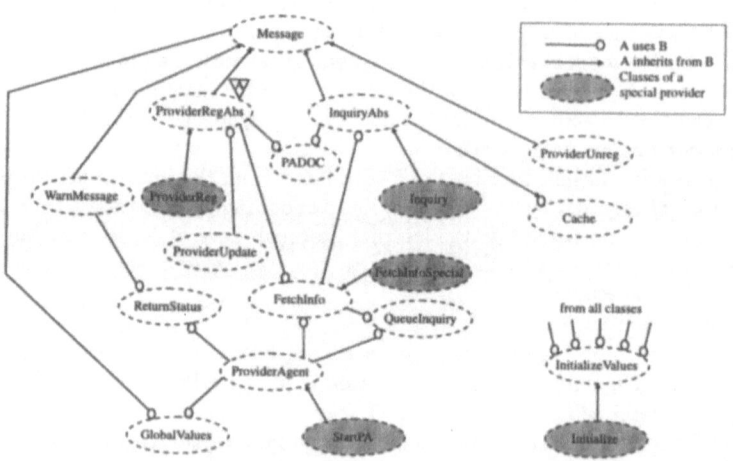

Fig. 4. The classes representing the provider agent

The figure shows the inheritance or subordination relations between classes as well as the functional relations between them characterizing which class invokes methods from which other class.

Class	Task
Cache	Intermediate storage for queries and corresponding answers
Fetchinfo	Creates orders for registration and other requests (queue administration)
GlobalValues	Providing global values for all objects
Initialize	Provides general initialization parameters
InitializeValues	Provides PA-specific initialization parameters
InquiryAbs	Basic methods for the query translation
Inquiry	PA-specific translation methods
Message	Top method processing a MeDoc Message
ProviderAgent	Represents the communication layer
ProviderRegAbs	Basic methods for registration
ProviderReg	Registration method for a special provider agent
ProviderUnreg	Cancellation of a registration
ProviderUpdate	Daemon supervising the time periods for registering
ReturnStatus	Treatment of incoming status messages
StartPA	Main class for starting a PA
WarnMessage	Generation of appropriate warning messages depending on the status

Table 1. Explanation of the most important classes

To create a new type of provider agent, two steps have to be taken:
- the abstract classes of the framework must be extended and
- the framework itself must be configured.
If a certain type of provider agent already exists, i. e. a certain external protocol is already implemented, only the configuration files must be adapted to create a special provider of this type. To build an extension for a new provider class, the first task is the implementation of the access methods typical for this provider class and integrating them into the framework. In that process, two different kinds of access are distinguished, which can be implemented independently of each other:

1. access to documents (treatment of queries)
2. acquisition of meta knowledge (the registration).

Treatment of queries. The two main classes, which are involved in the access to the provider data base, are *Inquiry* and *ProviderReg*. In order to deal with the document queries, the class *InquiryAbs* of the framework must be extended by a class named *Inquiry*. This new class implements the methods that are specific for a special provider agent. *InquiryAbs* is the class whose objects start the search for documents in the provider's data base (cf. fig. 4). The class *Inquiry* specializes the following three abstract methods of its superclass *InquiryAbs*:

- `GetAnswerFromProvider(query)`
  This method sends a query to the provider. The query has already been translated by the method *TranslatePhysicalToProtocol(term)*, which will be described later. The answer from the provider is translated back before returning it finally to the user agent.

- `TranslateAnswer(answ)`
  This method translates the answer received from the provider into a format required by the user agent. A so called DocRefList (a list of references to documents) is generated from the string returned.

- `TranslatePhysicalToProtocol(term)`
  This method translates the queries having been preprocessed by the general part of the PA into the protocol of the provider. More information about this topic can be found in [5].

These methods are necessary to send document queries to the provider and to transform the received answers. The next subsection describes the methods which must be supplied for the acquisition of information about the provider's data base.

Registration. The registration is a task that is different for every type of provider. It therefore has to be implemented separately for every provider that is to be included into the MeDoc service. There are mainly two classes involved in the registration process. The class *ProviderRegAbs* takes care of the registration of the provider agent with the broker. It supplies the latter with the necessary meta data of the provider.

Like the already mentioned class *InquiryAbs*, *ProviderRegAbs* is an abstract class. Hence the class *ProviderReg*, which extends it, specializes all methods of *ProviderRegAbs* having the modifier "abstract" in their designation. There are two special methods which must be implemented in *ProviderReg*:

- `GetAnswerFromProvider(request)`
  This method requests the sending of meta data from the provider to the provider agent. The answer is saved in a series of files. The method returns a string array that contains the names of these files.
  The meta data contained in the files must still be transformed. The method which is invoked next reads and interprets the received data from the above mentioned files.
- `TranslateAnswer(m_data)`
  This method transforms the meta data into so called ProviderDescriptors, the format in which the Broker expects the meta data to be represented.

3.4 The Z39.50 provider agent

The Z39.50 is an international standardized protocol for information retrieval in the Internet [12]. It is especially dedicated to the communication with library data bases. This rather complicated interface is not suited as a direct language interface to the end-user. It is a session-oriented protocol and comprises a query language (RPNQuery) as well as return formats for the bibliographic data. It has been an important decision to include Z39.50 provider agents into MeDoc because more and more libraries implement this protocol. The German activities in this respect are represented by the project DBV-OSI [1].

One of the design principles in developing a Z39.50 provider agent has been the usability of existing tools for the implementation of this PA. This design decision has been taken on the base of a comparison between the available access systems and implementation systems. In order to fulfill the needs of the PA, an access system has to support the functions **search** [4] as well as **scan** and **present** [5], and it has to be available on UNIX operating systems. Among the available choices, the free software package YAZ made by Index–Data [11] turned out to fit the PA's requirements best. YAZ provides an interface to the Z39.50 protocol using its own query language, and can be easily integrated into the provider agent to convert MeDoc messages into the Z39.50–RPNQuery language. The embedding of the YAZ component into the Z39.50 PA is shown in fig. 5.

---

[4] Functionality for searching documents.
[5] Functionalities for meta knowledge acquisition (registration) and presentation of results, respectively.

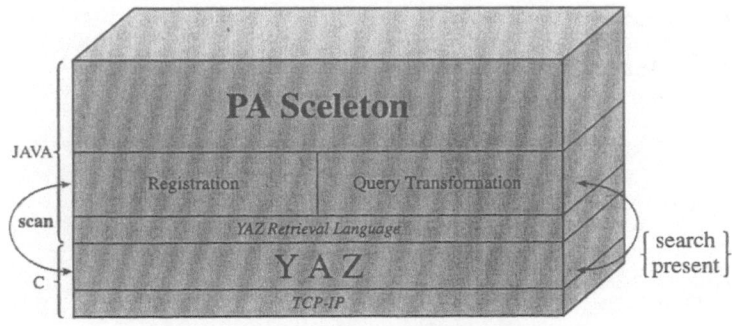

Formats for results: USMARC, UNIMARC, MAB

Fig. 5. Different layers of the Z39.50 provider agent

The YAZ tool provides the following services:

- communication via TCP with the Z39.50 server
- access authentification with the server
- transmission of meta data by means of the SCAN functionality
- transformation of queries from the YAZ query language into the Z39.50 protocol
- transformation of the answer format into formats "readable" by MeDoc.

The transformation of a query.

A document query in the MeDoc service is translated in three steps:

1. from the global to the conceptual level $\quad$ GL → CO
2. from the conceptual to the physical level $\quad$ CO → PH
3. from the physical to the protocol level $\quad$ PH → PR.

The transformations GL → CO and CO → PH are carried out within the PA skeleton; these steps are explained in detail in [5]. In this paper, we will concentrate on how a query term in MeDoc's physical level description is transformed into the YAZ query format. In order not to make things too complicated, MeDoc's physical level format is considered simply as an internal string representation of the query. Building the YAZ query is conceptually the last step in the query transformation, since all remaining tasks, the construction of the Z39.50 query, and the communication with the Z39.50 data base via TCP/IP, are effectively encapsulated in the YAZ tool. These functions are carried out by simply passing the YAZ query to one of the YAZ tool routines like *search()* or *present()*.

A query term is transformed into the YAZ format by dynamically building a corresponding object tree with each node representing a sub expression of the query; this is similar to building a parse tree if one were following a more traditional procedural approach. Fig.6 contains an example transformation which will be referred to in the following discussion; the sample query expresses the user request for literature about Java programming.

The transformation starts by simply creating a root object representing the whole (untransformed) input query (this is object "Oroot" at the top of fig.6). The root object, just like any other object that is created subsequently, evaluates the query term it contains as follows:

1. It localizes the outmost (leading) operator in the query term, which is "AND" in our example.

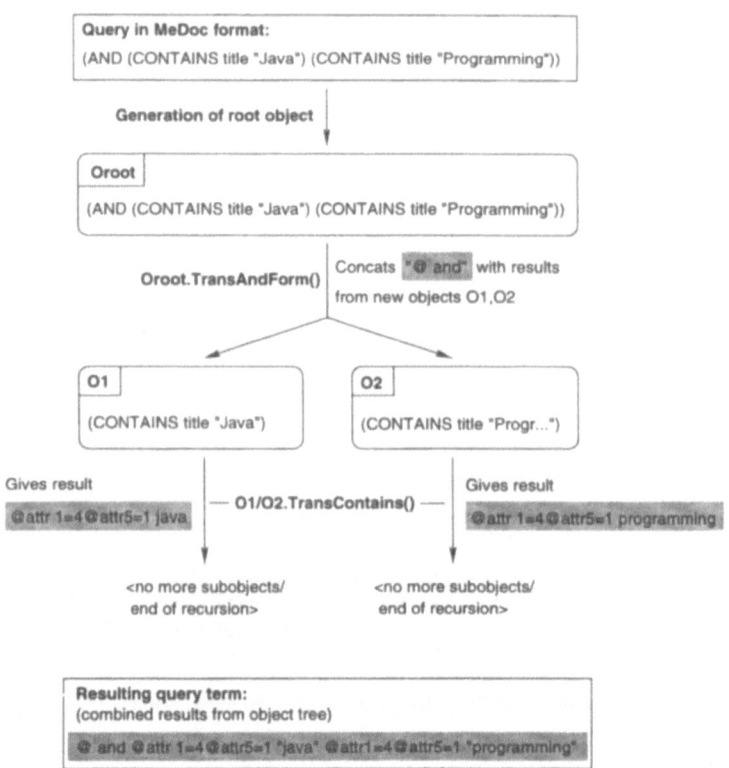

Fig. 6. The transformation of queries

2. The object dispatches the query term to the corresponding member class (*Oroot. Trans-AndForm()* in the example). Note that all objects in the object tree are omnipotent wrt. the possible set of operators, or in other words, all objects possess methods for parsing all operators allowed in the query.
3. The selected member class creates the proper output query fragment for its operator ("@ and" in the example), and locates any sub terms in the remaining expression. For each remaining subexpression, a new object is instantiated (these are "O1" and "O2" in the example), and query processing continues recursively by evaluating these objects.

The object recursion ends when no more subexpressions are found in the leaf objects; in that case, no more objects are generated and the query result is compiled as the recursion unrolls bottom-up. See the bottom of fig.6 for an example of a full query resulting from a completed recursion.

When the recursion has finished, the root node delivers the resulting query to the YAZ tool, which in turn generates the query format required by the Z39.50 protocol and transmits it to the Z39.50 data base.

Registration. The registration of the provider agent with the broker takes place either when the program is started using the option "-r" in the command line or when a predefined time has passed. The corresponding time period can be defined in the entry "update_days" in the configuration file. In both cases, the class *ProviderUpdate* puts the request for registration into the query queue. When this request is finally processed, an object of type *ProviderRegAbs* is created and the actual registration begins.

The registration can be divided into the following steps:

- The meta data is requested to be sent from the provider.
  For each attribute (e. g. keywords, authors), there will be one file. The number and the order of attributes that are requested to be sent from the provider to the PA can be written into the configuration file as a parameter to be initialized.
- After receiving the meta data, it is translated.
  The files created in the preceding step are read again. The data is translated into the MeDoc protocol and is then stored in smaller files in order not to send one large file to the broker (this might cause problems on the net). The size of the file can be defined in the initialization file.
- Further transformations possibly requested by the MeDoc format.
  According to the initialization file further transformation steps may take place, e. g. stemming of the keywords.
- A connection to the broker is established.
  A message indicating the beginning of the transmission of meta data is sent to the broker. If the broker is already receiving meta data from a different provider agent, the transmission can be postponed up to two hours. Meanwhile a request for the beginning of the transmission is sent to the broker once every ten minutes.
- The files with the meta data are transmitted.
- A message about the successful end of the data transmission is sent to the broker.

4 Interfaces to local reference data bases – Natural language access to relational data bases

4.1 General remarks

Entering user queries using natural language can be seen as a complementary - not a competing - approach to the form based method used in MeDoc (recall that in MeDoc, the user builds his query by filling in certain predefined input fields like "author", "title", etc. in a HTML based form). The natural language communication with information retrieval systems described below allows queries using full sentences ("Which books by Watson on neuronal networks have been published by Springer?") as well as using abbreviated forms like "books on neuronal networks". This approach gives the user the full expressiveness of his native language and simultaneously includes morphological and fully developed linguistic methods in the retrieval process which are superior to stemming algorithms generally used in retrieval methods.

In the previous sections of this paper, the work done in the MeDoc project which opens the access to digital libraries in the internet has been reported. Provider agents play the central role in connecting the user with the information in the internet libraries, by transforming queries represented in the internal MeDoc protocol (a formal language) into retrieval languages stipulated by the provider (e.g. the RPNQuery for Z39.50).

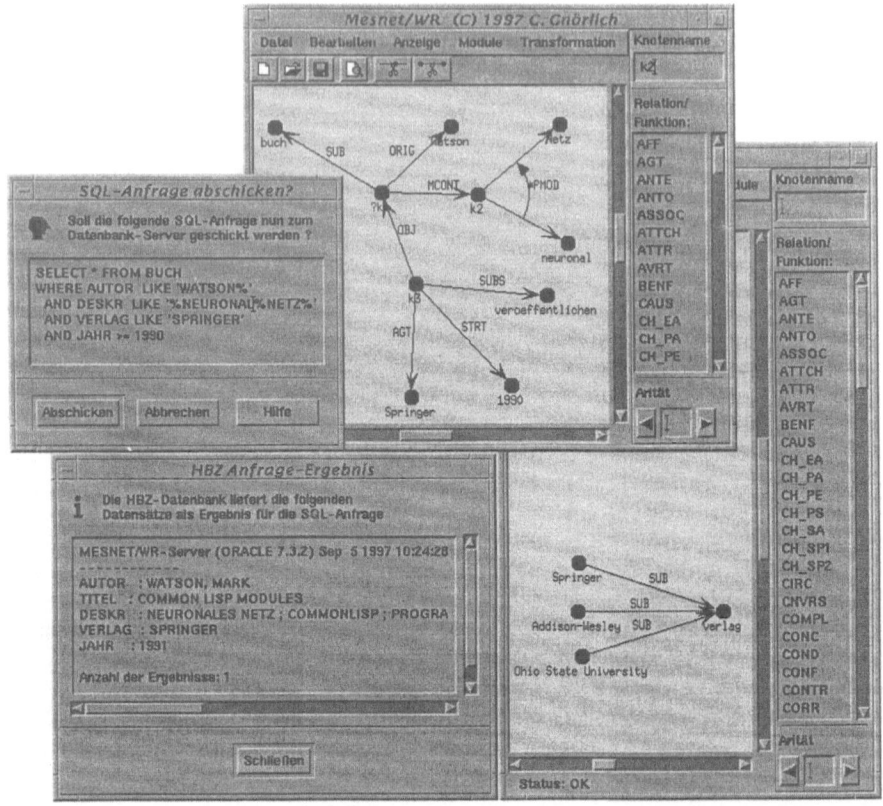

Fig. 7. Screenshot from the MESNET/WR system.

This chapter discusses a similar transformation process, this time starting with a meaning representation of a natural language query based on the MESNET[6] paradigm [9]. In this case, the target data base is a relational data base containing the bibliographic data of all scientific libraries in the Land North-Rhine Westphalia, courtesy of the HBZ Cologne. Here, the user queries are transformed into SQL, which is the standard query language for relational data bases.

It should be a comparatively small step to join these two lines of development and to realize a natural language access to Z39.50 providers as well. For this purpose, an analogous transformation process has to be installed to translate MESNET expressions into the YAZ protocol, the provider agent's front-end to the Z39.50 interface. The following discussion gives a short overview over the transformation of natural language queries, and outlines how natural language processing abilities could be incorporated into the MeDoc system.

---

[6] MESNET – Multilayered Extended Semantic Network

64

4.2   The transformation of meaning representations into SQL

The methods for translating natural language queries into semantic knowledge representations by means of a word-class controlled functional analysis are described in [8], and cannot be discussed here in detail. For the scope of this text, it is sufficient to state that methods exist which will create a MESNET representation from a given natural language query.

Figure 7 shows the result of the analysis for the sentence "Which books about neuronal networks by Watson have been published by Springer since 1980?" (upper window) together with some piece of background knowledge (right window), represented in the system MESNET/WR which provides a general knowledge representation and development platform based on the MESNET paradigm. The two windows on the left side of the screenshot show the corresponding SQL query generated by the transformation, and the search result respectively.

Working on the MESNET representation of the user's query, the transformation component employs a rule-based approach to interpret the user query. Fig. 8 shows the transformation of the meaning representation of the query " Books about programming in Java".

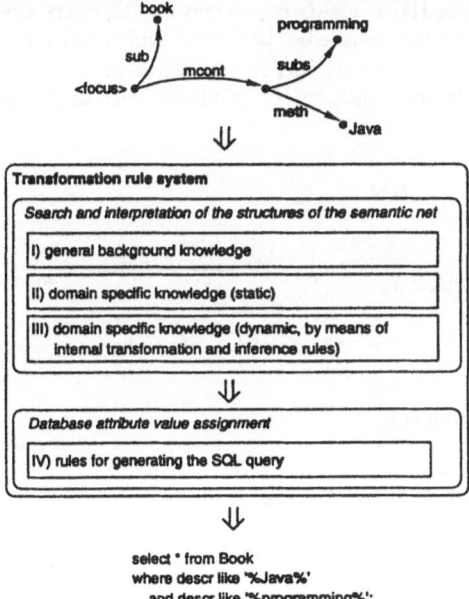

Fig. 8. General structure of the transformation rule system.

The rule system is divided into four stages, which represent different kinds of background and inferential knowledge in the system.

I. General background knowledge

These rules and facts contain background knowledge which is fully independent of the current context of rule application, e.g. by providing rules like

sub('Springer','Publisher')

indicating that "Springer" refers to a publisher.

II. Static domain specific background knowledge

Static domain specific background knowledge does not depend on the actual query context, but it represents a certain bias in the rule system, which might differ from a real-world scenario. E.g., if a certain target data base does not distinguish between books and volumes (both are subsumed under the data base attribute "book"), the following rule will mark both words as synonymous:

```
sub(Obj,'Book') :- sub(Obj,'Volume')
```

This way, a query regarding a "volume" will be correctly transformed into a query containing the data base attribute "book".

Another application of static domain specific background knowledge includes modeling the user's preferences. If the user is known to be a computer scientist, additional rules might be added to interpret the word 'Java' as the name of the programming language, and not the island, if no other disambiguating information is present in the current query.

III. Dynamic domain specific background knowledge

In contrast to rule system II), which typically consists of facts and rules with constant premises, rule system III) is highly dependent on the query context. Type III) rules are intended to augment the knowledge base with additional facts inferred from the query by finding and interpreting certain sub structures in the semantic network. E.g., let a semantic network describe that "N.N." publishes with an entity $k2$ which is a publisher (see fig. 9).

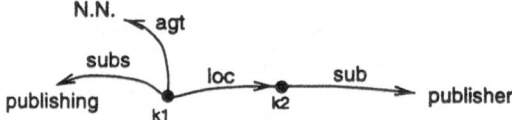

Fig. 9. Inferring the author.

By using the following rule,

```
sub(A,'publisher') :-
  agt(K1,A), subs(K1,'publishing'),
  loc(K1,K2), sub(K2,'publisher').
```

the system infers that "N.N." therefore must be an author, which will eventually guide the system to fill in the "author = N.N." part of the query later.

IV. Generating the SQL query

Generating the resulting SQL query is merely a matter of collecting the results from the previous stages, and assigning the found data base attribute values to the suitable places in the SQL statement. Some additional rules exist containing strategies for resolving conflicts when more than one potential filler has been proposed for a given database attribute.

5 Conclusion and further prospects

Summarizing, the system described above represents a prototype capable of accepting a natural language query, transforming it into an SQL expression, and delivering the results of the SQL query to the user in a tabular form.

A comparison with the MeDoc design shows that a possible integration with the MeDoc system would mostly hinge on introducing enhanced provider agents incorporating the natural language transformation abilities, plus some minor changes in the MeDoc user interface and internal data protocol.

Allowing natural language input would require an extension of MeDoc's user interface, e.g. by adding another form entry labeled "free form entry" for the natural language query. Some additional control logic is required so that the user can either activate the standard query attribute column for form-oriented queries, or the free-form text entry field, since a combination of both query methods does not make sense.

Adapting the transformation rule system to the YAZ protocol seems to be feasible and not too difficult. Basically, rule groups I) to III) which interpret the query will remain unchanged, while rule system IV) which is responsible for assigning values to the database attributes requires some changes. A comparison between the YAZ/Z39.50 database attribute set and the attributes used in the SQL data base reveals a great similarity. Therefore, the main effort in porting the rule system to generate YAZ format queries should consist of retargetting rule system IV) from outputting SQL queries to embedding the database attribute values into YAZ format queries.

Our strategic aim will be to combine these techniques within one system to realize a natural language access to local as well as to distant information resources in the Internet. One important task in that work is to overcome the language barrier and to warrant the multilinguality of the resulting information retrieval system.

References

1. Deutsche Bibliothek.
   (http://www.ddb.de/partner/dbv-osi_II.htm: German version),
   (http://www.ddb.de/partner/dbv-osi_ii_engl.htm: English version). Deutsche Bibliothek, 1997.
2. MAB committee. *MAB - Maschinelles Austauschformat.* Deutsche Bibliothek, Leipzig, Frankfurt, Berlin, 1993.
3. Andreas Barth et al. *The MeDoc Digital Library Project - Its Goals and Major Achievements.* this volume, 1997.
4. Dietrich Boles et al. *The MeDoc System - a Distributed Digital Library Facility.* this volume, 1997.
5. Kai Großjohann and Dirk Menke. *Query Transformation for Heterogeneous Provider Systems in MeDoc.* this volume, 1997.
6. Hermann Helbig. *Künstliche Intelligenz und automatische Wissensverarbeitung.* Verlag Technik GmbH, Berlin, 1996.
7. Hermann Helbig, H. Böttger, F. Ficker, P. String, and F. Zänker. The natural language interface NLI-AIDOS. *Journal of New Generation Computing Systems,* pages 221–246, 1990.
8. Hermann Helbig and Sven Hartrumpf. Word class functions for syntactic-semantic analysis. In *Proceedings of the 2nd International Conference on Recent Advances in Natural Language Processing (RANLP-97),* pages 312-317, Tzigov Chark, Bulgaria, September 1997.
9. Hermann Helbig and Marion Schulz. Knowledge representation with MESNET: A multilayered extended semantic network. In *Proceedings of the AAAI Spring Symposium on Ontological Engineering,* pages 64–72, Stanford, CA, 1997.
10. Brian P. Holt. *UNIMARC Manual.* British Library, London, 1987.
11. Index-Data. YAZ user's guide and reference. Technical report, Index Data, 1997. http://www.indexdata.dk/yaz/yaz.html.
12. Library of Congress. *ANSI/NISO Z39.50-1995 specifies versions 2 and 3 of the Z39.50 protocol.* Z39.50 Maintenance Agency, 1995. http://lcweb.loc.gov/z3950/agency/1995doce.html.
13. Cornell University. *NCSTRL-URL.* Cornell University, 1997. http://www.ncstrl.org/Dienst/htdocs/INfo/faq.html.

Provider Selection — Design and Implementation of the Medoc Broker

M. Dreger[1]
N. Fuhr[2]
K. Großjohann[2]
S. Lohrum[1]

[1] Institute for Computer Science, FU Berlin, Takustr. 9, D-14195 Berlin,
dreger@view.in-berlin.de, lohrum@inf.fu-berlin.de
[2] Institute for Computer Science VI, University of Dortmund, D-44221 Dortmund,
{fuhr,grossjohann}@ls6.cs.uni-dortmund.de

Abstract. One of the objectives of the Medoc system is transparent searching in heterogeneous distributed bibliographic and full text databases (information providers). For a sufficiently large number of information providers an automatic method for provider selection becomes necessary. We take a decision-theoretic approach: we estimate the cost for retrieving n relevant documents from each provider, then choose the combination which minimizes total costs. The main cost factor is the total number of relevant in each database; additional factors are the retrieval quality of the database, the costs for retrieving a document from the database, and the user-specific costs for retrieving a non-relevant or a relevant document, respectively. In this paper, we also describe a first implementation of the approach where each factor is made explicit so that the implementation can easily be adapted for specific situations.

1 Introduction and Motivation

The Medoc project aims at improving the access of Computer Science researchers and professionals to information relevant to Computer Science. This is done by providing them with easy access to heterogeneous, distributed information sources. By "information source" we mean a searchable collection of bibliographic data or fulltext documents that are relevant to Computer Science. In the following, an information source will be called "provider", and search and retrieval in the information is done using a "provider system". (Thus, the "provider system" is hardware plus software, the "provider" is the "provider system" plus the documents themselves.)

To enable users to transparently search these information sources, two functions must be provided. First, the providers appropriate for a given query must be automatically selected. Second, the query must be transparently (to the user) issued to the selected provider systems and the query results must be merged. The first function (provider selection) is the focus of this paper.

There are two alternatives to automatic provider selection. The first alternative is to let the user select the providers. The second is to broadcast the query to all providers. The first alternative does not remain feasible as the number of providers increases. Some providers charge money for processing queries, so the second alternative is not feasible, either.

Therefore, a mechanism for automatic provider selection is needed, which is based on (meta-)data that is automatically extracted from a provider system. (The project does not have the manpower necessary for intellectual extraction of metadata.)

In the following section 2, we will present a general framework for provider selection which is based on an extension of the Probability Ranking Principle. In section 3 we describe a specialization of the general framework. Finally, section 4 contains some considerations that arise when one wants to implement the model described in section 3.

2   General Model for Provider Selection

The Medoc System can be seen as a networked Information Retrieval (IR) system. As opposed to query processing in database systems, where the goal is to satisfy a given query condition, Information Retrieval aims at satisfying the information need of a user. That is, to retrieve those documents that are the most relevant to the user. The Probability Ranking Principle (PRP) [6] provides the theoretical justification for probabilistic IR models. The PRP assumes that retrieving either a nonrelevant or a relevant document incurs a cost for the user, and that the cost for retrieving a relevant document is less than the cost for retrieving a nonrelevant document. From this, it can be shown that in order to minimize total retrieval costs, the next document to retrieve should be the one with the highest probability of relevance amongst the documents not yet retrieved.

The PRP provides a framework only. While it says that the retrieval should be based on (an estimation of) the probability of relevance of the individual documents, it does not say how that estimate should be computed. In order to arrive at an estimate of the probability of relevance of the different documents, it is possible to make different assumptions, leading to different probabilistic IR models which "instantiate" the PRP.

Probabilistic IR models have a number of desirable features:

1. They have a theoretical justification, through the PRP.
2. The result ranking lists are based on (an estimation of) the probability of relevance of the documents.
3. The assumptions are made explicit and can each be tested for validity.

Also, probabilistic IR systems have performed well in tests of retrieval quality. We aim for a model of provider selection which is based on the PRP so that we gain these same advantages.

In order to apply this principle to networked IR, it needs to be generalized. The standard PRP takes the relevance of documents into account (by assigning different costs to relevant than to nonrelevant documents). For the provider selection problem, a number of other factors should be taken into account, too.

- Restrict querying to relatively few providers as opposed to querying all of them, as issuing a query to a provider may cost money in addition to the time spent.
- The cost for retrieving a document from different providers can be different. As an example, this is obvious if providers charge money for each document. But this cost amount could also take into account different response times of different provider systems, and other factors.
- Different provider systems provide different retrieval quality, and that should be taken into account when choosing providers, thus selecting providers with a high quality for a good overall result. The different retrieval quality may have one of several reasons. First, the indexing and/or retrieval algorithms used by the systems may differ (Boolean retrieval produces exceptionally poor results, for instance). Second, the expressiveness of the query language may vary (phrase search can be supported well or not so well, for example). Finally, there may be a mismatch between the schema used for formulating the query and the provider schema.

We deal with the first requirement by assuming that not only retrieving a document from a provider incurs some cost (as is done with the standard PRP), but also that there is a fixed cost for issuing a query to a provider. We deal with the second requirement by allowing the "cost for retrieving a document" parameter to be different for each provider. We deal with the third requirement by explicitly taking (an estimate of) the recall/precision curve of each provider into account.

As explained above, we assume that not only retrieving a document incurs some cost, but also that issuing a query to a provider incurs some cost. Let $C_i^d(s)$ be the cost for retrieving s documents from provider i. This can be expressed as follows:

$$C_i^d(s) = C_i^0 + s \cdot C_i^d ,$$

where C_i^0 is the cost for issuing a query to provider i and C_i^d is the cost for retrieving a document from provider i. As with the normal PRP, we distinguish between the costs for relevant and nonrelevant documents. Let C_i^N be the cost for retrieving a nonrelevant document from provider i and let C_i^R be the cost for retrieving a relevant document. Let r_i be the number of relevant documents retrieved from provider i, let s_i be the total number of documents retrieved from provider i. Clearly,

$$C_i^d(s_i) = C_i^r(r_i) = C_i^0 + r_i \cdot C_i^R + (s_i - r_i) \cdot C_i^N .$$

As in the PRP, the goal is to minimize the total retrieval costs. Given providers $1, \ldots, l$, the total costs $C^r(n)$ for retrieving n relevant documents from all providers are minimized:

$$C^r(n) = \min_r \sum_{i=1}^{l} C_i^r(r_i),$$ (1)

where $r = (r_1, \ldots, r_l)$ gives the number of relevant documents to retrieve from each provider and $r_1 + \cdots + r_l$ must equal n.

As explained above, we deal with the second requirement (that the cost for retrieving a document from different providers can be different) by varying the parameters C_i^R and C_i^N depending on the provider.

The third requirement, to deal with the different retrieval quality of different provider systems, is dealt with using the recall/precision curve of each provider. A measure for the effectiveness of an Information Retrieval system is the recall/precision curve. *Recall* is the ratio of the number of retrieved relevant documents divided by the total number of relevant documents. *Precision* is the ratio of the number of relevant retrieved documents divided by the total number of retrieved documents. One can express precision as a function of recall, giving the recall/precision curve $\mathcal{P}(\mathcal{R})$. Obviously, $s_i = r_i/\mathcal{P}(\mathcal{R}) = r_i/\mathcal{P}(r_i/R_i)$, R_i being the total number of relevant documents in Provider i.

Inserting this value of s_i into equation (1), we get

$$C^r(n) = \min_r \sum_{i=1}^{l} \left(C_i^0 + r_i \cdot C_i^R + \left(\frac{1}{\mathcal{P}_i(r_i/R_i)} - 1 \right) \cdot r_i \cdot C_i^N \right).$$ (2)

3 Specific Model

In order to be able to apply the model described above, two things are needed. First, one needs an algorithm for solving the optimization problem presented in equation 2. Secondly, an estimate of the different parameters of the model is needed. This section describes the algorithm, the parameter choices are described in the next section.

We describe a divide-and-conquer algorithm for computing the overall optimum cost function $C_i^R(n)$. Our algorithm is based on the following assumptions:

1. For each database, the costs per additional relevant document are monotonously increasing (i.e. for all i and all $k > 0$, $C_i^r(k+2) - C_i^r(k+1) \geq C_i^r(k+1) - C_i^r(k)$.
2. We do not consider fractions of (expected) relevant documents for individual databases. (E. g. a document with an expected precision of 0.5 would yield half a relevant document.)

The first assumption is essential for reducing the computational complexity of the algorithm. Without this assumption, it is shown in [2] that our optimizing problem is equivalent to the knapsack problem, and thus it is NP-complete. The second assumption keeps the algorithm simple.

```
TYPE listofdb: LIST OF database;
TYPE costfct = ARRAY[1:maxrel] of cfelem;
{cost function as array with #relevant docs as index}
TYPE cfelem = RECORD cost: integer;
                              gdl: LIST OF reqdoc
            END;
{cost function contains costs and list of document requests}
TYPE reqdoc = RECORD dbn: database;
                              numdocs: integer
            END;
{document request contains database id and # docs}


PROCEDURE costrel(db: database; r: integer; VAR cost, numret: integer);
{gives costs and number of docs to be retrieved for getting r relevant docs from database db,
yields infinity cost if r exceeds total number of relevant docs}


PROCEDURE ocf(S: listofdb; n: integer): costfct;
{computes optimum cost function for list of databases S}
VAR S1, S2: listofdb; C, C1, C2: costfct;
      gd: reqdoc; db: database; i, j1, j2, d1, d2, c12: integer;
BEGIN
C[0].cost := 0; C[0].gdl := empty();
IF length(S) = 1 THEN {single database}
  db = first(S); gd.dbn := db;
  FOR i := 1 TO n DO {compute elements of cost function}
        costrel(db,i,C[i].cost, gd.numdocs);
        C[i].gdl := insert(empty(),gd);
  OD
ELSE {>1 databases → divide and conquer}
  divide: split(S,S1,S2);
  conquer: C1 := ocf(S1,n); C2 := ocf(S2,n);
  merge: {merge cost functions}
  j1:= 0; j2 := 0; d1 := 0; d2 := 0;
  FOR i := 1 TO n DO
        IF d1 < d2 {determine point of equal cost difference}
        THEN j1 := j1+1; d1 := C1[j1+1].cost-C1[j1].cost;
        ELSE j2 := j2+1; d2 := C2[j2+1].cost-C2[j2].cost FI;
        c12 := C1[j1].cost+C2[j2].cost;
        IF c12 < C1[i].cost AND c12 < C2[i].cost
        THEN C[i].cost := c12; C[i].gdl := concat(C1[j1].gdl,C2[j2].gdl)
        ELSIF C1[i].cost < C2[i].cost THEN C[i] := C1[i]
        ELSE C[i] := C2[i] FI;
  OD;
FI;
RETURN(C);
END.
```

Fig. 1. Algorithm for computing optimum cost function

The algorithm is shown in figure 1. Here the procedure costrel gives us the database-specific costs $C_i^r(n)$ for retrieving n relevant documents from privder i. The overall optimum cost function is computed in procedure ocf. Given a list S of providers and a maximum number n of relevant documents to be retrieved, this procedure returns a data structure giving the vectors r and the costs $C_i^r(k)$ for $k = 1, \ldots, n$. The crucial point in this procedure is the merge step of the divide-and-conquer strategy: when we merge two cost functions C1 and C2, for each number of relevant documents, we test whether a single function or the combination of both C1 and C2 is cheapest. Here we exploit the fact that the cost differentials are monotonously increasing and that in case both arguments contribute to the optimum solution, the cost differentials must be equal. Since we have discrete cost functions, we consider the discrete cost differences d1 and d2 instead of the differentials and assume that at each point, the differentials lie between the corresponding two subsequent differences. An example for the application of this algorithm is shown in figure 2.

For retrieving n relevant documents from l providers, this algorithm takes $O(n \cdot l)$ time.

n	C1 cost	gdl	C2 cost	gdl	C cost	gdl
0	0	$\langle\rangle$	0	$\langle\rangle$	0	$\langle\rangle$
1	4	$\langle(2,1)\rangle$	5	$\langle(1,2)\rangle$	4	$\langle(2,1)\rangle$
2	7	$\langle(4,1)\rangle$	6	$\langle(3,2)\rangle$	6	$\langle(3,2)\rangle$
3	10	$\langle(6,1)\rangle$	8	$\langle(7,2)\rangle$	8	$\langle(7,2)\rangle$
4	13	$\langle(8,1)\rangle$	11	$\langle(13,2)\rangle$	11	$\langle(13,2)\rangle$
5	16	$\langle(10,1)\rangle$	15	$\langle(21,2)\rangle$	15	$\langle(21,2)\rangle$
6	19	$\langle(12,1)\rangle$	20	$\langle(31,2)\rangle$	18	$\langle(4,1),(13,2)\rangle$
7	22	$\langle(14,1)\rangle$	26	$\langle(43,2)\rangle$	21	$\langle(6,1),(13,2)\rangle$

Fig. 2. Example for computing optimum costs of two providers

As mentioned above, we have not considered that a provider also may yield fractions of (expected) relevant documents, which also could contribute to the requested sum of relevant documents (e.g. $r_1 = 1.4$ and $r_2 = 2.6$ for $n = 4$). Thus, our algorithm only yields an approximation of the optimum solution. An algorithm for computing the optimum should not restrict to integer values for the number of relevant documents r_i from each provider. The correct restriction would be to assume integer values for the number of documents selected, from which the corresponding fractions of relevant documents are derived. However, this approach affects the complexity of the merge step (which is now n), where all possible intermediate points between i and $i+1$ would have to be computed. In the worst case where we would have to retrieve (almost) all documents of a provider i in order to find the last relevant one, there would be an intermediate point for each document in the provider. Since different providers may yield different intermediate points, we would have to compute up to $N = \sum_{i=1}^{l} |D_i|$ points ($|D_i|$: number of documents in provider i). Thus, the the corresponding algorithm would take $O(N \cdot l)$ in the worst case. The corresponding algorithm is described in [2], along with a modified version which restricts the number of intermediate points between i and $i + 1$ to a given constant c by dropping additional points. Thus, the algorithm presented here corresponds to $c = 1$, whereas the correct optimum is computed with $c = \infty$.

4 Implementation Considerations

When we thought about implementing the database selection model, we knew that we would not have much time for experiments to find out specific parameters that would maximize the quality of the suggestions of the broker. Therefore, we tried to make all factors explicit, then restrict ourselves to a simple implementation in the project. This way, our work is not lost but can be improved on by future experiments which find better values for the parameters.

Given the cost model described in section 2 the following parameters need to be estimated: the number of relevant documents, the recall/precision curve, the costs for retrieving a relevant document from a provider (C_i^{R}), the costs for retrieving a nonrelevant document from a provider (C_i^{N}) and the costs for processing a query at a provider. The first parameter, the number of relevant documents, is described in the following subsection, the description of the other parameters is in subsection 4.2.

4.1 Estimation of Number of Relevant Documents

The goal here is to calculate $E(R)$, the estimated number of relevant documents, for which the following holds:

$$E(R) = \sum_{d \in D} \Pr(R \mid d, q)$$

$\Pr(R \mid d, q)$ can be interpreted as $\Pr(R \mid d \to q) \cdot \Pr(d \to q)$. (See [5] for a justification.) Plugging this into the above equation and factoring out we get

$$E(R) = \Pr(R \mid d \to q) \cdot \sum_{d \in D} \Pr(d \to q)$$

Thus, the estimation of the number of relevant documents in a provider takes place in two steps. In the first step, we estimate the number of documents found ($\sum_{d \in D} \Pr(d \to q)$), in the second step we estimate the probability of relevance of the documents thus found ($\Pr(R \mid d \to q)$).

Because of the impossibility of comparing retrieval status values from different providers[1] we assume binary indexing for all providers.

---

[1] Unless all providers use a probabilistic IR engine, of course; then the retrieval status values are (estimates of) the probability of relevance of the documents.

Let us discuss simple queries first. A simple query is a query of the form (CONTAINS *attribute-name* "*value*") (the other comparison operators are treated similarly). We assume that, for each term and each field and each provider, the Broker stores the number of documents where the term occurs. Therefore, the number of documents found can be directly read from the Broker database.

For easier explanation, in the following we will assume that there is only one field. With this assumption, a simple query consists of just a term t_j.

For a simple query t_j, the estimate of the number of documents found is simply f_j, the number of documents that contain the term, and it is read from the metadata stored in the Broker.

The next question is what is the estimate w_j of the probability of relevance of the documents thus found. Our estimate is based on the global inverse document frequency. Let N be total number of documents in all providers. The global inverse document frequency, then, is $\log(N/f_j)$. We normalize this number so that it is never greater than 1:

$$w_j := \text{normalize}\left(\log\left(\frac{N}{f_j}\right)\right)$$

For normalization, we could declare w_j to be 1 for those terms that occur in exactly one document in all the providers. Another plausible choice would be to use 1 for those terms that occur in exactly one document in the largest provider. In the current implementation, the former alternative is used.

After discussing the simple queries, let us come to the conjunctive queries. This is a query of the form $q = t_1 \wedge t_2$ (without loss of generality we assume binary connectives in this presentation, the implementation does not have such a restriction). Let f_1 and f_2 be (the estimates of) the numbers of documents found for the queries t_1 and t_2, respectively. Assuming that the occurrence of the terms t_1 and t_2 in the same document is stochastically independent, we arrive at the following estimate for the number of documents found for the query q:

$$f^{\text{indep}} := \frac{f_1}{N} \cdot \frac{f_2}{N} \cdot N = \frac{f_1 f_2}{N}$$

Assuming a maximum correlation between the occurrences of t_1 and t_2, we arrive at the following estimate:

$$f^{\text{max}} := \min(f_1, f_2)$$

The independence assumption has been used with success in probabilistic IR systems. However, it was then applied to the occurrence of any two terms in a document. Here, the situation is slightly different. As an example, consider a user formulating a query specifying both the author (say, Norbert Fuhr) and a title word (say, "probabilistic"). It is plausible to presume that, most of the time, there will be a correlation between the two query conditions in the sense that the given author is more likely to write about that subject than most other authors. After all, the user wouldn't use these two together in a query if there was no reason to assume that this author has written about the indicated subject. On the other hand, clearly the maximum correlation scenario is at least as unlikely as the independence scenario. Therefore, a middle ground must be achieved.

We do this by defining a parameter p_r and defining

$$f := p_r (f^{\max} - f^{\text{indep}}) + f^{\text{indep}} \ .$$

The next step is to estimate the probability of relevance of a document thus found. We choose the following estimate:

$$w := w_1 + w_2$$

This is reasonable because $w_1 = \Pr(\text{rel} \mid t_1)$ and $w = \Pr(\text{rel} \mid t_1 \wedge t_2)$. Just extending this from two terms to many more makes this clear: if a document contains t_1 and t_2 and ... and t_{20} it is almost certain that this document is relevant, i. e. its probability of relevance is near 1 and thus $w \approx 1$. The formula given above does this.

Let us now come to the disjunctive queries. The query language contains a *weighted sum* operator. This means queries of the form $q = t_1 \ _{\alpha_1} + _{\alpha_2} \ t_2$. Again, we distinguish between a maximum correlation scenario and an independent scenario. With maximum correlation, we get

$$f^{\max} := \max(f_1, f_2) \ ,$$

with independence, we get

$$f^{\text{indep}} := f_1 + f_2 - \frac{f_1 f_2}{N} \ .$$

For the estimate of the probability of relevance of the documents thus found we get

$$w := \frac{\alpha_1 f_1 w_1 + \alpha_2 f_2 w_2}{f}$$

where f is defined depending on p_r as in the conjunctive case.

Using the definitions above, the whole query can be processed in a bottom-up fashion. When that is done, we estimate the number of relevant documents as the number of documents found (f) times their probability of relevance (w).

Please note that this procedure for estimating the number of relevant documents in each provider differs from the one shown in [1]. The procedure shown there does not deal with term weighting, and it is restricted to linear queries. The rest of the provider selection mechanism, however, is used unmodified, as described in said article.

The mechanism for estimating the number of relevant documents described above leads to two more parameters that have to be chosen.

Relative correlation for AND. This parameter reflects the fact that two conditions joined with AND cannot be expected to be stochastically independent. Nor can they be expected to maximally correlate. Instead, a middle ground has to be achieved. We do not know the value of this parameter (we just assume it to be 0.2). Nevertheless, introducing such a parameter makes the assumption explicit so that we know what to do if we want to improve the effectiveness of the broker algorithm. In the description above, this parameter was called p_r.

Relative correlation for WSUM. This is similar to the parameter described above, but applies to weighted sum queries. We chose 0.8 in this case.

4.2 Other parameters

Recall/precision curve. Nothing was known about the retrieval effectiveness of the provider systems connected to the Medoc system. We did not have time during the project for empirical investigations in this regard. Also, we did not have time to gather empirical data indicating how much retrieval effectiveness degraded when there were mismatches between the schema used in the query and the schemata used by the providers. Therefore, we chose the same value for all provider systems as a crude approximation, though ideally, the curve should vary according to the provider system and according to the actual query:

$$\mathcal{P}_i(\mathcal{R}) := 1 - \mathcal{R}$$

Costs for processing a query at a provider. This includes
1. the money charged by the provider for issuing a query,
2. the time needed to contact the provider, and
3. the time needed for the provider system to process the query.

The exact value of this parameter does not matter; only the relation between the different cost parameters is important. None of the providers connected to the Medoc system charge money for processing a query. We did not have any information about the time needed for the querying, therefore we assumed:

$$C_i^0 := 1$$

Costs for retrieving a relevant document. This parameter includes
1. the knowledge benefit to be gained by reading the document,
2. the time spent in reading the document, and
3. the money needed for the purchase of the document.

At the time of the implementation, nothing was known about the price of documents. Therefore, that part of this cost parameter was assumed to be zero. It is plausible that the knowledge benefit and the time spent cancel each other out. Therefore, we chose:

$$C_i^R := 0$$

Costs for retrieving a nonrelevant document. This parameter includes
1. the time spent in reading the document,

2. the money needed for the purchase of the document, and

3. the user's disappointment of having read a useless document.

We did not take into account the latter parameter. We also did not take into account the money needed, as nothing was known about the pricing structure of the providers at the time of the implementation. Because the parameter C_i^0 did not take into account the financial aspect, either, we had to choose whether the time spent for processing a query is more important than the time wasted in reading nonrelevant documents. We decided that the time spent reading was to be weighed higher than the time spent waiting for the query processing. It is not at all clear that a nonrelevant document from one provider should incur more (or less) cost than a nonrelevant document from another provider, with respect to the time spent reading it. Thus, we chose the same value for all providers:

$$C_i^N := 2$$

5   Related Work

The databases group at Stanford has developed GlOSS [3, 4] which also automatically selects providers according to a user's query. There, a "goodness" parameter is calculated for each provider and all providers are ranked according to this parameter. The user may then issue the query to any of the providers mentioned. GlOSS does not deal with structured data, however (documents are presumed to be a sequence of terms only), and it does not provide for querying the selected providers automatically. The goodness parameter computed for each provider is based on the contents of the provider, not on an estimation of its retrieval quality nor on costs for issuing a query or requesting a document from the provider. Whereas our method directly refers to the user satisfaction (relevance), the GlOSS method only refers to fulfillment of the query.

6   Conclusion

We have presented a mechanism for automatic provider selection which works, though it leaves room for improvement. The mechanism is based on a theoretical approach which makes all parameters explicit; though we had to use crude approximations to many of these parameters during the project, this approach is a good basis for further investigation and improvement.

In addition to the problem of estimating the parameters well, there are additional issues of a more practical nature pertaining to the deployment of the provider selection mechanism.

Index size. Preliminary experiments have shown that the metadata stored by the Broker (basically, the number of documents that contain a given term) is about half as large as the index data of the connected providers themselves. This opens questions of scalability. We do not have certain results yet but we assume that we can reduce the size of the metadata substantially.

Heterogeneity of Providers. In principle the approach described above can deal with heterogeneous provider schemata (both with respect to the data stored and with respect to the query operators provided). The validity of the approach has not been tested, though.

Miscellaneous Problems. In some cases, we have to deal with problems very specific to the software systems and environment that is actually used. While these problems are important for deployment of such systems, they can't be planned for in a general framework, they must be dealt with as they occur.

References

1. Fuhr, N. Optimum Database Selection in Networked IR. In Callan, J. and Fuhr, N., editors, *NIR'96. Proceedings of the SIGIR'96 Workshop on Networked Information Retrieval*, 1996. http://SunSite.Informatik.RWTH-Aachen.DE/Publications/CEUR-WS/Vol-7/.
2. Gövert, N. Datenbankselektion in vernetzten Information-Retrieval-Systemen. Diplomarbeit, Universität Dortmund, Fachbereich Informatik, April 1997. (http://ls6-www.cs.uni-dortmund.de/~goevert/diploma/).
3. Gravano, L., Garcia-Molina, H., and Tomasic, A. The Effectiveness of GlOSS for the Text Database Discovery Problem. In Snodgrass, R. T. and M., W., editors, *Proceedings of the 1994 ACM SIGMOD. International Conference on Management of Data.*, pages 126–137, New York, 1994. ACM.
4. Gravano, L. and a Molina, H. G. Generalizing GlOSS to Vector-Space Databases and Broker Hierarchies. In *Proceedings of the 21st VLDB Conference*, 1995.
5. Nie, J. An Outline of a General Model for Information Retrieval Systems. In Chiaramella, Y., editor, *11th International Conference on Research & Development in Information Retrieval*, pages 495–506, Grenoble, France, June 1988. Presses Universitaires de Grenoble.
6. Robertson, S. The Probability Ranking Principle in IR. *Journal of Documentation*, 33:294–304, 1977.

Query Transformation for Heterogeneous Provider Systems in Medoc

K. Großjohann[1] and D. Menke[2]

[1] Institute for Computer Science VI, University of Dortmund, D-44221 Dortmund,
grossjohann@ls6.cs.uni-dortmund.de
[2] Institute for Computer Science VII, FernUniversity Hagen, D-58084 Hagen,
dirk.menke@fernuni-hagen.de

Abstract. One of the objectives of the MeDoc system is the possibility of querying distributed heterogeneous provider systems. This paper describes how the MeDoc system deals with this heterogeneity. We take an approach of multiple layers. The users formulate their queries with respect to the global schema which is then transformed into the conceptual schema, then further into the physical schema, and finally into the protocol of the provider system. This transformation process does not require equivalent schemata of the connected provider systems, a best-match approach is chosen instead, so as not to unecessarily restrict the information sources that can be added to the system.

1   Introduction and Motivation

The Medoc project aims at improving the access of Computer Science professionals to information relevant to their work. To do this, the Medoc system has been implemented which enables transparent access to distributed, heterogeneous information sources on the Internet. We assume that these information sources are fulltext or bibliographic databases ("providers"), and transparent access means automatically selecting the right database for a query and transparently querying all selected databases. To facilitate this, the user should be able to input one query which is valid for all providers, and the system should take care of automatically transforming the query into the form suitable for each provider.

In order to keep the process of query transformation sufficiently modular, we distinguish between different layers and transform the query step by step from one layer to the next.

In the following section, we describe the query language to be used in the Medoc project. We then go on to describe the approach for the query transformation. We distinguish between different levels of abstraction from the idiosyncrasies of each provider system. After a short overview of these levels in section 2.1, each level is described in detail in a separate section, starting with the most provider-specific and finishing with the least provider-specific level. Together with each level, we describe how to transform a query from it to the next more provider-specific level. Section 3 deals with the implementation of the transformation steps between the levels. The paper finishes with a short section giving an outlook on future work.

1.1 Related Work

In [3], a different approach to a similar problem is presented. The authors deal with Boolean systems only. For each provider system, they generate a query which is equivalent to or more general than the original user query and thus retrieve more documents than should be found. There is an additional filtering step when integrating the results. The whole system works with bibliographic data only, not including the full text of the documents.

The approach presented in [3] is not appropriate for our context because we expect that provider systems may request money for queries and for documents. Our system could benefit from a post-processing approach as taken by Chang, however; for us, this would translate to a re-ranking of the results. It is not clear, however, how to do that if the query refers to the full text of the documents but the results presented by the provider systems contain bibliographic data only.

In addition to this, there is a great number of works about schema integration, schema transformation, and schema equivalence by the federated databases community. There, the emphasis is on equivalence of schemata in order to allow updates and the like, whereas we need to deal with schemata that are not equivalent.

2 Query Language

For the design of the Medoc query language we focused on the features required by searching bibliographic and fulltext databases. An informal survey of some bibliographic databases accessible via the Internet showed that the schema used is based on BibTeX [8, 6]. Also, consider that the schema is important mainly for formulating queries. Thus, BibTeX seems to be a reasonable basis because it is powerful enough for queries yet not so unwieldy as to confuse potential users.

These databases usually use a fairly simple data model where a database consists of a set of documents and a document consists of a set of fields. Fields may be multi-valued (such as the list of keywords of a document). Most fields are textual, but there are numerical fields as well (viz. publication year). In addition, documents can have different types (journal, journal article, proceedings volume, article in proceedings, and so on), and they can be classified (in the field of computer science the ACM Computing Classification System [1] makes sense). For this, we introduce two fields "object (or document) type" and "classification". These fields are different from both the textual and the numeric fields. They can assume one of a predefined set of values.

Therefore, we support a number of fields from BibTeX, as well as a few extra fields resulting from the fact that we store fulltext documents in addition to bibliographic data and from the additional information we want to store. The following fields are supported by the Medoc query language:

Author, booktitle, editor, institution, journal, keywords, organization, publisher, school, series, title, year (all from BibTeX); objecttype (modeled in BibTeX as separate object types); classifications (according to the ACM Computing Classification System); and fulltext (for fulltext documents).

For each kind of field, the usual operators are defined. Textual fields support a **CONTAINS** operator which allows for searching for the occurrence of a term in a field (including linguistic operations such as stemming, where appropriate). The numeric field supports the usual **LE**, **EQ** and **GE** operators. The two special fields **objecttype** and **classifications** allow for searching for a match using the **MATCH** operator.

Conditions on fields can be combined with the **AND** and **WSUM** operators. The meaning of **AND** should be clear, but **WSUM** perhaps deserves some attention. Some of the databases can be expected to be equipped with Boolean retrieval systems whereas others might provide a ranking facility. We use **WSUM** for the latter type of system, but this operator can also be used for Boolean systems, substituting the "or" operator.

In principle, all combinations of the conditions on fields with **AND** and **WSUM** are possible, but the implementation is restricted to trees of height two. Please refer to Fig. 1 for a summary of the query syntax.

querycond	::=	*term*
term	::=	*factor* | *and-term* | *all-term* | *wsum-term*
and-term	::=	(AND *querycond querycond$^+$*)
all-term	::=	(ALL *querycond querycond$^+$*)
wsum-term	::=	(WSUM *wfactor$^+$*)
factor	::=	(*comp-op field value*)
wfactor	::=	*weightfactor*
comp-op	::=	*num-comp-op* | *text-comp-op* | *gen-comp-op*
num-comp-op	::=	EQ | GE | LE
text-comp-op	::=	CONTAINS
gen-comp-op	::=	MATCH
field	::=	(attribute name)
value	::=	(attribute value, must match the data type)
weight	::=	(floating point number w, $0 < w \leq 1$)

Fig. 1. Query language syntax

2.1 Overview of Layers

For query transformation, we use an approach based on layers as known from federated database systems. There, users see a view of the database based on the *global*, or *external*, schema. The *conceptual* schema contains the semantic operators and the attributes stored in the database. The *physical* schema contains the physical operators used by the database system to implement the semantic operations from the conceptual schema. We add an additional layer, the *protocol* layer, for improved modularity.

2.2 Global Schema

Users interact with the system based on the global, or external, schema. It contains semantic operators and all available attributes and is thus provider independent. The conceptual schema contains only those attributes actually available in the given provider system. The global schema contains all attributes available in at least one provider system. For the transformation from the global schema to a conceptual schema, attributes are replaced based on semantic similarity. This semantic similarity is expressed using an *attribute hierarchy* (see Fig. 2 for an example). Such an attribute hierarchy is a tree where the nodes are attribute names. This tree specifies a specialization/generalization relationship. The root of the tree is the most general attribute of all, the leaves of the tree are the most special attributes.

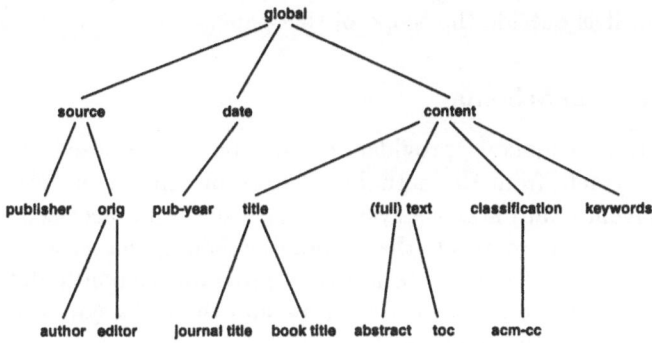

Fig. 2. Example attribute hierarchy (excerpt)

Transforming a query from the global schema to a conceptual schema now works as follows. Each factor of the query is considered one at a time. If the attribute specified in the query is also present in the conceptual schema, nothing needs to be done. If the attribute specified is not present, we search for attributes that are more special and substitute a disjunction. I. e. if the query specifies attribute a but the conceptual schema only contains attributes b and c, both of which are specializations of a, then the query is rewritten to contain a disjunction, $b \vee c$. If the search for more special attributes is not successful, more general attributes are searched for. I. e. if the query contains attribute a but the provider only knows attribute g which is a generalization of a, then the query is rewritten to search for g.

In the latter case, where an attribute is replaced with a more general one, there is one additional problem. Namely, not all documents that will be found can be expected to be relevant to the original query, because the rewritten query is more general. We have implemented a very simple-minded approach to this by restricting the number of generalization steps in the hierarchy (possibly to zero). There is a need to work on more comprehensive solutions.

An earlier implementation of this kind of transformation (albeit restricted to freeWAIS-sf databases) is described in [7].

Such a straightforward substitution of one attribute with another is not appropriate for all cases, however. As an example, consider a user specifying an ACM Computing Classification in the user's query, and a provider which does not know about this attribute. If this provider knows about the **keywords** attribute, it makes sense to substitute the query for a certain ACM classification with a query for suitable keywords.

For the general case, we associate each attribute with a data type. The **keywords** attribute conveniently has the data type "content-text", the **acm-cc** attribute has "classification-ACM". For transforming from one data type to another, then, we invoke a specific procedure. In the example described above, there would be a procedure for the transformation from classification-ACM to content-text. It is a separate problem how to find the right keywords for each classification, it is outside the scope of this paper.

2.3   Conceptual Schema

The conceptual schema is provider-specific, but as opposed to the physical schema it abstracts from the actual operators present in the provider system. Whereas conventional database systems can usually be accessed based on the conceptual (to be more exact, the external) schema, this is not true for most information retrieval systems. Rather than providing semantic data types, they require users to choose the right data type and the right syntactic operator for the semantic operation aimed at.

Let us illustrate these issues with an example. Consider the data type *proper name*. Users wish to be able to specify searches for the last name, the first name, or an initial, and the search specification should not depend on the data representation used by any given provider system. An additional operation that should be supported is phonetic similarity search. Users wish the system to abstract from the specific procedures that are implemented in the system to implement the operators, and they wish the system to abstract from the specific data representation used.

It is possible to represent the name "John Smith" like this, or as "Smith, John", or even "Smith, J." or "J. Smith". It is the job of the transformation from the conceptual to the physical schema to rewrite the query such that the right representation for each provider system is used.

As to the operators, the operation phonetic similarity search can be implemented directly using the Soundex or Phonix algorithms, or it can be approximated by using a string similarity algorithm based on the Damerau-Levenstein metric or on n-gram similarity. It is the job of the transformation from the conceptual to the physical schema to choose the right procedure for each provider system.

As a second example, consider the data type *natural language text*. Users wish to be able to specify searches for words without having to know the grammatical context where the word is used, i. e. they wish to search for stems. Stemming can be supported directly, using the Porter algorithm or a lexicographical method, or it might need to be approximated using wildcard and truncation operators. Another query operation that needs to be supported is phrase search. If the system does not offer a direct support using some linguistic method (e. g. parts of speech taggers), it needs to be approximated using proximity operators, for example.

For the implementation of this transformation from the conceptual to the physical schema, two different methods can be used. The simpler method consists basically of query rewriting, such as substituting "Smith, J." for "John Smith", or substituting the Soundex operator for the phonetic similarity operator. The more complex method, we call it "simulation", consists of implementing functionality that is missing from the provider system itself in the Provider Agent. It can be applied to the stemming operation, for provider systems which do not support stemming themselves. Given that the Provider Agent has a list of words that occur in the data base of the provider, it can compute the stem of each of the words itself. A query for a stem is then rewritten into a disjunction of all the words with the given stem.

2.4 Physical Schema

The physical schema abstracts from the actual syntax used for issuing queries to the system. Queries with respect to the physical schema basically "look like" those in the query language described in section 2, except that the operators and attributes might of course differ from those defined there.

The physical schema is provider-specific. It comprises those attributes that actually appear in the given provider, as well as those operators that actually appear there.

Please refer to section 3 for information on the implementation of the transformation from the physical schema to the protocol.

2.5 Protocol Layer

Each provider system to be connected must be accessible from the outside. Of course, each system uses its own protocol. We separate the protocol layer from all the other layers in order to achieve better software reuse. Two provider systems using the same protocol can use the same module, regardless of all the other differences the two systems might have.

One example of such a protocol is Z39.50 [2], an ISO protocol. Libraries are beginning to replace their proprietary OPAC systems with ones based on Z39.50, or to equip their existing OPAC systems with Z39.50 gateways.

Another example is SQL. The Ariadne system [4] developed within the Medoc project uses an SQL database for data storage.

Quite a few databases already have Web interfaces, often using CGI scripts. In particular, freeWAIS-sf databases can easily be equipped with a Web interface by using SFgate. (See [9] for more information about freeWAIS-sf and SFgate.) We have written a module for this special Web interface.

3 Implementation

When users issue queries to the system with respect to the global schema, several transformation steps are required to be able to process the query at a particular provider system. Namely, transformation from the global to the conceptual schema, from the conceptual to the physical, and from the physical schema to the protocol. For the former two transformation steps, we take a rule-based approach; for the latter step we rely on the inheritance feature provided by Java.

3.1 Rule-based transformation

For the transformation from the global to the conceptual schema, it might be nice to have a mechanism that automatically traverses a given attribute hierarchy (see Fig. 2) and transforms the query as specified by that hierarchy. For easier implementation, we adopted a different approach, which is at the same time more flexible. This flexibility allows us to use the same approach for the transformation from the conceptual to the physical schema.

A transformation step for a given provider is controlled by a configuration file which contains rules. There are two kinds of rules; the first kind applies to factors, the second kind to terms that are not factors (see 2 for an explanation of "term" and "factor").

Let us discuss factor rules first. A factor rule is composed of a left-hand side and a right-hand side, separated by an equals sign, as follows:

$$factor\text{-}rule ::= comp\text{-}op \:/\: field = func\text{-}name(\,,arg)^*$$

Factors are triples, consisting of an operator, an attribute name, and a comparison value. Thus, the left-hand side of such a rule specifies a number of factors that the rule applies to. (The *field* part of a left-hand side may also be equal to * which matches all attribute names.) The right-hand side of a rule specifies a Java function to call for transformation, and an optional list of arguments to pass to the Java function.

The other rules (for terms that are not factors) are similar to the factor rules, but the left-hand side is different:

$$term\text{-}rule ::= factor\text{-}rule \:|\: nf\text{-}op = func\text{-}name(\,,arg)^*$$

where $nf\text{-}op ::= \text{AND} \:|\: \text{ALL} \:|\: \text{WSUM}$.

Rules are applied according to the following algorithm. The input of this algorithm is a query condition, in its tree representation. The root of the tree is then matched against all of the rules. If a rule matches, the function specified by it is called with the parameters given in the configuration file, in addition to the query condition itself. If the query condition is not a factor, the function will usually first apply the algorithm recursively to its children, then combine the thus transformed children according to some rule.

A number of prewritten functions exist to be used in configuration files. The transformations supported are:

- the identity (do-nothing) transformation,
- the removal of a subtree from the query condition,
- the rewriting of proper names (first name first, last name first, or last name plus initial),
- simulation of stemming,
- replacement of AND by WSUM,
- substitution of one attribute name by another, and
- substitution of one attribute name by the disjunction (WSUM) of several attribute names.

The latter two kinds of transformations are used for the transformation from the global to the conceptual schema.

Other kinds of transformations can be added by writing new Java classes. No modification nor recompilation of existing source code is necessary, but the newly written classes have to implement two methods. The first of them, setParms(), is called with the list of (comma-separated) strings given in the configuration file; thus, the transformation process can be customized for each instance of the Provider Agent. The second method does the transformation itself.

3.2 Transformation into Protocol

For the transformation from the physical schema into the protocol, a generic mechanism, such as the rule-based transformation described above, cannot be used because the code needed to access the provider system differs widely. Therefore, we rely on the inheritance mechanism provided by Java for this transformation step.

There is a framework for Provider Agents. In the framework, the transformation from the global to the conceptual schema and the transformation from the conceptual to the physical schema are already implemented, one only needs to provide the right configuration files. For the transformation from the physical schema into the protocol and for acutally connecting the underlying provider system (including authentification, for instance), as well as for transforming the results into the MeDoc format, the framework is not developed as well. It only provides "hooks" where the functions needed for new provider systems can be added. In part, this lack of a more general structure comes from the fact that there is no similarity between different systems which can easily be exploited: an SQL database is accessed in an entirely different way than a Z39.50 database which in turn is accessed differently than a freeWAIS-sf/SFgate database. But in part, this lack of structure comes from the fact that we did not have time to "do it right". Mostly, this is true for the conversion of the results into the MeDoc format.

4 Outlook

As can be seen above, we have devised a mechanism for query transformation which is rather flexible and can accomodate quite a large number of uses. Essentially, it is a framework for fitting in any rule that might be needed for transforming the queries.

It does not adequately implement the idea for attribute matching, though. It would be nice if there was a mechanism which just needed the attribute hierarchy as a parameter and which would automatically substitute attributes as appropriate, following the specialization and generalization hierarchy.

We have not implemented a mechanism for dealing with the problem of transforming queries into ones with attributes that are more general than the original query. Some ideas on this problem can be found in [5].

References

1. ACM Computing Classification System. Online unter der URL http://www.acm.org/class/, 1991.
2. ANSI. Information retrieval (z39.50): Application service definition and protocol specification (ansi/niso z39.50-1995). Technical report, NISO Press, Bethesda, MD, 1995.
3. Chang, C., Garcia-Molina, H., and Paepcke, A. Boolean query mapping across heterogeneous information sources. In *IEEE Transactions on Knowledge and Data Engineering*, August 1996.
4. Dreger, M., Lohrum, S., Schweppe, H., and Ziegler, C. D. Ariadne, an interactive navigation and search system for computer science information in the world-wide web. In *Digital Libraries in Computer Science: The MeDoc Approach*, Lecture Notes on Computer Science. Springer-Verlag, Heidelberg, 1997.
5. Fuhr, N. Object-oriented and database concepts for the design of networked information retrieval systems. In Barker, K. and Özsu, M., editors, *Proceedings of the Fifth International Conference on Information and Knowledge Management*, pages 164–172, 1996.
6. Goossens, M., Mittelbach, F., and Samarin, A. *The LATEX Companion*. Addison-Wesley, 1994.
7. Gövert, N. Information Retrieval in vernetzten heterogenen Datenbanken. In Krause, J., Herfurth, M., and Marx, J., editors, *Herausforderungen an die Informationswirtschaft. Informationsverdichtung, Informationsbewertung und Datenvisualisierung. Proceedings des 5. Internationalen Symposiums für Informationswissenschaft (ISI'96)*, volume 27 of *Schriften zur Informationswissenschaft*, pages 133–142, Konstanz, 1996. Universitätsverlag Konstanz. (http://ls6-www.cs.uni-dortmund.de/~goevert/ISI96/).
8. Lamport, L. *LATEX—A Document Preparation System*. Addison-Wesley, 1994.
9. Pfeifer, U., Fuhr, N., and Huynh, T. Searching structured documents with the enhanced retrieval functionality of freewais-sf and sfgate. In D. Kroemker, editor, *Computer Networks and ISDN Systems; Proceedings of the third International World-Wide Web Conference*, pages 1027–1036, Amsterdam - Lausanne - New York - Oxford - Shannon - Tokyo, April 1995. Elsevier.

The MeDoc Communication Protocol

Markus Dreger[1], Stefan Lohrum[1], and Peter Müller[2]

[1] Institut für Informatik
Freie Universität Berlin
Takustr. 9
D-14195 Berlin
[2] Konrad-Zuse-Zentrum für
Informationstechnik Berlin (ZIB)
Takustr. 7
D-14195 Berlin

Abstract. This article describes the communication within the MeDoc
System, which can be divided into two major parts: two-staged query
processing and MeDoc fulltext server integration.

Communication for query processing requires two steps: In a first step,
user queries are channeled through user agents to brokers which reply
with a set of possibly relevant information sources. In a second step,
queries are sent to provider agents which encapsulate these sources and
which reply with a set of relevant document references.

For the communication with the MeDoc fulltext server additional functions are defined which allow document retrieval with authentication and
content based navigation.

Finally, this article describes the MeDoc communication protocol which
was designed and implemented to meet these communication requirements.

1 Introduction

As described in [3] the MeDoc System is an open and distributed mediator
system that leads users to relevant information sources on the Internet and provides transparent access to them. To achieve this goal a uniform query language,
schema and protocol are needed. This article deals with the communication requirements and the protocol in the MeDoc System.

Fig. 1 gives an overview of the architecture. *User agents* [4] encapsulate different user clients and provide user specific services. *Provider agents* encapsulate
heterogeneous provider systems and provide a well-defined interface within the
MeDoc environment. One task is to map incoming MeDoc queries into queries
understood by the associated provider system and to map results back into the
MeDoc environment. Another task is to provide a *content description* of their
associated provider system. This description is registered with *brokers* [5] which
are responsible to match incoming queries to possibly relevant provider agents.

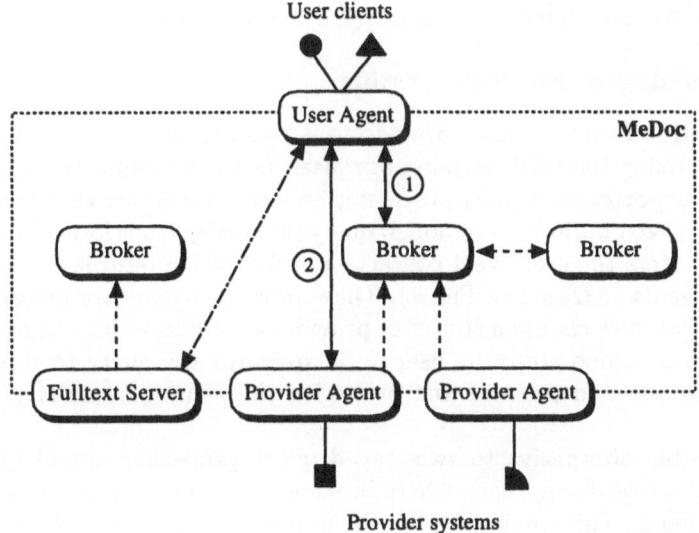

Fig. 1. Overview of MeDoc components.

The MeDoc fulltext server [7] provides the interface of a usual provider agent. Therefore it can register with brokers and participate in query processing. However, it offers additional functions regarding document delivery and content based navigation.

It makes sense to position the user agent close to users and to place provider agents close to their associated provider systems to improve interaction with users and provider systems, respectively. Additionally, response times highly depend on the availability of brokers, hence, it should be possible to replicate them. Consequently, the MeDoc System is a distributed system with the need to communicate between its components.

There exist two major parts handled by communication in the MeDoc System. The first part covers processing of queries based on a two-staged procedure (Sect. 2). The second part handles communication with the MeDoc fulltext server. Here specific messages have been identified (Sect. 3). Each of these parts define additional communication needs which arise due to requirements defined by the particular functions. For example, query processing cannot be done without information about available provider systems. Additional communication is necessary to propagate this information. We discuss these additional communication needs within the respective section.

Section 4 discusses the implementation of the MeDoc protocol. Section 5 presents a short discussion about implementation decisions. Finally, the paper concludes with section 6.

2 Communication for Query Processing

2.1 Two-staged Query Processing

In the MeDoc System, query processing is realized following the ODP trader model [1]. Using the ODP terminology, user agents are importers and provider agents are exporters of a query processing service. Brokers are then traders which mediate between both. In this model, query processing is performed in two steps. In the first step, the user agent contacts a broker which returns a set of relevant provider agents (Arrow 1 in Fig. 1). These provider agents are presented to the user, who can now choose a subset of provider agents to which the query should be sent. In a second step, the user agent forwards the query to this subset of provider agents and presents the user with the returned results (Arrow 2 in Fig. 1).

A possible alternative to two-staged query processing would be to use a "store-and-forward" approach where brokers are responsible to contact relevant provider agents. This would simplify the user agent, because in this case brokers are responsible to merge results.

However, there are several problems associated with this approach. One problem is additional communication overhead to enable users to follow the status of their query processing. This would require to add user management facilities into the broker.

Another major problem is the loss of cost control. A design requirement of MeDoc is to allow commercial information providers to participate. This type of provider charge users for information retrieval tasks. If the broker would autonomously forward queries to every relevant provider there would be no chance for the user to monitor access to commercial provider systems.

To sum-up, two-staged query processing offers the following advantages:

- Prior to sending the query to provider agents, the user can influence their selection. This allows better control of resulting costs (regarding access to commercial provider agents), the load of the system can be reduced (because only those provider agents are contacted which the user ranked best) and the final result set can be reduced to a manageable size (because only few provider agents are contacted).
- The user agent is aware of how many provider agents are involved in query processing and, hence, can determine how many result sets should be returned.
- Functionality of brokers gets simpler because there is no need to forward queries.

2.2 Query Processing Messages

For query processing the following message types have been defined:

- *paref-query*. This message is sent from the user agent to the broker to request a list of relevant provider agents for a query.

- *paref-list*. This message is returned by the broker upon receipt of a *paref-query* message.
- *docref-query*. This message is sent from the user agent to a provider agent to request a list of relevant documents for a query.
- *docref-list*. This message is returned by a provider agent upon receipt of a *docref-query* message.

Both pairs of messages (<*paref-query*, *paref-list*> and <*docref-query*, *docref-list*>) implement the two-staged query processing procedure.

Additional Query Processing Messages

To enable complete user-defined query processing, the user agent can send a request to list all known provider agents of a broker (*paref-all*). The corresponding response message is just a *paref-list* message, containing every known provider agent.

Additionally, a user agent can request a list of replications of a specific broker (*broker-all*). The broker returns a list (*broker-list*) that enables user agents to switch to another replication in case of a broker breakdown.

2.3 Provider Agent Registration

Query processing requires that brokers have some knowledge about the content of their associated provider agents. For that reason, provider agents must *register* with a broker. Consequently, they must also have the possibility to *withdraw* their registration. Therefore two messages were defined in the first prototype of the MeDoc System:

- *provider-registration*. Provider agents register with a broker by sending their content description as well as some attributes for administrative purposes.
- *provider-withdrawal*. Registration of a particular provider agent can be withdrawn with this message.

Since content descriptions of provider agents may get very large, the registration process was split into the following messages in the second extended prototype:

- *provider-reg-init*. Provider agents wishing to register with a broker initiate their registration request.
- *provider-reg-metadata*. Once a registration request is initiated, the provider agent sends its content description with multiple messages of this type.
- *provider-reg-finish*. This message successfully terminates a registration request. The broker enters the collected meta data in its internal registration database.
- *provider-reg-abort*. In case of an error, the provider agent can abort its registration request. The broker simply discards all received meta data.

3   Communication with the Fulltext Server

The development of a fulltext server within the MeDoc project makes it necessary to define messages suitable to access the additional functionality.

Functionality in this system can be roughly divided into two parts: *document delivery* and *content navigation*. Every part requires that the user is "known" to the fulltext server. For that reason users must authenticate themselves with the server using passwords.

For document delivery this leads to the following messages:

- *document-order*. The user agent requests the delivery of a specific document.
- *password-query*. Upon receipt of a *document-order* message the fulltext server replies with a *password-query* to request the password of the user.
- *password-content*. The user agent requests the password from the user and sends it back to the fulltext server.
- *document-component*. If the password matches the one stored with the fulltext server, the requested documents (or part of it) are returned.

Content navigation is driven by the user agent which keeps state information about the *navigation space*. This navigation space is defined as a set of attributes which, in turn, are determined by the fulltext server. User agents simply send messages containing information about the current position of the user in the navigation space and the user's choice to the fulltext server, which returns an updated set of attributes (the new position of the user in navigation space). This updated set now becomes the current set of the user agent. Thus, we have the following messages:

- *navigation-query*. The user agent sends the current position of the user in the navigation space and his/her choice to the fulltext server. In case the user just starts the navigation, there is no actual current position. This is reflected in the very first message by setting special attributes.
- *navigation-attribute*. The fulltext server returns the new position in navigation space with this message.

Once the user reaches a position where real documents are identified, the fulltext server returns a *docref-list* message as described in section 2.2.

Finally, an increasing number of documents is also available electronically and referenced in retrieval systems for information retrieval purposes, like the fulltext server. The electronic versions of the documents are available through their URL. Consequently, the user agent must have the ability to request and retrieve the URL of an electronically available document from the fulltext server:

- *browse-url-order*. The user agent requests a URL for a specified document.
- *browse-url-content*. If the user is authorized to access the URL, it is returned by the fulltext server with this message.

Authorization is done similarly to document delivery by first requesting a password (*password-query*).

4 Implementation

The implementation of the MeDoc protocol was driven by the following requirements:

- *Simplicity.* To simplify integration of provider agents of new provider systems, the protocol must be simple to implement.
- *Extensibility.* Updating a system whose components are widely distributed requires that new components (especially new communication features) can be added without updating every existing component at once.
- *Robustness.* Corrupted or unknown requests must not break the overall functionality of the system. Also, long communication duration (eg. caused by network latencies) should not lead to long response times.

This lead to an asynchronous communication model based on a synchronous transport layer.

4.1 Component Structure

Every component can be divided into three layers: *component layer, communication layer* and *transport layer.* The component layer acts on *objects* which are sent and received with help of the communication layer. The communication layer transparently maps objects to data streams which are then passed to the transport layer for actual transmission. Communication layer and transport layer form the *communication component* (Fig. 2).

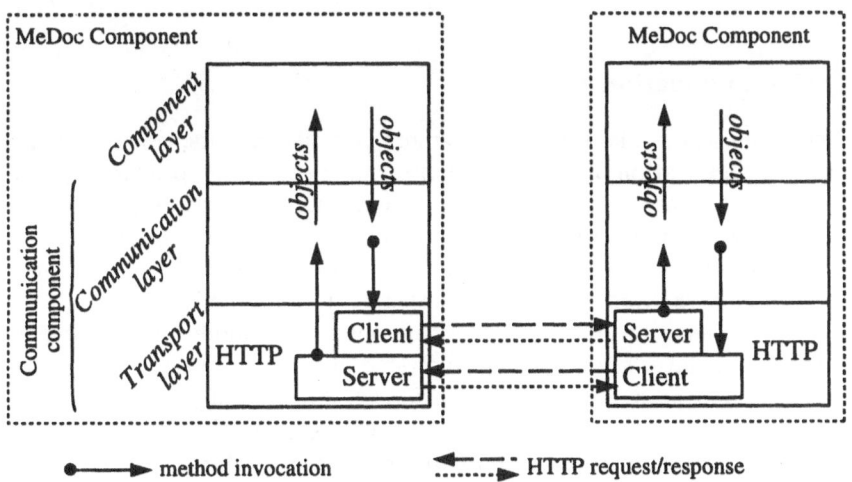

Fig. 2. Layers of MeDoc components.

Communication components define an interface which is used by other parts of the MeDoc component to send and receive objects. This interface defines methods to actually send messages. It also provides declarations of methods to handle incoming messages. These methods must be defined by the particular part of the MeDoc component. They are called by the communication component each time a message arrives. Fig. 3 shows an example interface definition of the communication component for a user agent. `UAReceiver` is an abstract interface description of methods which the particular MeDoc component must provide to handle incoming messages appropriately. On the other hand, `UACommunicationComponent` is a class already providing functionality to send messages used by user agents[1].

```
public interface UAReceiver{
  public void receive(PARefListMsg paref_list_msg);
  public void receive(DocRefListMsg docref_list_msg);
  public void receive(StatusMsg status_msg);
}

public class UACommunicationComponent{
  public UACommunicationComponent(UAReceiver receiver);
  public void send(URL address,
                        PARefQueryMsg paref_query_msg);
  public void send(URL address,
                      DocRefQueryMsg docref_query_msg);
}
```

Fig. 3. Interface of the communication component for the user agent.

4.2 Communication Layer

Particular messages like queries to remote provider agents, document delivery requests or registration of provider agents, may need a long processing time. For example, in the case of query processing network latencies or provider system outages may cause particular providers to not reply immediately. However, others may already have been able to send their response. It should be possible for users to view already existing results while other requests are still open.

For that reason an asynchronous communication model was chosen at the communication layer's level which allows to close a particular communication channel as soon as a message is transferred. Additionally, response messages need not necessarily take the same way back as their corresponding requests. This is an advantage in case of forwarded queries, which may be useful for further extensions.

The communication layer is responsible to map objects to and from data streams. For that reason every MeDoc object that is sent to other components

---

[1] We only present methods necessary for the query processing part. Actual implementations also include methods for provider agent registration and to communicate with the fulltext server.

offers methods to generate a string representation (`ConvertToString()`) and to initialize itself from a string (special constructor) (Fig. 4).

```
public class Query
  // constructors
  public Query(int count, Date date,
               QueryCondition query_conditon)
  public Query(Query query)
  //
  // Initialize object from 'stream'
  //
  public Query(String string)

  // methods
  public setQueryCondition(QueryCondition query_conditon)
  public setCount(int count)
  public setDate(Date date)
  public QueryCondition getQueryCondition()
  public int getCount()
  public Date getDate()
  public boolean equals(Query anotherQuery)
  //
  // Convert object to 'stream' representation
  //
  public String ConvertToString()
}
```

Fig. 4. Example of a MeDoc object.

4.3   Transport Layer

The transport layer is based on the synchronous HTTP protocol [2]. Each (asynchronous) MeDoc request/response pair is mapped to two separate HTTP requests (Fig. 5). For that reason, the transport layer implements an HTTP client and server as shown in Fig. 2. The HTTP client sends requests to other MeDoc components and receives status messages as normal HTTP responses. The server part receives messages from other MeDoc components and forwards them to the communication layer. If the message is valid and syntactically correct, a message object is created. Eventually this message object is passed to the appropriate method as defined by the MeDoc component. In case of an error, the communication component denies the message and returns an error message.

Once a MeDoc message is constructed (ie. its string representation generated) the transport layer invokes an HTTP request containing the actual MeDoc message in its body part. The type of the message is indicated using the *Content-type* field of the HTTP header information (Fig. 6).

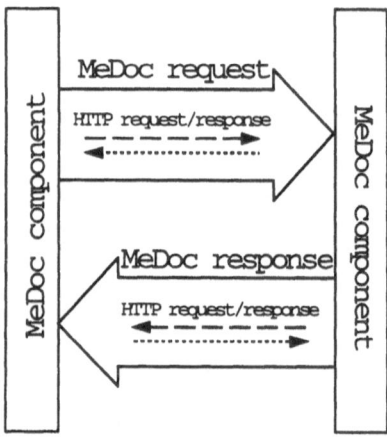

Fig. 5. Using HTTP as transport protocol for asynchronous MeDoc request/response pairs.

```
POST / HTTP/1.0
Date: Wed, 12 Jun 1996 14:03:46 UT
From: dreger@inf.fu-berlin.de (Markus Dreger)
Referer: http://medoc-ua.inf.fu-berlin.de:12345/
Content-length: 424
Content-type: application/x-medoc; type="docref-query"

Message-Id: "dreger.1234.medoc-ua"
Hit-Count:
Date: Wed, 12 Jun 1996 14:03:23 UT

(ALL (CONTAINS title "distributed")
     (CONTAINS title "database")
     (GE year 1994)
)
```

Fig. 6. Message at the transportation layer.

The recipient of a message receives an HTTP request and first analyzes the *Content-type* field. If this field indicates a MeDoc message suitable for the recipient the request is accepted. Otherwise an HTTP not accepted response message is returned and the transfer is aborted.

In a second step, the transport layer hands the received MeDoc message over to the communication layer which tries to create a message object using appropriate constructor calls. If object construction fails an error message is returned, otherwise the object is passed to the MeDoc component which actually implements the receive method and a positive acknowledge is sent back. Thus, the request is only accepted and passed to the component layer if the contained MeDoc message object is valid.

5 Discussion

Due to tight time constraints in the project it was necessary to provide a communication component as early as possible to allow testing of MeDoc component interaction.

For that reason, we took a pragmatic approach in designing and implementing the MeDoc communication protocol. Once that the communication model and primitives were identified it was decided to use HTTP as transportation protocol because of the following reasons:

- HTTP is a very simple but flexible protocol. In its syntax it mainly follows other well known Internet protocols such as FTP, SMTP, Telnet or NetNews.
- Due to its significance in the Internet, many software libraries are available which can be immediately used to realize MeDoc communication.
- HTTP already provides mechanisms for multipart messages.
- Functionality of HTTP is well understood.

However, it should be noted that the MeDoc System is only a prototype implementation and that the concepts discussed for the communication protocol can be easily adopted to different, existing protocols. Especially, adoption is possible for the communication layer as well as transportation layer.

A possible alternative for the communication layer comes from the domain of software agents and is discussed in the following section. Section 5.2 discusses possibilities to use Z39.50 as protocol to implement communication and transport layer. In section 5.3 we briefly go into particulars of using CORBA as an alternative implementation platform.

5.1 KQML

KQML [6] is a communication language defined for interaction of autonomous software agents. It defines messages (called *performatives*) which cover a broad range of communication primitives. KQML allows several basic communication models including synchronous and asynchronous communication.

Agents are not expected to implement all defined performatives. There exist performatives to indicate receipt of unknown performatives. However, KQML assumes existence of special agents, called *facilitators*, which provide functionality for mediating between other agents.

The MeDoc protocol could be mapped to KQML as follows:

1. MeDoc defines its own set of communication primitives, hence, it is necessary to define a MeDoc ontology.
2. Brokers play the role of facilitators.
3. Some MeDoc communication primitives can be directly mapped to KQML performatives. For example, the available documents of a provider form its "knowledge base". A MeDoc query request (*docref-query*) is mapped to a KQML *ask-all* performative. This performative returns all objects of the receiver which are true for the performative's content. The query itself is put into the content part of the performative[2].
4. Some MeDoc communication primitives require definition of additional KQML performatives.

5.2 Z39.50

Z39.50 is a standardized retrieval protocol defined within the domain of library science. It assumes a client/server approach where the client requests service from the server during a session, and hence, Z39.50 uses a synchronous communication model.

Although Z39.50 provides enough flexibility to integrate the MeDoc communication primitives, it would introduce several disadvantages:

1. Z39.50 is not designed for provider agent mediation or content based navigation. These services must be implemented using the extended service facility.
2. MeDoc defines its own set of attributes and its own query language. Although it is possible to extend already existing Z39.50 attribute sets as well as query language types, this would deminish the main advantage of Z39.50, its interoperability.
3. To actually send a MeDoc message it would be necessary to establish a Z39.50 session. This introduces additional communication overhead.
4. To be Z39.50 compliant, every MeDoc component must implement some services which are not necessary within the MeDoc environment. This introduces additional implementation overhead.
5. Finally, MeDoc defines an asynchronous communication model. As a consequence, every MeDoc component would have to implement Z39.50 client *and* server functionality.

The advantage of using Z39.50 would be that provider systems which implement Z39.50 could be directly accessed by user agents. However, they must also

---

[2] Here the MeDoc ontology comes into account. The query semantics is only understood within the MeDoc environment.

provide extended services to register with brokers or to provide content based navigation (in case of fulltext servers). Consequently, providing a specialized provider agent which maps incoming MeDoc queries into "normal" Z39.50 messages would be necessary, because it is not always possible to change existing provider systems.

5.3 CORBA

One important part of communication in distributed systems is the mapping of data structures into data streams and *vice versa* (*marshalling* and *unmarshalling*, respectively). Using HTTP, these mappings must be separately defined. In this case, implementations based on other technologies like CORBA [8] would be more advantageous, because marshalling and unmarshalling are performed transparently to the application programmer. An experimental implementation of a subset of the protocol based on CORBA has shown that the main advantage is the higher level of abstraction. On the other hand one is faced with constraints regarding CORBA availability on different platforms and for different languages. However, distributed communication environments require that every MeDoc component is provided with a corresponding communication component. Regarding the state of current available implementations of distributed communication environments this introduces technical and organizational problems, because different CORBA implementations may not be compatible.

6 Conclusion

The decision to use HTTP as transport protocol for the MeDoc protocol has shown to be very practical. New message types to enhance the protocol can be easily integrated. Additionally, implementation in different programming languages is very simple, because there already exist HTTP software libraries for most common languages. During the project, we have implemented it in both Java and Python for different provider agents using available libraries for the HTTP protocol.

The design decision to realize the communication in a separate component which can be integrated as a module in various MeDoc components eases the implementation effort and leads to a very robust communication.

References

1. Bearman, M.: ODP-Trader. In: Proceedings of the IFIP TC6/WG6. First International Conference on Open Distributed Processing Berlin, Germany (1993) 181–191
2. Berners-Lee, T., Fielding, R., Frystyk, H.: Hypertext Transfer Protocol – HTTP/1.0. IETF Request for Comments, RFC 1945 (1996)
3. Boles, D. *et al.*: The MeDoc System – a Digital Publication and Reference Service for Computer Science, in this volume.

101

4. Boles, D. *et al.*: Conception of the User Agent – the User Interface of the MeDoc System, in this volume.
5. Dreger, M. *et al.*: Provider Selection – Design and Implementation of the Broker, in this volume.
6. Finin, T., Labrou, Y., Mayfield, J.: KQML as an agent communication language. to appear in: Bradshaw, J. (ed.): Software Agents, MIT Press (1997)
7. Meyer, J., Appelrath, H.-J.: Design and Implementation of the MeDoc Fulltext System, in this volume.
8. Object Management Group (OMG). The Common Object Request Broker: Architecture and Specification. Revision 2.0 (1995)

The MeDoc Library: Security Aspects

A. Brüggemann-Klein, C. Haber

Technische Universität München,
Institut für Informatik,
D-80290 München,
email: {brueggem,haber}@informatik.tu-muenchen.de

Abstract. The MeDoc Project aims at building a digital distributed full text library containing high quality computer science literature. Since the MeDoc library contains electronic editions of classical paper books and journals, accounting and security aspects are of considerable importance in this project.

The basic concepts for the MeDoc service have been identified in a requirements analysis phase. This paper describes the security requirements and their implementation within the MeDoc prototype.

The MeDoc billing facilities imply the implementation of security mechanisms into the MeDoc service. Therefore security tools and implementations of cryptographic algorithms have been evaluated as to their suitability for the MeDoc service. Communication channels are now secured by transparent encryption mechanisms based on SSL. The prototype admits only registered users to the MeDoc library. The users are authenticated via password and can be charged via accounts.

1 Introduction

The MeDoc library offers high quality computer science literature in full text over the Internet accessible via common WWW clients. The basic concepts of the MeDoc library have been identified in a requirements analysis phase [5]. The library contains besides non commercial contents the electronic versions of classical paper books and journals. As the production of these documents is with costs their use cannot be offered for free. To ensure that the right person/institution is billed, security measurements have to be implemented. Since information like passwords transmitted over the Internet can be overheard easily, measurements against unauthorized listening are of interest. Another topic is the integrity of the messages.

The first section of this paper describes the attacks to communication over the Internet and the security services designed for detecting or preventing these attacks. Section 3 deals with the MeDoc business model and deduces the security services needed within MeDoc. The next section discusses existing security systems and their suitability for the MeDoc library. Finally we describe the integration of SSL into the MeDoc service.

2 Security attacks and services

In a networked environment, there are different attacks against the communication channel.

2.1 Security attacks

We distinguish between passive and active attacks. Passive attacks are listening on, or monitoring of, transmissions. The goal of the attacker is to obtain information that is being transmitted. Typical passive attacks are *eavesdropping* and *traffic analysis*. Since avoiding traffic analysis is not in the scope of this project, measurements against it will not be discussed in this paper. Active attacks involve modification of the data stream or the creation of a false stream. They can be divided into four categories: Interruption, Interception, Modification and Fabrication. *Interruption* means that no communication is possible any more. This may be caused by cutting the communication line or destroying one of the communication partners. Avoiding interruptions lies in the responsibility of the system and network administrator. *Interception* means that an unauthorized party listens to the communication. *Modification* implies that messages are modified during the transfer and *fabrication* is the insertion of counterfeit objects into the system.

2.2 Security services

Security services enhance the security of the communication over an open network by counteracting security attacks. Computer and network security research have focused on Authenticity, Integrity, Confidentiality, Nonrepudiation, Access Control and Availability as general security services.

Authenticity guarantees that the sender of a message has not been faked and therefore helps to avoid fabrication. Authenticity can be realized with the help of passwords or biometrics like fingerprints, iris scan, ... The *Integrity* service ensures that the message has not been modified on the way. It prevents modification attacks. The integrity of a message may be checked with one way hash codes. *Confidentiality*, which ensures that no one except the sender and the receiver of a message can understand the message, is realized by encrypting the message. Confidentiality of a message is attacked by interception. *Nonrepudiation* requires that the sender cannot deny having sent the message. Digital signatures ensure the authenticity of a sender and make sure that the sender cannot deny the transmission. *Access Control* guarantees that only authorized users can access a service. Access Control can be realized with the help of access control lists. *Availability* requires that network services are available any time. Attacks on availability are usually active attacks like cutting a transmission line.

Availability has to be ensured by the network administrator and access control is managed by the system administrator. They are not within the scope of MeDoc.

3 MeDoc security requirements

The MeDoc project aims at building a distributed database of structured full texts, as well as providing access to existing, external full text and bibliographic databases. It was therefore important to have an open system, where existing databases may be integrated easily. This is apparently contradictory to the security requirement for a billable service. The contradiction is resolved by securing only sensitive information e.g. actions/communications that invoke costs. Hence in order to understand the security mechanisms in MeDoc, it is important to know the MeDoc business model.

3.1 MeDoc business model

The MeDoc business model defines the relationship between the producer, the provider and the user of a document [3]. The only thing one has to know concerning security issues is that searching the MeDoc library is free and viewing documents may cause costs. Initially, only registered users are admitted to the library, so they can be charged via accounts. If a user wants to view a document, the user or the institution the user belongs to needs a license for that document. The licenses and the cost models are described in [4] in more detail.

3.2 Requirements on security services in MeDoc

The business model has some impact on the security requirements in MeDoc. As access to billable documents is restricted to registered users that have a license, the authentication of these users is very important. Next in the priority list is the confidentiality service. In the MeDoc environment confidentiality means, that unauthorized listeners shall not be able to reconstruct billable documents passed to the user. Confidentiality regarding the interests of a user, i.e. the user's queries is in conflict with the requirement of MeDoc being an open system where any database provider may offer documents. To ensure the second type of confidentiality, the communication between user and database provider would have to be encrypted and a key exchange between user and provider would have to be implemented (either exchange of public keys, or of a private key). This key exchange is organizational overhead that prevents spontaneous participation of database providers in the MeDoc system and therefore contradicts the MeDoc philosophy. Moreover the main users of the MeDoc system are researches and students at educational institutions and their research interests usually are not kept secret. The integrity service will gain importance the moment pay per view models are integrated in the MeDoc system. Right now all users are registered users and they or the institution they belong to have licenses for some of the documents. Now the worst thing to happen is that users cannot access documents they have a license for or they will get a wrong document. Both possibilities should be prevented, but at least no costs for a document may be caused for a user if the messages between user and provider are modified. Therefore the integrity service is not the most important one within MeDoc. The same applies to the nonrepudiation service. As no costs are involved if a user repudiates a query or a document order nonrepudiation is not very important. The availability of the MeDoc Service can only partly be ensured by the developers. If the system is stable, the availability depends on the availability of the network connection and thereupon the developers have no influence whatsoever. Access control is a similar problem. We may restrict access to the MeDoc system to authorized users, but we have no means to ensure, that no users may get the documents by logging in on the provider's computer bypassing the MeDoc system. Therefore part of the access control lies with the system administrators of the MeDoc system and not only with the developers.

The MeDoc service being to the widest possible extent based on existing tools known security systems have been evaluated as to their suitability for the MeDoc service.

3.3 Evaluation criteria for security systems

There are different criteria for the suitability of security systems to be used in MeDoc. One very important aspect are the security services supported. To decide on one tool it is not sufficient to list those services. The realization of the services, the cryptographic algorithms supported and the key length must be considered. Other criteria are the portability of the tool, its costs including support, resources, ... and the time required for integrating the tool into the MeDoc environment. Last but not least the security mechanisms should be transparent to the user in the sense that the user does not need to bother about security.

4 Evaluation of existing security systems

After having developed a criteria catalogue existing security tools were evaluated against it. There are a number of *cryptographic algorithms* to ensure authenticity, integrity, confidentiality and nonrepudiation. We evaluated the following implementations of cryptographic algorithms: Crypto libraries, Kerberos, PGP, SHTTP and SSL.

4.1 Crypto libraries

Java 1.1 has a security API and there are some Crypto libraries e.g. SECUDE [9] that offer implementations of different cryptographic algorithms like DES, triple DES, IDEA, RSA, Diffie-Hellmann, ... These cryptographic algorithms may be used to realize the authentication, confidentiality, integrity and nonrepudiation service. The problem with these libraries is that they offer only the encryption facilities. There is no protocol managing the encryption (which messages are when encrypted using which encryption algorithm?). Crypto libraries are one way to secure the communication in MeDoc, yet this way would require considerable additional effort for the implementation of the security protocol. An existing tool that has the protocol already implemented is preferred to Crypto libraries.

4.2 Kerberos

Kerberos [6] was developed at the MIT for the project Athena. It is a well known protocol for trusted third party authentication. Kerberos provides secure network authentication, allowing persons to access machines over a network. It is based on symmetric cryptography (DES). As the communication between the components may be encrypted, Kerberos supports the confidentiality service. With Kerberos every entity on the network shares a different secret key with a central authentication server. Knowledge of the secret key is used as proof of identity. Figure 1 shows the sequence of the Kerberos protocol that takes place if a user for the first time requires a service. One major disadvantage of Kerberos

1. Request for a ticket granting ticket
2. Ticket granting ticket
3. Request for a service ticket
4. Service ticket
5. Service request

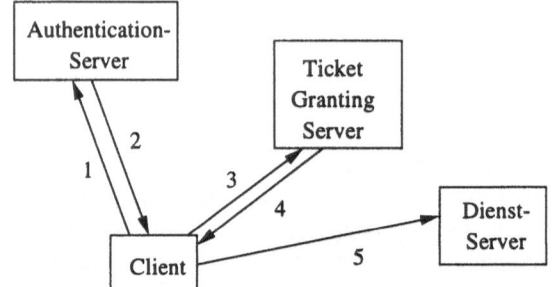

Fig. 1. Kerberos service request

are the central components (authentication server and ticket granting server). All document providers (e.g. publishing houses) need to trust the institutions where the central components are installed and maintained. In a distributed project like MeDoc it is hard to find such an institution. Non commercial project partners where the central components could reside are universities and there the maintenance and administration of the components cannot be ensured after the project ends. Another disadvantage of Kerberos is the complexity of the installation, administration and integration into the MeDoc system. The last disadvantage to mention is the usage of time stamps in a distributed system. Time stamps are used within Kerberos to limit the validity of ticket granting tickets and service tickets. The usage of time stamps implies that the clocks of all systems involved need to be synchronized which is hard to achieve. Advantages of Kerberos are the well known protocol and the availability of the source code which is public domain. Because of the central components and the time stamps Kerberos cannot be used to secure the MeDoc system.

4.3 PGP

PGP (Pretty good privacy) [15] is an application layer protocol that is primarily used to secure email messages. PGP uses symmetric cryptography (IDEA) for data encryption, asymmetric cryptography (RSA) for key management and MD5 as a one-way hash function. It supports data encryption and digital signatures, i.e. the authenticity, confidentiality, integrity and nonrepudiation service. In order to implement the security services needed within MeDoc, the MeDoc messages will have to be encrypted and signed. PGP is easy to install and maintain, well designed, public domain, and the source code is available. A disadvantage of PGP is that by default it is not transparent to the user. This transparency could be achieved (programmed) with the integration of PGP into the MeDoc system. There is some discussion about PGP's approach to key management, the so called web of trust. With PGP you need to decide which public keys you trust to really belong to the owner. If you know the owner of a key and got the public key from the owner directly, you will believe that the key belongs to the owner. You may then sign the key to say that this key really belongs to the person who claims to be the owner. If you get a key signed by a person you trust, you may decide that as you trust the person who signed the key, you trust that the key truly belongs to whom it appears to belong. PGP assumes that if a key is signed by several persons you half trust, then these "half trusts added" result in full trust in the key. Those trusts, half trusts, ... build the web of trust. The evaluation of PGP showed that PGP could be used to secure the MeDoc system.

4.4 SHTTP

SHTTP (Secure Hypertext Transfer Protocol) [13] is an application layer protocol. As the name suggests, it is based on HTTP. With the help of SHTTP the user can decide which messages are to be encrypted and/or signed and which encryption algorithm to use. At the time of the evaluation there was only one reference implementation of SHTTP by EIT (Enterprise Integration Technologies) [14] and this implementation was subject to the US export restrictions. Besides, SHTTP is not transparent to the user. As there was no implementation of SHTTP that may be used in Europe, SHTTP was no alternative for securing the MeDoc system.

4.5 SSL

SSL (Secure Socket Layer) [8] is a protocol layered between TCP and HTTP. It may be used to secure any communication based on the TCP/IP-Protocol. One goal of SSL was to ensure authenticity, confidentiality and integrity of messages sent over the Internet regardless of the protocol and the software used. Existing application software shall be usable as without SSL. With respect to application layer protocols SSL has the same functionality and interface as TCP and to TCP SSL looks like an application layer protocol. The usage of cryptographic algorithms is transparent to the user. SSL allows for different sessions with different cryptographic algorithms. Each session may contain several connections. In a handshake protocol, the encryption algorithms are negotiated, a secret key for the communication is computed on the basis of a PreMasterSecret that is exchanged and the communication partners may be authenticated using certificates. The data is then transmitted over a secure transmission channel.

We decided to use SSL for the MeDoc System, because it supports the important security services, is transparent to the user, supports different Crypto algorithms (DES, triple DES, IDEA, RSA, Diffie/Hellman, ...), is rather easy to install/administer and is the tool easiest to be integrated into the MeDoc service, as the communication protocol in the MeDoc system is based on HTTP [7]. SSLeay [11], the implementation we choose, is an Australian implementation of the SSL protocol that supports full key length, is not subject to export restrictions and may be used commercially. The support for SSLeay is rather good and there are some SSLeay mailing lists.

5 Implementation of the security features

Before we can discuss the integration of SSL into the MeDoc system it is vital to know the MeDoc architecture.

5.1 MeDoc architecture

The MeDoc system supports providers by offering documents in full text and users by finding information in heterogeneous, distributed databases with the help of an information brokering system. As the MeDoc architecture is discussed in detail in [2], we will focus on the parts where security measurements need to be taken. This parts are shown in figure 2.

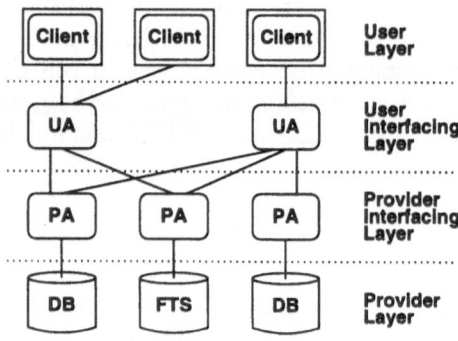

Fig. 2. Architecture of the MeDoc System

User Agents (UA) are the User Interface to the MeDoc System [1]. The user logs in at the User Agent via a common WWW Browser. The User Agent forwards user queries to the Provider Agents and stores the query results received from them.

Provider Agents (PA) transform the query from the MeDoc query language to the provider specific query language [10] and forward the query to the provider database (DB). They transform the results received from the database back into the MeDoc language. The Full Text Server (FTS) is a special server where the full texts of the documents converted as part of the project are stored.

The communication between User Agent and Provider Agent follows the MeDoc-Protocol, which is a proprietary protocol based on HTTP [7]. As the user accesses the MeDoc system with ordinary WWW browsers like Netscape or Internet Explorer (Client), the communication protocol between Client and User Agent is HTTP. The communication between Provider Agent and Provider Database is not standardized. If possible, the WWW interface of the database is used, but there is an implementation for a Z39.50 interface as well.

In section 3.1 we introduced the business model in MeDoc. For the implementation of the security services in MeDoc we need to have a closer look at the realization of the business model and the information flows in the MeDoc system where sensitive information is concerned.

5.2   Information flow

As stated in section 3.1 queries are for free in the MeDoc system. The only user actions with restricted access i.e. where the user has to be authenticated are requests to view a document. This authentication is realized with passwords. We assume that the user got a list of document references in reply to a query to the Provider Agent. Having displayed the document reference list in the browser, the user may decide to view one document at the WWW-Server of the provider with the help of a BrowseRequest or to order the document with a DocumentOrder message. The document order message causes the document to be packed and sent the User Agent where it is stored locally to enhance the access time for future viewing requests.

In the following we will discuss the security relevant interfaces in the MeDoc system that are concerned with viewing a document. The first interface to be discussed is that between User Client and User Agent.

Client - User Agent In the MeDoc-System, clients are common WWW-Clients. The User Agent is an ordinary WWW-Server using scripts. As it was one requirement that there is no need for users to install special software to participate in MeDoc, only mechanisms integrated in existing clients can be employed. We intend to use a SSL capable Web Server in the User Agent so that the user can secures the communication via SSL. We cannot enforce the usage of SSL without loosing many spontaneous users (those using non SSL capable browsers). Prior to using the MeDoc library, the users have to login at the User Agent. After login and password are transmitted, the session is assigned a session password that can be used for all further transactions. This is a rather weak security mechanism, but at least the user password has to be transmitted but once, and the validity of the session password is limited to 16 hours.

The next interface to consider is that between User Agent and Provider Agent.

User Agent - Provider Agent Users can only view documents they have a license for. The dialog sequences for viewing a document are shown in figure 3.

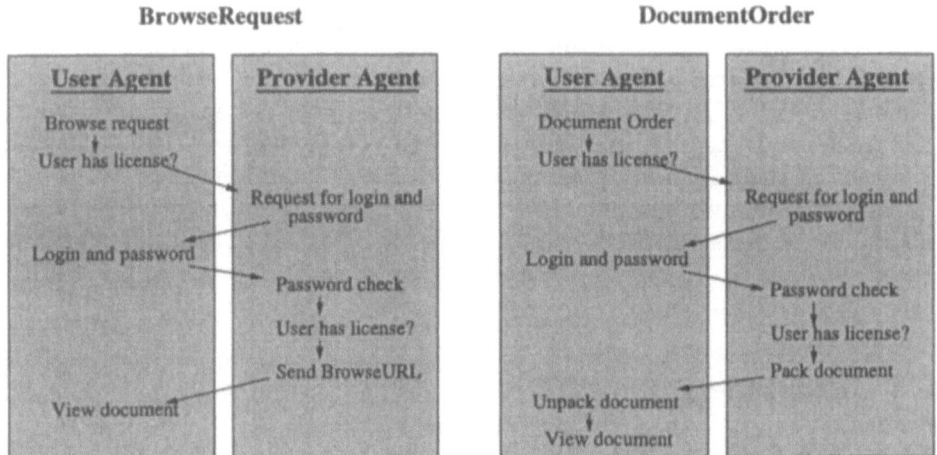

Fig. 3. Typical dialog sequences

As the dialog sequences for the BrowseRequest and the DocumentOrder are very similar we will only discuss the BrowseRequest but the same applies to the DocumentOrder. To access documents at a provider site, the user sends a BrowseRequest to the Provider Agent. Prior to sending the BrowseRequest the User Agent checks whether the user has a license for the document in question. If a license is available the query is forwarded to the Provider Agent, if not an access denied message says where to get a license. The Provider Agent answers with the request for a login and password. This password is stored locally in the User Agent and is sent to the Provider Agent. If the password is valid, the Provider Agent sends the User Agent a BrowseURL, a temporary URL containing a session key granting access to the document. Passwords being sensitive information that is not to be send over the Internet in plain text the message containing the password needs to be encrypted. To ensure that only MeDoc Provider Agents can ask for a user password, the Provider Agent has to be authenticated before its password request is answered. Therefore the password request is encrypted so that the sender of the password request (the Provider Agent) is authenticated via an SSL certificate before being sent the actual password.The next message that is secured is the BrowseURL. The BrowseURL contains a session key. Without this session key the user cannot view the document. The duration of the session key may be configured by the administrator of the Provider Agent.

Up to this point we have discussed which messages are encrypted before they are transmitted and why these messages are encrypted. We ensured that the right persons are billed (authenticity of the users) and that only authorized persons may gain access to billable documents. There is one more security aspect to be considered at this interface, concerning the privacy of a user. As the MeDoc project aims not only at single users but at whole institutions as MeDoc users, it is not sensible to make every single user within an institution known to the provider. For a provider it is sufficient to know, that the user belongs to an institution, that has a license for the document. This grouping of users according to their institution has two effects. On the one hand the provider has less users to administrate (only the institutions), on the other hand, the provider has no data about the search and document requests of one user but only about the institution of the user. Therefore two users of the same institution cannot be distinguished. After a BrowseRequest is sent by the user, the Provider Agent asks for the user's login and password. The User Agent answers with the login of the user's institution at the provider site and the corresponding password. The Provider Agent checks the validity of the password and either send the user a BrowseURL or denies the service.

Provider Agent - Database Provider Agents encapsulate the underlying databases. We distinguish existing databases and databases built up as part of the MeDoc project (full text server) [12]. Existing databases are not part of the MeDoc-system and therefore no security mechanisms can be enforced. As the databases built up in the project are supposed to be on the same server as their Provider Agent, there are no special security requirements for the interface.

Client - WWW-Server of provider With the help of a BrowseURL users may view documents at the provider's site. Viewing of documents is no longer controlled by the MeDoc system for performance reasons. To ensure the communication between the WWW-Server of the provider and the client of the user, we use a SSL-capable WWW-Server at the provider's site that supports https only. We stated, that we cannot enforce SSL secured connections between User Client and User Agent as we would loose spontaneous users using non SSL capable browsers. This seems contradictory to requiring SSL between clients and WWW-Servers at provider sites. As anybody shall be able to spontaneously use the parts of the MeDoc system that are for free, we cannot force users to use a special browser, but we can ask the users of billable information to do so in order to access the information. At the interface between user client and User Agent the risk lies with the users not using SSL as others may impersonate them, at the interface between user client and WWW-Server of a provider the risk would lie with the provider as unauthorized persons might access their documents.

The security measurements at the different interfaces are shown in figure 4.

5.3 Integration of SSL: Implementation details

The integration of security mechanisms into the MeDoc system resulted in the so called secure communication component.

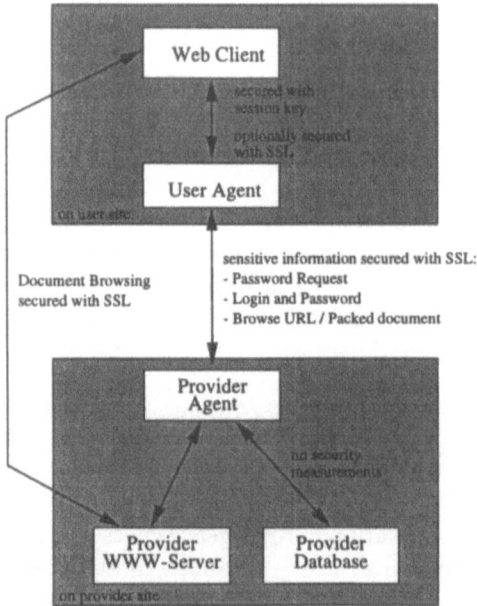

Fig. 4. Security relevant interfaces in the MeDoc system

The MeDoc prototype is implemented in JAVA, the SSLeay code to be integrated is written in C. The easiest way to integrate these two was to integrate the SSL software as native code. In order to avoid changes to the existing communication component, we implemented SSL sockets that have the same functionality as ordinary sockets. SSL sockets are enhanced to support client and server authentication and various encryption algorithms. To prevent invoking the handshake protocol for each message existing communication channels may be reused within their lifetime

6   Experiences and Conclusion

The security of the MeDoc system focuses on the authorized viewing of documents. No unauthorized users shall gain access to billable documents and with the pay per view model it is vital to charge the right persons. The privacy of the user is not ensured as the queries are not encrypted while they are sent over the Internet. The interface between user client and User Agent is the weakest point if the user does not use SSL to contact the User Agent. Anybody overhearing the communication between User Agent and client and grabbing the user password may impersonate this user and take advantages of the original user's license. Wherever possible, the transmission of passwords over the Internet is encrypted, but it is only as safe as the encryption algorithms used with SSL and the implementation of SSLeay.

One way to a "secure library" would have been to have a special MeDoc application, but then spontaneous usage of the MeDoc library without any installation requirements for the user would not have been possible. So far, the encryption is working and there is hardly any administration needed. Responsibility for the communication between Client and User Agent lies with the user.

Security is a problem within the WWW that is not solved yet, but it is of growing importance as the WWW turns into an electronic marketplace.

References

1. D. Boles et al.: Conception of the User Agent – the User Interface of the MeDoc System, in this volume.
2. D. Boles et al.: The MeDoc System – A Digital Publication and Reference Service for Computer Science, in this volume.
3. M. Breu, A. Brüggemann-Klein, C. Haber, and R. Weber: The MeDoc distributed electronic library - accounting and security aspects. In *ICCC/IFIP Conference on Electronic Publishing*. University of Kent, Canterbury, April 1997.
4. M. Breu and R. Weber: Konzeption der Abrechnung in MeDoc (in German). Technischer Bericht, TU München, 1996. http://medoc.informatik.tu-muenchen.de/publications/abrech.ps.
5. A. Brüggemann-Klein: MeDoc Pflichtenheft. Technischer Bericht, TU München, June 1996.
6. B. Bryant, J. Steiner, and J. Kohl: Kerberos Installation Notes. DRAFT Initial Release plus later patches through patch level 7.
7. M. Dreger, S. Lohrum, and P. Müller: The MeDoc Communication Protocol, in this volume.
8. A. O. Freier, P. Karlton, and P. C. Kocher: The SSL Protocol Version 3.0. Internet Draft, March 1996, expired 9/96.
9. Gmd security technology - secude-5.0. SECUDE Webpage: http://www.darmstadt.gmd.de/secude/secude.html.
10. K. Großjohann and D. Menke: Query Transformation for Heterogeneous Provider Systems in MeDoc, in this volume.
11. T. J. Hudson and E. A. Young: SSL Programmer Reference. SSL Programmer Reference.
12. J Meyer and H.-J. Appelrath: Design and Implementation of the MeDoc Fulltext System, in this volume.
13. E. Rescorla and A. Schiffmann: The Secure Hypertext Transfer Protocol. Internet Draft expired Jan 96.
14. W. T. Wong: Secure NCSA httpd Reference Manual. Draft.
15. P. Zimmermann: Dokumentation zu PGP 2.6.2. The documentation kit for the current MIT release of PGP, Version 2.6.2.

Cost Models and Accounting in MeDoc

R. Weber, M. Breu, A. Endres

Technische Universität München, Institut für Informatik, D-80290 München,
E-Mail: weberr@informatik.tu-muenchen.de
FAST e.V., Arabellastr. 17, D-81925 München,
E-Mail: breu@fast.de
Universität Stuttgart, Inst. für Informatik, Breitwiesenstr. 20/22, D-70565 Stuttgart
E-Mail: endres@informatik.uni-stuttgart.de

Abstract. The German digital library project MeDoc offers a wide range of billable digital books and journals contributed by the participating publishing houses. Operating a digital library has important economical aspects, as the contents of a digital library are information merchandise just as paper books or journals bought in a book store. Therefore suitable business models have to be defined and new innovative cost models, like floating licenses or fine grained usage-based pricing become both necessary and feasible in network based digital libraries. According to the MeDoc business model the user has to pay for services rendered. Initially only registered users are admitted to the MeDoc library, so the users can be charged via accounts. Currently a Clearing Center handles the actual invoice process for the MeDoc service. Cost models offered in MeDoc are various forms of subscription and usage-based pricing. The mechanisms described have been implemented and are being evaluated in the MeDoc prototype.

1 Introduction

With the transition from classical libraries to digital libraries, the distribution of responsibilities between publishing houses, library organizations and end users is changing. When providing electronic versions of classical paper books or journals on the Internet, the traditional business models have to be reconsidered and new cost models for the usage of electronic documents must be applied. Electronic books and journals not only have new properties that provide added value (e.g., full text searching, audio-clips, video animations), but electronic editions on the World Wide Web also have potentially a far larger audience.

MeDoc (Multimedia electronic Documents) [14] is a German digital library project that brings together publishing houses on the producer side and universities and industrial user institutions on the user side. For an overview over the organization and aims of the project MeDoc see [1]. The MeDoc library provides a distributed electronic full text library of high quality computer-science literature. This library can only be furnished with high-quality commercial products, if the usage is billable and protected. This requires the development and installation of a commonly accepted business model and the implementation and evaluation of a variety of cost models to charge for the usage of the services of the MeDoc library [4] [5]. A requirements-analysis phase [6] has identified the basic concepts and models for accounting and a security policy for MeDoc. The scope of this paper are the cost models and accounting realized in the MeDoc prototype.

There are several digital library initiatives that deal with aspects of a billable digital library, like the United States initiative [11] (with [7]), the British initiative [20] or another German initiative [16], also dealing with the billing and charging issues. Several expositions are the subject of pricing electronic services, like [8] [9] [12] [18] or [21]. Others are dealing more generally with commercial infrastructures for digital libraries like [19]. A few projects deal with the the the aspect of integrating electronic payment systems into digital libraries like Copinet [17] or IterPay [7]. But there is still no comprehensive foundation of business and cost models for digital libraries on which to base the pricing.

In this paper we first introduce the business model of the MeDoc service. Based on this business model a variety of cost models can be applied. A basic taxonomy of these cost models is discussed. We give details on what cost models are currently applied in the MeDoc digital library. The implementation of the MeDoc billable digital library is described. We describe the workflow when ordering and using licenses and the price modeling facilities.

2   The Business Model

On the Internet there are typically two basic models to finance a service: one can be compared to TV financed by commercials and the other to Pay TV. Many services on the Internet (e.g. Yahoo, Lycos) finance themselves through advertisements. The end user gets the service for free. This is the same model that most commercial TV stations use. These Internet services are quite successful and have considerable value for the end user, but there is no guaranteed quality of results and searching can get tedious. This business model gets around the problem that there is still no feasible way to collect (typically very small) fees for each usage of such a service from a world wide and mainly anonymous auditorium. MeDoc, like a variety of other Internet services, has adopted a business model that is more like Pay TV. The user has to pay for the service delivered. For this the user is guaranteed a certain quality of contents and service. Figure 1 shows this business model.

On one side we have the *producers* of electronic documents, typically publishing houses or data base providers, but also universities or research institutes with their variety of technical reports, teaching material, theses, etc. The main role of a producer is to provide the documents with a guaranteed level of quality. The producer has to provide the documents in a suitable electronic format together with the meta data (e.g., title, authors, formats, abstract, table of contents) of the documents.

On the other side are the *users*. They use the service either to search or to retrieve documents. The main target users for the MeDoc project are (for

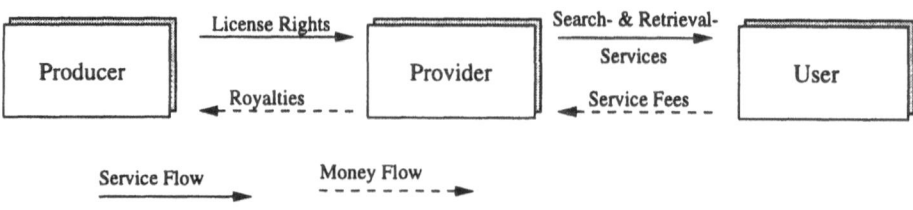

Fig. 1. The Business Model of the MeDoc System.

the time being) computer scientists, students and computer professionals of the pilot user organizations. None of them wishes to spend much time with tedious searching among irrelevant contents and each of them wants to be assured to have retrieved relevant data. These users are typically grouped by their institutions or companies.

The *providers* operate as a link between producers and users. Besides providing the basic technical service they add value to the offer of the producers: They bundle the offers of a variety of producers, enable inter-producer search, and act as a financial clearing house between users and producers. Currently the MeDoc consortium itself acts as the provider running several distributed servers, but in principle of course there could be several competing providers. The provider acquires from the producer the license rights to offer the electronic document as a service to the user. In exchange, the user is charged service fees. Right now the MeDoc project forwards the service fees directly to the producers (minus some handling fee).

The business model from Figure 1 has to be refined, because MeDoc would encounter the problem of collecting fees from potentially some 100,000s of (German) end-users. Contractual partners for the provider is currently not the individual end-user but mainly the end-user institution, representing a group of users (Figure 2).

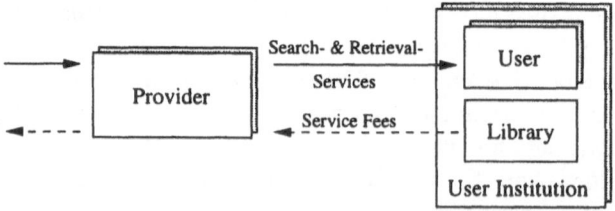

Fig. 2. The Refined Business Model

These end-user institutions are called "libraries", because the conventional university libraries could be such user groups representing their members, although they need not necessarily be libraries in that general sense. Their main responsibility is the administration of local users, the control of copyright restrictions, and perhaps the reimbursement of usage fees from their members. No end user needs to enter financial relations with the provider. The libraries represent their individual users to the provider and are responsible for the payment of the service fees. They subscribe to various services (e.g. books and journals) and allow their users free or reimbursed access. How that reimbursement is done is outside the scope of this paper.

3 Cost Models

MeDoc provides information brokering services free of charge, but document delivery or browsing of commercial documents is with costs.

3.1 User Requirements

The choice of an adequate cost model for a digital library or any billable service for that matter is an important and difficult task. The applied cost models strongly influence the acceptance of the service. Until now there is little experience with cost models for digital libraries and electronic documents. Due to its simplicity, the most common cost model in the Internet besides free access is the individual subscription of a single user to a service for a fixed fee (usually via login and password). Not only is the simple login&password solution for larger providers difficult to manage and tedious for the users, but also users have different needs for digital documents and they have different usage patterns. Therefore for the same product we need a set of different cost models to satisfy those different requirements.

In addition to the basic requirement of price worthiness from the users point of view other aspects are also important. There is the request for *clarity*. The cost model must be clear and simple. This is essential for user acceptance. *Predictability* is the other important issue. The user needs to be able to predict the cost of a service usage. This must apply not only to the cost of a single user action but also, more importantly, for budget tied users or user groups, to the cost of a complete time period, e.g. a budget year. A further requirement factor when selecting a cost model is the amount of *administration* involved. A low administration level is regarded mandatory by the MeDoc pilot users.

3.2 Taxonomy

To meet the requirements defined in the previous section various cost models have been developed [5] and tried in pilot studies. The following presents a taxonomy of cost models. We discuss basic rate, subscription and usage-based pricing models and their variations used in MeDoc.

Basic Rate A basic rate allows general access to the digital library. Some of the service components may be used without further charges, others may be subject to additional fees. With basic rates, services can be financed that cannot be charged for directly, e.g., long-term archiving or statistics.

Subscription A service can be subscribed to by a fixed fee for a limited period of time. This is quite often applied to large document bases such as, for example, journals, dictionaries or encyclopedias that contain information that is regularly maintained or extended. Subscriptions allows access to complete document bases or parts thereof. Subscription to an electronic journal differs significantly in one aspect from a paper journal: If a subscription expires, you still have the old paper copies of that journal that you can keep. But what about an electronic journal? If the provider ceases to recognize you as a registered user the information might no longer be accessible at all. This is the reason why publishing houses quite often link the subscription of the electronic edition to a subscription of the paper (or CD-ROM) edition.

Subscription models are employed if there is to be continuous usage of a document base, or if the pricing of each individual usage is not adequate or user-friendly. Subscription models usually are favored by users and providers and to a lesser degree by producers due to their easy handling, usage independence and predictability. Typically, standard HTML multi media documents only support subscription models, because to compute the value of a composite document in advance is difficult and with subscriptions, no advance report of charges prior to document delivery is required.

In MeDoc we distinguish the following basic license types that can be subscribed to:

- *Individual licenses* are assigned to individual persons. A special case of individual license is the anonymous license, where the identity of the user is unknown. In general, anonymity requires instant payment methods (e.g. electronic cash).
- *Group licenses* are assigned to a group of persons; each member of the group has the same right to use the service. This is typically connected with discount rates as opposed to several individual licenses. The number of group members is fixed in advance. For each additional member another license fee is required. Usually larger groups are granted higher discounts.
- *Campus licenses* are assigned to institutions and are valid for all their members; each member has the right to use the service. The number of group members is not known exactly in advance and new members (within reason) will not incur additional costs.

One disadvantage of the pure group license model is it's inflexibility. Once the number of group members is complete, no further users can be admitted even if some group members made use of their license right just once and since then lost all interest in it.

Floating licenses are a variation of group licenses where there are more group members than licenses. These licenses are shared by the members of the group. A license is assigned to a group member for a limited period of time. Once all licenses are assigned a subsequent user has to wait until one of the licenses is released. This model is quite common with software products like compilers or databases. Since standard World Wide Web technology does not support the session concept, licenses cannot be returned automatically, because there is no definite end of usage, as in the Web users do not log out explicitly. Instead, a license has to be released on a time out. The shorter the assignment period, the more users of a given group can use the same license. Advantage of the floating license model is it's easy administration. Unused licenses can be used by other group members, manual reassignment of unused licenses becomes unnecessary.

Usage Based Cost Models In usage-based cost models, each service usage gets billed as opposed to the flat fee system of the subscription cost models. Service usage in a digital library usually entails the retrieval of documents or fragments thereof or a search in document data bases. Every document (or a set of related documents) of the document base gets assigned an individual price. Each access to the document base is charged for separately. "Pay per view" models can be applied to the delivery of documents, as well as to information searching. There exists a wide variety of usage parameters: for example, size of the document or document fragment, time of access or number of query terms.

Usage-based cost models are offered as an alternative to subscription if the access of the user to the document base or service is infrequent and the user is generally not interested in subscribing to the complete document base, for example when requiring a single article of a certain journal. Especially with encyclopedias it makes sense to charge for subdocuments so the user does not need to pay for a huge document when only requiring a single entry. Usage-based cost models are suitable to meter - and to charge justly for - the usage of a document base or service.

One basic problem of usage-based cost models is the lack of predictability of the costs for the user. This applies not only for the total usage cost of a digital library for a period of time, but also to the costs of each individual service. It is not always possible to compute the costs prior to service execution. So for user acceptance it is mandatory to keep the usage parameter system clear and to enable the user at least to estimate the incurred costs easily.

3.3 Pricing

The MeDoc service has already started as a prototype. A total of 64 books and 7 journals from 14 publishing houses are currently (15/11/97) available. Further books are still converted into an appropriate format for licensing and presentation on the Web. The pilot users can order the books and journals on a paper order sheet or online via protected web order forms.

Table 1 gives an overview of the different cost models applied in the MeDoc digital library. Currently group licenses for books can be ordered at 7.5 % of the paper version. These licenses grant the right for viewing only, not for printing. The license is personal, i.e. it must be assigned to a specific person. The transfer of the license to another person must happen infrequently, e.g. after six months. An individual license may be ordered for any of these books with a surcharge of 1.33 times the group license price, that is 10 % of the price of the paper copy.

Table 1. Cost Models Applied in MeDoc

Cost Model	Group Size	Applied To	Fee per user in % of Book Store Price	Typical Fee + VAT
Individual License	1	Books	10 %	DM 5.30
Group License	small	Books	7.5 %	DM 4.00
	large	Reference B.	1-2 %	DM 0.60
Campus License	∞	Journals	0 %	free with library copy

Group licenses for very large groups are available at a yearly subscription rate. The yearly subscription fee is between 1 and 2 % of the price of the paper version per individual user. This model should give a library the chance to provide all its members with a license. One publisher has consented to try this cost model with two reference books.

Although granting group and individual licenses corresponds best to the sale of a book, the problem is that if sold once, the service basically should be provided for an arbitrary time. The agreement with our pilot users limits the licenses until the end of the project, but they are subject to be extended if the project is extended. Technically these licenses are handled as floating licenses with a long assignment period, so a transition to real floating licenses is possible whenever the license granting publishing houses agree to it. Electronic journals are offered as a campus licenses as free add-ons to the library paper version. There are also plans to introduce a pay-per-view model to access single articles of unsubscribed journals. The technical prerequisites for the application of this cost model are available, but our pilot users are very reluctant to accept this model, because they cannot control the expenses incurred by their end-users, i.e. the predictability of this cost model is not given. For the time being the publisher in question has agreed to accept the campus license cost model and be satisfied with extensive usage statistics.

Libraries order a bunch of licenses for each book in advance. Users of such a library can request a license for their personal use. No more than the number of ordered licenses can be assigned. If more users want to access a book, additional licenses must be ordered.

4 Implementation Approach

In accordance with the participating publishing houses and our pilot users subscription and usage-based pricing have been implemented for the MeDoc digital library.

4.1 Architecture

A detailed overview over the MeDoc digital library architecture is given in [3]. The MeDoc User Agent [2] and the MeDoc Full Text System [15] deal with the issues raised by the fact that part of the MeDoc offer is with costs. The special functionality of the MeDoc digital library making possible the billability of the MeDoc offer is sketched in figure 3.

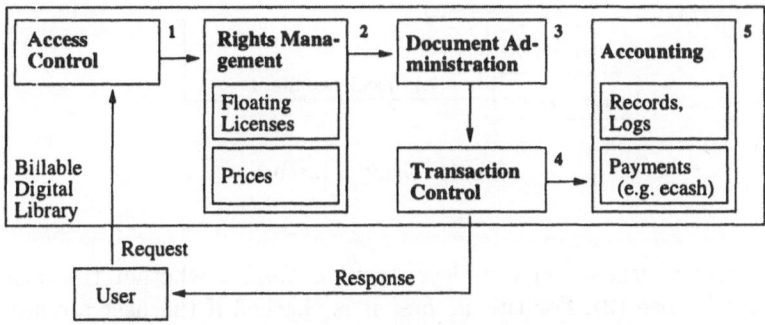

Fig. 3. Basic Architecture of a Billable Digital Library

Access to the MeDoc library is controlled and restricted (1). Only known users belonging to predefined user institutions may use services that are with costs. The license and price administration (2) manages the task of making documents accessible via licenses or charging usage-based prices for them. The document offer (3) is organized in a tree-like structure according to the MeDoc document model [13]. This allows for the definition of licenses and usage-based prices for subdocuments. The transaction control (4) ensures that neither the user is charged for services rendered incorrectly nor the user can deny the reception of correctly rendered services. For a description of the protocol idea see [22]. Incurred costs can be billed via accounts or charged for via electronic payment systems (5). For anonymous users such digital cash facilities are prerequisites which are not yet integrated in the MeDoc library. All rendered services are recorded via log files and user's accounts. The actual handling of invoices is done by the FIZ Karlsruhe that acts as Clearing Center.

4.2 Using a License

The MeDoc Full Text System [15] cooperates with the MeDoc User Agent [2] to implement the license models. This minimizes the administration requirements as well as the necessary message traffic, because the individual end users are known to the User Agent already. The Full Text System relies on the User Agent for the authentication and authorization of the users and their grouping. Therefore the Full Text System has auditing rights at the User Agent as described in [6].

Figure 4 shows the workflow when using a license in this cooperation scenario. We assume that the user has logged in at the User Agent successfully and has obtained a list of document references. When the user tries to access a document

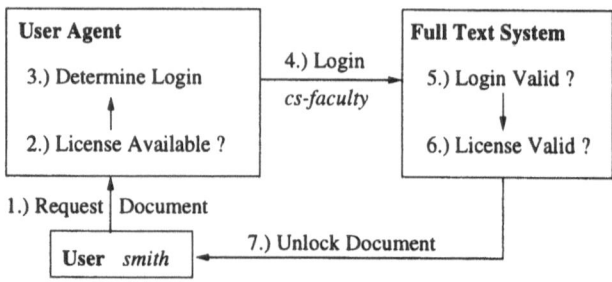

Fig. 4. Using a License

that requires a license (1) the User Agent evaluates whether the user can be assigned a license (2). For this at first it is checked if the user already owns a corresponding license. If this is the case that license can be used for the access request. If not, it is examined if a license with a suitable scope of validity is available. If this is the case the user is assigned that license. Then the User Agent evaluates what login is to be used to retrieve the document from the Full Text System (3). This login is used to contact the Full Text System with the document request (4). If the Full Text System accepts the login as valid (5) and a corresponding valid license is present (6), the document is released via a temporary URL (the MeDoc Browse URL [15]) and displayed to the user (7).

4.3 Ordering a License

Figure 5 shows the workflow when ordering a new license based on the current implementation.

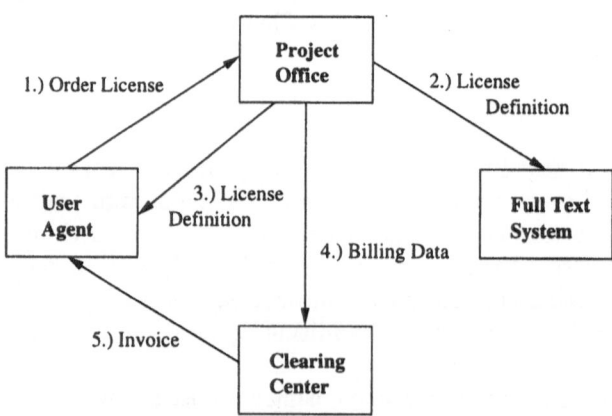

Fig. 5. Ordering a License

When ordering a new license the administrator of the User Agent contacts the MeDoc Project Office (1) via protected Web order forms or a paper based order sheet. The MeDoc Project Office generates the necessary license administration data. These data are forwarded as database statements via signed email to the Full Text System (2) that hosts the document subscribed to and the User Agent (3) ordering the license. They both have to install the new license after verifying the signature by executing the database statements. This process can be automated with email filters like procmail. The MeDoc Project Office generates billing data for this order and forwards them to the MeDoc Clearing Center (4). The Clearing Center executes the invoices to the administrator of the User Agent (5). Manual interference of the User Agent administrator can be restricted to the actual ordering and contract signing. Manual interference of the Full Text Server administrator is not necessary when ordering a license.

4.4 Modeling Usage Based Prices

Usage-based prices can be defined in the MeDoc Full Text System for document clusters as well as for subdocuments defined according to the MeDoc document model [13]. Prices may be attached not only to documents but also to certain document features. Document features are e.g. document format (PDF, HTML, ...) or document type (article, chapter, ...). Prices can apply to all users or only to special users. Prices can be defined absolute or relative to base prices. If neither a usage-based price nor a license applies, the Full Text System refuses to release the document. This means that free document offers must be defined explicitly.

Price definitions are resolved from special to general definitions, meaning definitions referencing a special user precede those pertaining all users and definitions for specific document subtrees are taken into account before more general ones regarding common document features are evaluated. The MeDoc price modeling technique allows for an efficient and flexible pricing of complex document offers, but requires great care in the definition process to avoid contradictory or ambiguous definitions.

5 Conclusion

The MeDoc service is still in a field test period. But the project already exceeds standard research approaches for digital libraries. That is, the MeDoc service is tested under (nearly) real conditions to be able to get forecasts for running the real service. MeDoc started with several basic cost models for electronic books and journals and a first suggestion for pricing services with these cost models.

The project MeDoc set up a running prototype in very short time that takes into account or at least addresses many aspects of electronic publishing of billable books and journals, like document access models, security, cost models, accounting, user and group concepts and system distribution. Therefore not all aspects could be dealt with in necessary depth. Unlike Decomate [10] MeDoc actually performs accounting of billable services which is essential when offering commercial books and journals. If results from projects like Copinet [17] or Iter-Pay [7] that deal with digital payment systems, were integrated into MeDoc we could deal with anonymous users as well.

Due to the usage of Postgres95, Fulcrum and Java the MeDoc system has some performance problems at evaluating complex pricing and license definitions. Memory cashing mechanisms and other workarounds have helped to ameliorate this problem but a thorough reimplementation based on more efficient tools is necessary to reach a stable and efficient system. Presently the administration support is very basic and requires much expert knowledge. To set up a comfortable administration environment including efficient monitoring facilities further work is necessary that unfortunately could not be done within the project term anymore.

The MeDoc system is well prepared to evaluate further cost models. Floating licenses in particular are favored by our pilot users as they hope for better exploitation of their licenses combined with very low administration requirements. The handling of floating licenses can start as soon as the publishers agree to it. Usage-based pricing and account-based handling of incurred costs can be put into action as soon as required as well.

The experiences with the MeDoc digital library prototype have proven so far that the cost model and accounting concept of MeDoc is valid and practical. Our pilot users and especially their administrations indicate that the most important issue is the transition from investment-based thinking ("buying a book") to a consumer-based thinking ("using a service"). Feedback from the pilot users shows they accept that a digital library is subject to charges, provided the quality of service is adequate and handling is user friendly and easy.

References

1. Barth A. and others . The MeDoc Digital Library Project: Its Goals and Major Achievements. In *Digital Libraries in Computer Science: The MeDoc Approach*, Lecture Notes on Computer Science. Springer Verlag, Heidelberg, 1997.
2. Boles D. and others . Conception of the User Agent – the User Interface of the MeDoc System. In *Digital Libraries in Computer Science: The MeDoc Approach*, Lecture Notes on Computer Science. Springer Verlag, Heidelberg, 1997.
3. Boles D. and others . The MeDoc System – A Digital Publication and Reference Service for Computer Science. In *Digital Libraries in Computer Science: The MeDoc Approach*, Lecture Notes on Computer Science. Springer Verlag, Heidelberg, 1997.
4. Breu M., Brüggemann-Klein A., Haber C., and Weber R. The MeDoc distributed electronic library - accounting and security aspects. In *ICCC/IFIP Conference on Electronic Publishing*. University of Kent, Canterbury, April 1997.
5. Breu M. and Weber R. Charging for a digital library - the business model and the cost models of the medoc digital library. In *Contribution to the First European Conference on Research and Advanced Technology for Digital Libraries*. Pisa, Springer-Verlag, September 1997.

6. Brüggemann-Klein A. MeDoc Pflichtenheft. Technischer Bericht, TU München, June 1996.
7. Cousins S. and others . InterPay: Managing multiple payment mechanisms in digital libraries. In *DL '95 proceedings*, 1995.
8. Day C. Economics of electronic publishing. In *JEP*, 1994.
9. Day C. Pricing electronic products. In *JEP*, 1994.
10. Dijkstra J. Decomate. Online http://decomate.lse.ac.uk.
11. Griffin S.M. Digital library initiative der usa. Online http://dli.grainger.uiuc.edu/national.htm.
12. Gupta A., Stahl D.O., and Whinston A.B. Pricing of services on the internet. Technical report, University of Texas at Austin, 1996.
13. Haber C., Meyer J., and Weber R. Aufbau und Realisierung des MeDoc-Volltextspeichers. In *Proceedings zum Workshop digitale Bibliotheken*. Springer Verlag, Heidelberg, 1997.
14. MeDoc . Home Page. Online http://medoc.informatik.tu-muenchen.de, 1996.
15. Meyer J and Appelrath H.-J. Design and Implementation of the MeDoc Fulltext System. In *Digital Libraries in Computer Science: The MeDoc Approach*, Lecture Notes on Computer Science. Springer Verlag, Heidelberg, 1997.
16. Neubauer K.W. Ibis - Internetbasiertes Elektronisches Bibliotheksinformationssystem. Online http://www.ub.uni-bielefeld.de/ibispro.htm, 1996.
17. Richards D. Requirements analysis for library accounting systems. In *Elektronisches Publizieren und Bibliotheken*. Bibliothek der Universität Bielefeld, February 1996.
18. Sairamesh J., Nikolaou C., Ferguson D., and Yemini Y. Economic framework for pricing and charging in digital libraries. *D-Lib Magazine*, February 1996.
19. Schutzer D. A need for a common infrastructure digital libraries and electronic commerce. *D-Lib Magazine*, April 1996.
20. UKOLN . Electronic libraries programme (elib) resources and projects. Online http://www.ukoln.ac.uk/elib.html, 1996.
21. Varian H. Pricing electronic journals. *D-Lib Magazine*, June 1996.
22. Zwissler S. *Methodischer Systementwurf für den elektronischen Handel*. PhD thesis, Universität Karlsruhe, April 1996.

Ariadne, an Interactive Navigation and Search System for Computer Science Information on the World-Wide Web

M. Dreger[1], S. Lohrum[1],
H. Schweppe[1] and C. D. Ziegler[2]

[1] Freie Universität Berlin, Institut für Informatik,
{dreger,lohrum,schweppe}@inf.fu-berlin.de
[2] FIZ Karlsruhe, Abt. Mathematik & Informatik, Berlin,
cdz@zblmath.fiz-karlsruhe.de

Abstract. Ariadne is a tool for interactive production and distribution of specialized information on computer science on the World-Wide Web. The key element of the Ariadne concept is the interaction between user and system. While most WWW information services can only be used passively, Ariadne enables users to decide on the contents and quality of the system and to obtain network-based, distributed scientific information on computer science.

The Ariadne concept is based on a combination of navigation and search methods for information retrieval, and on the users' contributions for information storage. Users have two options for maintaining their standards for the quality of the service: by entering information in the Ariadne database and by checking the quality of the information stored in it. Indexing and classification of the entries are used to ensure that Ariadne provides a red thread through the labyrinth of computer science information in the WWW.

Users have easy access to this information by combining navigation and search in given, but freely selectable parts of the Web. About changes of the information users can be informed by setting up profiles.

1 Introduction

The development of worldwide communication networks, distributed systems and tools for electronic publishing has provided the technical means for offering information, knowledge, new discoveries and inventions via open computer networks, and for retrieving and exchanging them without delay. The available information on scientific and technical activities in computer science is far beyond the contents of traditional bibliographic databases. Just by clicking, users are given access to the original documents, which increasingly are also available not only as text documents. The World-Wide Web [1] has become an important instrument for scientific communication and scientific publishing. However, it has also generated an enormous and highly heterogeneous mass of scientific and technical information which has never been recorded systematically, and which can only be accessed by browsing or by navigation of hyperlinks.

In the case of printed publications on computer science, the references in the established bibliographic databases and in the data compilations of the World-Wide Web [2] [3], together with libraries and document delivery services, are useful tools. An up-to-date bibliography of the most recent developments in computer science is hardly possible with bibliographic databases such as CompuScience [12] and Inspec [13] by FIZ Karlsruhe. The high quality standards of FIZ with regard both to correctness of the citations, and to the publication process for printed publications, are an obstacle to maximum up-to-dateness. On the other hand, in a dynamic discipline like computer science it is essential to have information about, and access to published expert information immediately. Every scientist knows that subject-specific workshops are more profitable in this respect than big standard conferences, which in turn are more up-to-date than journals. Increasingly, the results, discussions and papers of such events are published in digital form via the World-Wide Web in order to avoid the problems encountered with printed publications.

In view of all this, it will become necessary, in addition to the bibliographic description of publications in traditional form, to facilitate access to knowledge published on WWW sites in the form of hypertext, pictures, graphics, or as multimedia documents. This is demonstrated by the increasing number of WWW search engines and information services in the last few years [4].

The WWW navigation and search system Ariadne [1], developed in the context of MeDoc [14], is a service that differs from the common WWW search engines and robots in that Ariadne is intended to produce and supply high-quality information on computer science at low cost.

The Ariadne concept is based on a combination of navigation and search methods for information retrieval, and on the users' contributions for information storage.

Users have two options for maintaining their standards for the quality of the service: by entering information in the Ariadne database and by checking the quality of the information stored in it.

In contrast to other services and systems, Ariadne offers its users the possibility of contributing to the contents and quality of the services offered.

Indexing and classification of the entries are used to ensure that Ariadne provides a red thread through the labyrinth of computer science information in the WWW and serve as a standardized entry gate to information sources worldwide.

2 The Ariadne Concept

2.1 Publishing and Searching in the World-Wide Web

The World-Wide Web consists of a large number of heterogeneous, distributed hypertext documents. A document is found by navigation/browsing through the net via hyperlinks and/or by searching in one or several of the well-known Web

---

[1] http://ariadne.inf.fu–berlin.de:8000/

Search Engines. Browsing is a time-consuming technique and may get you lost in hyperspace, but searching with the aid of search engines is problematic as well.

A user must be acquainted with the available search engines (there are now more than a dozen). He must know about their strong and weak points and the idiosyncrasies of their query interfaces. Up to a point, the problems can be minimized by using so-called multiple search engines like SavvySearch [5] or Metacrawler [6].

Another problem is caused by the indexers' strategies for storage of bibliographic references in the basic database.

All indexers use robots or spiders which will index any page they encounter, with the intended goal of indexing the whole Web. The indexers used by the systems are not intelligent, and neither are the robots: In consequence, even the most irrelevant sites will be stored in the database. Together with the limited information content of the query interfaces, which are designed for intuitive access, browsing through the Internet will then lead to browsing through a list of several thousand hits in order to find the desired ten citations or so. Completeness is attained at the expense of quality.

In addition, indexing of the Web is a time-consuming procedure, even with the most efficient hardware available, and in consequence the ability of the search engines to keep their databases up-to-date leaves much to be desired. Months may pass before new pages are found, deleted pages are removed from the index, or page changes are indicated.

There is also another more serious problem: Publication on the Internet will largely severe the connection between address and content or between content and context.

To put this more clearly: To scientists, the journal or series in which a publication appears provides information on its quality, content, and formal context. 'Selective browsing' in journals with peer reviews, and in conference papers with expert opinions and selection procedures, is used to keep up to date in one's special field of interest. For publishing on the Web there exists no comparable filter function. To some extent, the establishment of electronic journals with editorial boards, peer reviews etc., and of scientific committees whose role is to recommend the publication of an electronic journal on a server (see Electronic Library of Mathematics of the European Mathematical Society (EMS) [15]) may counteract this situation, but there is still no connection between the hyperlink address (called URL or 'Uniform Request Locator') [18] and its contents. Of course, in principle, subsets of hyperlinks may be used for creating sub-webs with well-defined structures and topologies, i.e. the webs of theoretical computer science, software engineering, object-oriented programming, computational geometry. Information services like Yahoo [4], Dino [4], Lycos [4] and Harvest [4] attempt to structure their information in this manner.

Structures and topologies of this kind cannot be generated with the currently available tools and also cannot be used with the available query techniques, owing to the fact that navigation and search are still two completely separate processes. Navigation is used for constructing an index which can then be searched with a query formulation. The content, context and internal structure of the documents are left out of account. Selective browsing or navigation through the complete stock of documents is not possible on the Web.

Printed publications, especially journals, are published at regular intervals or on the occasion of special events, i.e. their date of appearance is more or less known. From that date, they are available in libraries, and can be searched for relevant contributions.

In contrast, publications on the Web are not linked to dates and events and in many cases they are preliminary versions or electronic preprints of printed material which will only appear after a considerable delay. There is no possibility of searching selectively for new publications, and in spite of the many efficient search engines, it is difficult to keep up to date. Furthermore a lot of Web-publications are of less value and noisy.

The development of the Ariadne system in the framework of MeDoc is an attempt to solve the above problems by combining the well-established methodology of the documentation sector with the ideas and technical options of the World-Wide Web.

2.2 Ariadne

Ariadne collects URLs, similar to the WWW information services. However, in order to prevent the quality problems described above, the URLs are not entered in the database automatically. Instead, they must be entered by the users, subject to a process of typing, classification and indexing. Ariadne enables interactive production and distribution of the computer science information available on the World-Wide Web.

Users have easy access to this information by combining navigation and search in given, but freely selectable parts of the Web.

Navigation and search Searching for information on the Web is quite different from the process of searching in information and database systems. Although the number of documents on the Web is finite, it is also undetermined. It is not possible to list all documents available on the Web at any time. For this reason, there are only two ways of finding documents on the Web: Either by starting navigation from a known document, following hyperlinks, or by querying the Web information systems. Both methods are unsatisfactory.

The Ariadne concept therefore proposes to restrict navigation and search to those parts of the Web that are relevant to computer science and to combine searching and navigation in order to organize an 'area-specific database search' [7] [8]. As the navigation and search area is defined by the ACM Computing Classification System [9], the Web sites that are relevant to computer science can be arranged in well-defined subwebs according to their contents.

Each node of the classification tree corresponds to a subject area of computer science. The information of a subject area can be retrieved by navigating through the classification system and/or by querying. With the option of guided or controlled navigation, a user can browse in his special fields of interest or else make a selective search in the subnets described by the navigation levels. Navigation in the classification system then corresponds to a depth-first-search, while querying the database for a subtree corresponds to a breadth-first-search.

Searches are carried out in a database which comprises WWW references (URLs) that have been typed (type of information object), classified (classification code of the classification scheme indicating the subject field of computer science to which the information object belongs), indexed (descriptors or controlled terms describing the contents of the information object), and described by an abstract, comment, or summary.

The context of documents (and to a certain extent also their internal structure) is taken into account by assigning classification codes, index terms and object types. By using the metadata in this way, the information is placed in a content-related context which can be used both for navigation and for searching (and also for judging the information content of the reference).

The quality of the references can be compared with the quality of entries in a bibliographic database. Production of high-quality entries is a considerable intellectual effort. Producers of bibliographic databases therefore have a large scientific staff. In contrast, the Ariadne concept relies on the users to ensure the information quality. The success of the concept therefore depends on intensive active cooperation of its users.

Active participation in Ariadne The key element of the Ariadne concept is the interaction between user and system. While most WWW information services can only be used passively, Ariadne enables users to decide on the contents and quality of the system and to obtain network-based, distributed scientific information on computer science. Users are to be integrated in two ways: The development and maintenance of the interactive review database, for information objects and services from the Web, is to take place with the active participation of the users, thus providing a tool for information supply to which the users have contributed. The database will list the network addresses (URLs) of scientifically relevant information, as well as the comments and a bibliographic description (descriptors, controlled terms, classification codes, abstract, summary), which are provided by the users. Compared with the many existing systems which automatically index WWW sites, this concept has the advantage that references will only be made to pages which others have found useful. The descriptions by the users is more informative than the indexing methods of the WWW information services. The interactive review database is an important supplementation to the passive WWW services.

Another way in which users can participate actively in system development is by checking up on the quality of the information contained in the Ariadne database, i.e. by deciding whether an item should be contained in the database at all, and whether the bibliographic description must be supplemented or corrected.

Active cooperation of the users in the establishment and operation of the system can help to establish contacts between scientists working in related fields, as well as between science, publishing houses and industry, and it can also contribute to the rapid distribution of new ideas, findings and problems. The network will catalyze scientific and technical cooperation. Scientific information will arise from scientific communication, and it will be the scientific community itself that ensures that its members obtain selective, structured and up-to-date scientific information of high quality.

Scientific information with Ariadne   Scientific information on computer science is abundant on the World-Wide Web. The problem is one of information overload rather than of scarcity, as is illustrated by the vast number of technical report servers, bibliographies, data compilations and bibliographic databases. However, the services offered vary greatly with regard to their quality and cost, and most of their references are to printed publication. High-quality bibliographic description and recording of the knowledge available on the WWW, and low-cost access to this knowledge, is a problem that still needs to be solved.

The quality of a scientific information service is influenced decisively by the following parameters:

- Completeness
- Up-to-dateness
- Depth of the subject description
- Correctness of the bibliographic information
- Consistency of addresses (URLs)
- Reliability, availability and response times of the system
- Easy access to the system and easy use.

Bibliographic databases like CompuScience and Inspec meet all of these quality criteria, although they are lacking in up-to-dateness, completeness and easy access.

They set a quality standard in the depth of the subject description, with index terms, classification codes, controlled terms, abstracts, summaries and meta-information.

Production of bibliographic references with this high quality standard requires high scientific competence, for which producers of bibliographic databases have an experienced scientific staff.

In contrast, the data compilations and bibliographies in the WWW have the advantage of being more comprehensive and up-to-date, free of cost, and unbureaucratic and easy to search.

On the other hand, the information is highly heterogeneous, and the formal description of the references is often incomplete and unreliable. The bibliographic description hardly covers more than a few bibliographic data.

While completeness, up-to-dateness, consistency and formal correctness can largely be ensured by computer programs, high-quality subject description cannot be done automatically with the same degree of reliability.

Ariadne's retrieval concept, i.e. navigation combined with searching, can be successful only with high-quality bibliographic description of the documents. Documents without or with insufficient classification cannot be found by navigation. Documents without descriptors or controlled terms are difficult to access, and the relevance of documents without abstract, summary or comment can hardly be judged.

For this reason, we developed the concept of network-based distributed production or participation.

This means that computer science information available on the Web should be made available via Ariadne. Any computer science specialist can improve the quality of the service by entering information he considers relevant or by correcting, commenting and abstracting information contained in the system.

This concept bridges the gap between producers and users which is characteristic of bibliographic databases and other specialized scientific information services. Scientific information is made available on the basis of the expert competence of the whole scientific community, and at low cost.

Apart from their detailed bibliographic description, bibliographic databases also contain meta-information, i.e. on language, country, document type, characterization of contents, conference data, etc.

We have taken over this concept in Ariadne for classifying information objects. The concept ensures that only information that can be classified is stored in the system and not just any WWW site. Information on object types enables the user to restrict his/her search to the objects that interest him/her most.

Ariadne supports the following object types:

- Document   – Scientific texts
- Software   – Algorithms, programs, software
- Service   – Data compilations, bibliographies, information systems
- Event   – Meetings, workshops, conferences
- Organization   – Enterprises, institutes, associations
- Person   – Authors, scientists
- Picture   – Graphics
- Video, Sound   – Self-explanatory

---

3 Functionality of Ariadne

Ariadne is a tool for interactive production and distribution of specialized information on computer science on the World-Wide Web.

Ariadne users can obtain network-based specialized computer science information with World-Wide Web clients like Netscape and Mosaic.

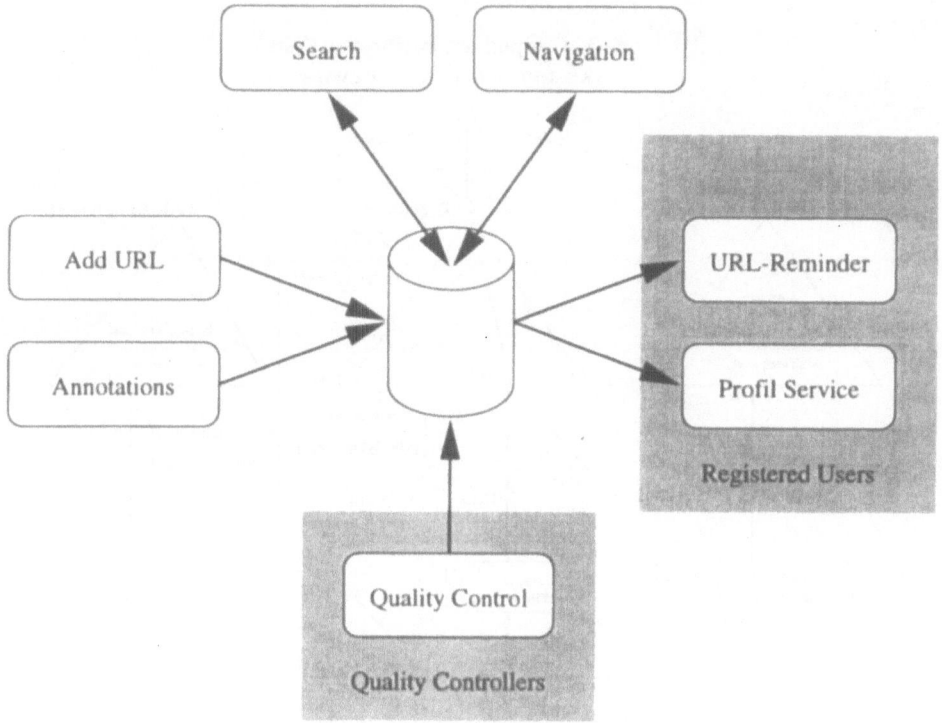

Fig. 1. Ariadne's Functionality

The information available on the Web is managed in a central database. The initial stock of about 8000 URLs was compiled mostly with the aid of existing data compilations [2] [3] and Information and Resource Discovery Systems [4]. The URLs were classified and indexed by the Ariadne administration.

Ariadne also provides access to other information sources and services, e.g. databases, data compilations, bibliographies, libraries, publishing houses, software libraries, Technical Report Servers and Document Delivery Services.

3.1 Navigation and Search

The Ariadne navigation tool is the ACM Computing Classification System. Users navigate virtually on the World-Wide Web by traversing the tree established by the classification system.

The numbers next to the classification codes indicate the number of entries in this subject field contained in the Ariadne database, and also the number of entries whose bibliographic and formal descriptions have been checked.

If the number of documents obtained by navigation is still too large, it can be reduced by searching. For this reason, each subtree of the classification system, represented by a browser page, permits a search for the root node of the subtree which denotes a subject area of computer science.

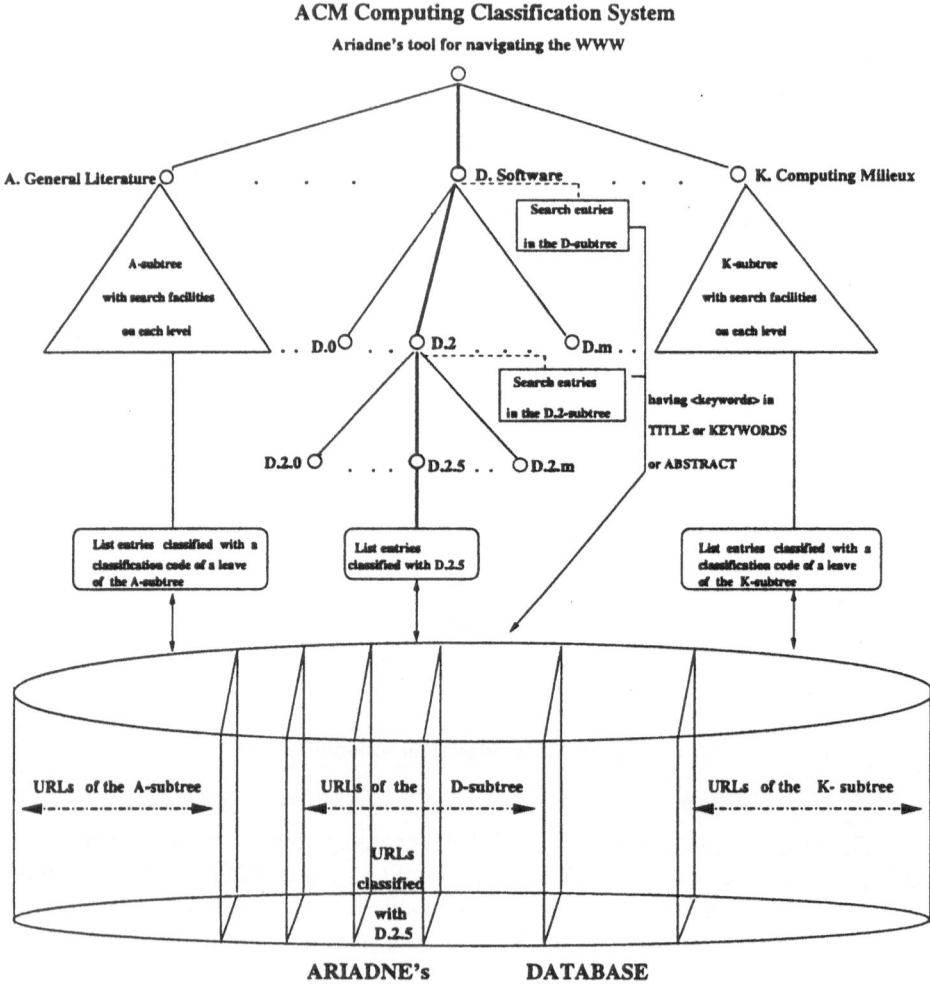

ACM Computing Classification System

Ariadne's tool for navigating the WWW

Fig. 2. The red thread through the web to Computer Science

Information can be retrieved selectively by entering search terms in a search form.

If more than one search term is entered the search is performed as a Boolean OR combination of the search terms. Variations of search terms are taken into account if search terms are reduced to their word stems or are entered in truncated form.

Search terms may occur in the document title, in the controlled terms or in the abstract, summary or comment of the document. Users can specify what category of a document should be searched. If no specifications are made, search terms are looked for in all categories.

The search for object types is organized in the same manner.

The search result is presented in the form of a list, sorted either by the date the objects were entered in Ariadne, or according to their order of relevance, as calculated by Ariadne.

3.2 Compilation and recording of information

Ariadne organizes active, structured, indexed and commented compilation of computer science information from the World-Wide Web, inviting all users to fill in the relevant fields in a form and forwarding the form to the Ariadne administration. Indexing and classification of the information is supported by offering a window in which controlled terms and classification codes from the ACM Computing Classification System can be selected. The URL and a classification code are mandatory.

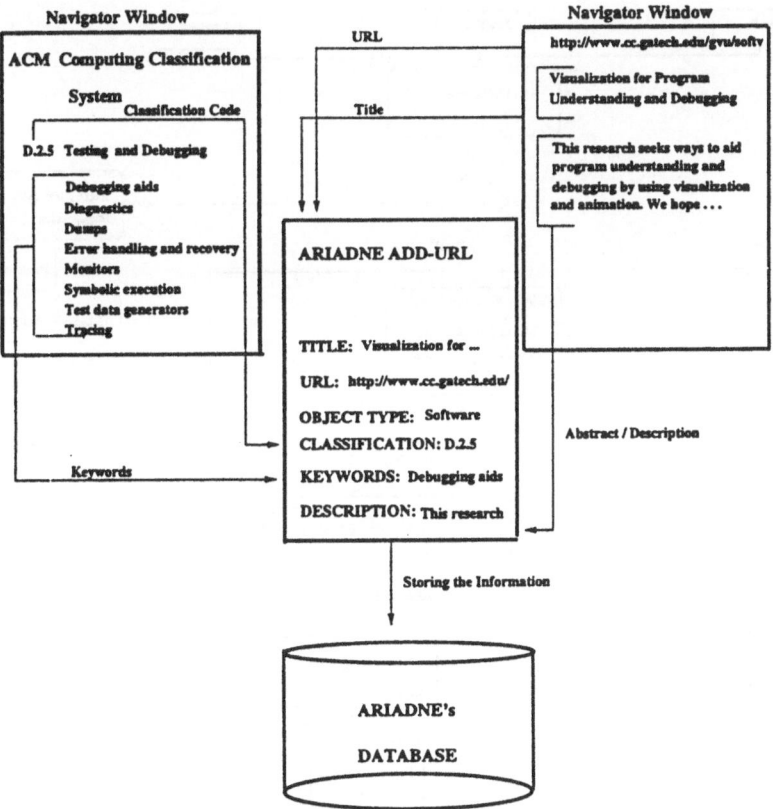

Fig. 3. Adding Information to Ariadne's Database

3.3 Quality control

Quality control is necessary if one intends to provide high-quality specialized information on computer science on the basis of 'spontaneous' contributions, unorganized and without fixed responsibilities. For a number of reasons, we decided in favour of interactive quality control for the Ariadne database.

On the one hand, we intended to ensure that only those documents, whose relevance to computer science was agreed upon by many computer science experts, could be found in the database. On the other hand, the concept of navigation and search depends on the quality of bibliographic description.

There are many instances in which the classification of a document is a matter of opinion. Documents often have interdisciplinary aspects and may be classified into several subject areas of computer science. The structure of classification schemes is hardly ever fine enough to account for the dynamics of a subject area. It is therefore important to have wide acceptance for the 'final' classification of documents.

Interactive quality control can also help to develop an awareness of the importance of specialized information, an awareness which has had a long tradition in other areas of science, especially mathematics.

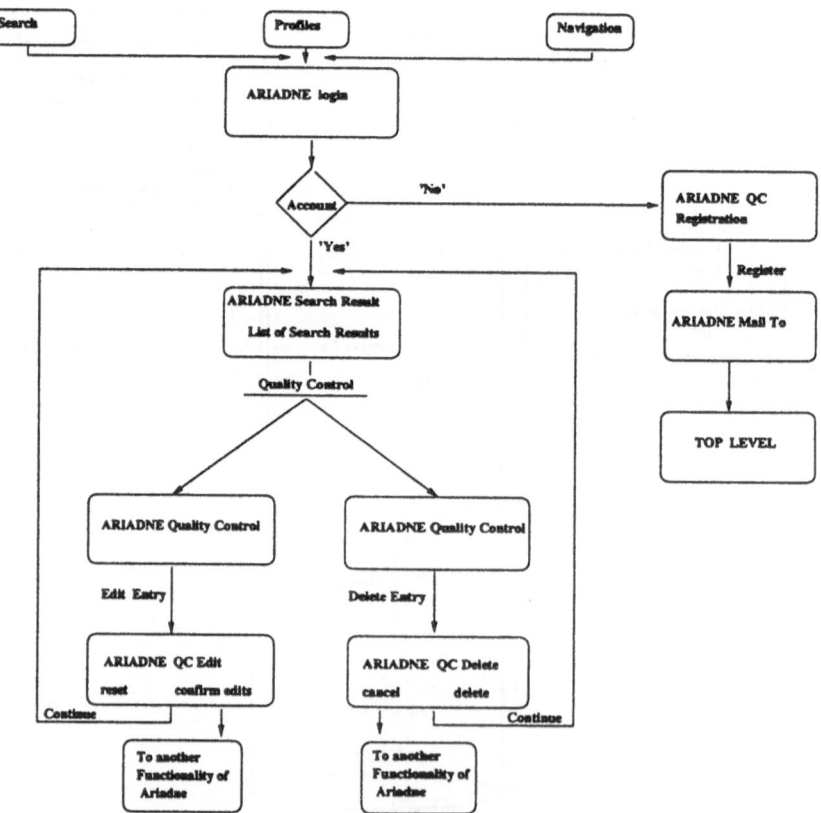

Fig. 4. The Process of Quality Controlling in Ariadne

The user acquires the permission to make quality checks by registering with the Ariadne administration as a quality controller for certain fields of computer science.

All entries in the Ariadne database comprise status information, i.e. whether or not an entry has been quality-checked, whether the URL of the entry is accessible, and the date of the last consistency check.

All new entries must be checked, and it must be decided whether the entry should remain in the database at all, or whether descriptive data require supplementation or corrections.

3.4 SDI profiles service

In the case of bibliographic databases, regular information on changes in a user's field of interest is provided by a service organized in the form of so-called SDI profiles (Selective Dissemination of Information). In view of the above-mentioned difficulties in obtaining information on activities, events and current research on the World-Wide Web, we consider the establishment of an SDI service as necessary and useful.

Profiles are long-term search queries stored by Ariadne and carried out at regular intervals. A user can set up an SDI profile by specifying his search query and modifying it until the search provides the expected results. The system will inform him via e-mail about changes made in the documents stored or about new documents added to the set. Users can also get information on their profiles and on the search results of the profiles interactively.

Ariadne will check and store the URLs of WWW sites on whose modifications a user wants to be informed. There are two ways of storing interesting URLs. First, URLs can be sent directly to the Ariadne Administration using the mail tool of the WWW browser. The titles under which the URLs will be stored in Ariadne are taken from the Email Subject. Secondly, URLs and their titles can be stored or removed interactively from the browser page.

With the URL check-up, users can have their bookmarks administrated by Ariadne.

4 Implementation of Ariadne

4.1 Architecture

Ariadne has been implemented as a typical 3-tier client-server application (see Fig. 5). In the user interface layer all standard WWW browsers can be used. This is a very important criterion for user acceptance and a necessity for instant access to referenced objects on the World-Wide Web. Persistent data storage and data integrity is guaranteed by a relational database system. The application logic is provided by several programs. This includes

- the generation of the different screen masks for navigation, search and display of results,
- the user-specific functions (*login* , *SDI profiles, quality control*),
- the integration of system services (e.g. *Email*), and
- the correction of errors.

For client access to the application programs a HTTP server with a standard CGI interface is used. The application programs themselves are written in the Python programming language. The client/server connection is made by the Hypertext Transfer Protocol (HTTP) [17]. Ariadne was developed under the UNIX operating system and was ported to Windows NT. Underlying database systems are Sybase or Oracle, which are encapsulated by a specific database module that provides transparent database access. This database module allows easy migration to other database systems.

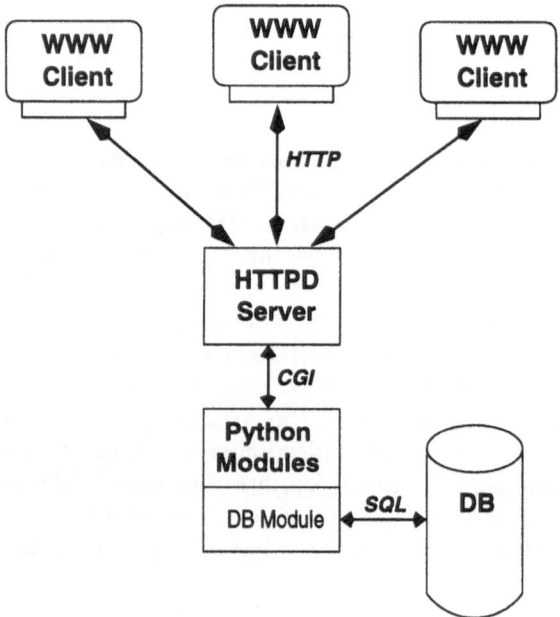

Fig. 5. Architecture of the Ariadne system

4.2   Data storage

Records, user data and profiles are modeled in a relational scheme. Each record has at least one title, at least one classification code, several descriptors, and a short description (abstract or comment). The formal description is based on the URL and the object type. In addition, further status information is recorded for each entry, e.g. the date of entry in the database, the last update, the date at which the validity of the URL was last checked, and a note on the results of this check. Descriptors and classification codes are stored in separate tables because of the 1-n relationship.

The user information comprises the user's name, corporate address, password, and the Email address as key. The table also contains information on whether the user wants to be informed via e-mail, and whether he has registered as a quality controller.

User SDI profiles are administered in still another table. Data integrity is ensured by formal checks with triggers and database constraints and via referential integrity.

4.3 Indexing and searching

When entering a new reference into the Ariadne database, terms are automatically extracted from its title and description. These terms are used for searches in addition to the user provided keywords and controlled terms derived from classification codes. In the database all terms are stored in the given form and as stems. For stemming the Porter algorithm [19] is used. This algorithm is designed for English terms, but in spite of the problems it has with other languages we decided to use it, because most of the computer science literature is published in English, particularly on the Web.

Each term is marked with the part of the description it is derived from, so that different weights can be assigned to the terms of the title and the user provided keywords for example (see table 4.3). These weights can be used to rank search results.

Term source	Code	Weight
term extracted from description	1	1
term generated from classification	2	5
term extracted from title	3	6
keyword given by a user	4	10

Table 1. Term weights of Ariadne's database

Searches can be made in the Ariadne database for a list of keywords/word stems, for a list of classification codes, and for object types. The keywords or classification codes within a list are combined disjunctively, while the search for different attributes is combined conjunctively. The above table permits either an exact search for word stems or a prefix search for keywords. The results can be weighted and listed in order of importance, or, alternatively, in chronological order.

4.4 Consistency check

At regular intervals, Ariadne checks the validity of the URLs by requesting that entry. On the basis of protocol information, Ariadne finds out whether the document is accessible, and when it has been modified last time. This information is recorded and displayed to the user. A document which was not found several times is no longer listed as an Ariadne entry.

4.5   Parameterization

To provide an easy way to adapt Ariadne to the needs of different scientific disciplines, several parts of Ariadne are exchangeable to provide an easy way to adapt it to the needs of different communities. This is possible for the classification scheme, which is the basis of the navigatorial access to the information, the stopword list and the algorithm for word stem reduction. Last but not least, the term weights used for ranking the results are configurable.

5   Experience with Ariadne

The concept of distributed creation and maintenance of up-to-date databases with references to scientific information on the Web is promising. The mix of functions integrated in Ariadne, particularly the active components, have shown to be interesting and helpful. This is expressed by the encouragement we've received from the users, the judgement in scientific publications on digital libraries [10] and the porting of the system by IZ Sozialwissenschaft. Moreover, the ACM concept for a digital library [16] comprises interactive SDI profile services, interactive distributed quality control and brokering services, functionality that can also be found in Ariadne.

Nevertheless the Ariadne project has encountered technical and particularly organizational problems in establishing such a service.

The completeness, number and quality of the entries in Ariadne is not up to the users' requirements. In order to get a wider acceptance for Ariadne's passive component, Ariadne must have a 'critical mass' of high-quality entries. To computer scientists who want to contribute information to Ariadne, the system will not be interesting unless they can expect to reach a large number of users this way; to passive users, on the other hand, the database is interesting only if it comprises a large store of information.

This fact is closely related to the problems of high-quality information (indexing, moderation, quality) and information acquisition. The technical implementation of these functions is still insufficient. The current version 4 of Ariadne is still a prototype in which the principles described in this publication have been implemented. The user who wants to classify and index entries is still given too little support. Input into the Ariadne database is a lengthy procedure, and quality control cannot be used for professional application of the system in the present form. Active use of the system is hampered by the fact that information cannot be entered into the Ariadne database from a given browser page unless a new window is opened which contains the page for information input. These problems must be solved with the aid of new tools and solutions if the system is to be successful on a long-term basis.

In order to ensure continuous updating and quality control, it is recommended to form Editorial Boards for all subject areas. These Editorial Boards should then be made responsible for information acquisition and quality assurance in their special area.

To conclude, Ariadne is a valuable experimental system and can form the basis for further developments and ideas in the field of digital libraries. Technological progress might help to solve some of the technical problems we have encountered in implementing Ariadne [11]. But the main challenge in gaining broad use and acceptance of such a service is an organizational one.

References

[1] Berners-Lee, T.; Cailliau, R.; Luotonen, A.; Frystyk Nielsen, H.; Secret, A.: The World-Wide Web. Communications of the ACM 37 (8), 76-82 (1994)

[2] Databases & Logic Programming. A bibliography server by Michael Ley, Universität Trier, Germany.
http://www.informatik.uni-trier.de/ ley/db/index.html;

[3] The Collection of Computer Science Bibliographies. A bibliography server by Christian Achilles. Universität Karlsruhe, Germany.
http://liinwww.ira.uka.de/bibliography/index.html

[4] AltaVista: http://www.altavista.digital.com
Lycos: http://www.lycos.com
Yahoo: http://www.yahoo.com
Open Text: http://www.opentext.com
Infoseek: http://guide-p.infoseek.com
Dino: http://www.dino-online.de
Harvest: http://mordor.transarc.com

[5] Dreilinger, D.: Savvysearch home page (1997)
http://www.cs.colostate.edu/ dreiling/smartform.html

[6] Selberg, E.; Etzioni, O.: Multi-service search and comparison using the Metacrawler. In: Proceedings of the 4th International WWW Conference, Boston, December 1995
http://www.w3.org/pub/Conferences/WWW4/Papers/169
http://www.metacrawler.com/

[7] Ullmann, Jeff: Web will change the role of journals. Computing Research News Online (May 1996)
http://www.cra.org/CRN/html/9605/opinions/ju.2_2_t.shtml

[8] Preparata, Franco P.; Savage, John E. : Publishing in journals still important. Computing Research News Online (May 1996)
http://www.cra.org/CRN/html/9605/opinions/fpp_jes.2_2_b.shtml

[9] Coulter, N.; Finermann, A.: ACM Computing Classification.
http://www.acm.org/class/1991/.

[10] Binder, Wolfgang: Die virtuelle Bibliothek ist Internet-Realit"at: Neue Rollen f"ur reale Bibliotheken. NfD 47, 215-224 (1996)

[11] Mendelson, Alberto O.; Mihaila, George A.; Milo, Tova: Querying the World Wide Web. International Journal on Digital Libraries Vol. 1 (1), 54-67 (1997)

[12] CompuScience. A bibliographic database in the field of computer science.
http://www.zblmath.fiz-karlsruhe.de/cs/computxt.html;
http://stneasy.fiz-karlsruhe.de/
http://www.zblmath.fiz-karlsruhe.de/cs/WWW2STN.html

[13] INSPEC Information Services.
http://www.iee.org.uk/publish/inspec/inspec.html;
http://stneasy.fiz-karlsruhe.de/

[14] Breu, B.; Brüggemann-Klein, A.: Das MeDoc-Projekt: Ein Überblick. Informatik/Informatique - Zeitschrift der schweizerischen Informatik Organisationen, Zürich (1997).

[15] http://www.emis.de/

[16] http://www.acm.org/dl

[17] Berners-Lee, T.; Fielding, R.; Frystyk, H.: Hypertext Transfer Protocol - HTTP/1.0. *Request for Comments*, 1945, May 1996.

[18] Berners-Lee, T.; Masinter, l.; McCahill, M.: Uniform Request Locators (URL) - HTTP/1.0. *Request for Comments*, 1738, May 1994.

[19] Porter, M. F.: An algorithm for suffix stripping. Program. (July 1980) vol. 14, no. 3, p. 130-137

Grey Literature and Multiple Collections in NCSTRL*

S. Adler[1], U. Berger[2], A. Brüggemann-Klein[3], C. Haber[3], W. Lamersdorf[1], M. Münke[1], S. Rücker[1], H. Spahn[1]

[1] University of Hamburg, Department of Computer Science, Distributed Systems Group, Vogt-Kölln-Str. 30, D-22527 Hamburg,
{4adler,lamersd,muenke,1ruecker,4spahn}@informatik.uni-hamburg.de,
[2] University of Stuttgart, Faculty of Computer Science, Breitwiesenstr. 20/22, D-70565 Stuttgart, Uwe.Berger@informatik.uni-stuttgart.de,
[3] TU Munich, Institute for Computer Science XI, Arcisstr. 21, D-80290 München, {brueggem,haber}@informatik.tu-muenchen.de

Abstract. One of the goals of the MeDoc project is to make computer science literature, e.g. Technical Reports and project and master theses of different authors and institutions available online through a single user interface. Therefore, we evaluated existing Technical Report servers as to their suitability as a basis for an electronic library and chose NCSTRL. The *Networked Computer Science Technical Reports Library* (NCSTRL) is a world–wide, distributed collection of computer science Technical Reports and other relevant materials. It is a well established system, but there are some deficiencies that need to be taken into account. This paper presents two different enhancements to the NCSTRL system to overcome those deficiencies. The first adapts NCSTRL to support not only the publication of Technical Reports but of other *grey literature* like course materials and theses as well. The second extension allows for the utilization of NCSTRL as a general tool for the online–publication of and search for electronic documents in multiple collections.

1   Introduction

As the research related material available on the Internet is rapidly growing, scientist are faced with the problem of efficient resource discovery and access. Traditionally, many institutions offer their publications online via FTP– or WWW–servers, but without any further support, finding relevant documents is still a cumbersome activity . In the last few years a number of different systems have been developed to support the user in searching and the provider in offering Technical Reports and other relevant documents. These systems range from simple lists of (hyper–) links to servers of publishing institutions to sophisticated distributed index and search servers. However, these systems were not designed to

---

* This work was partly sponsored by the German Ministry for Education, Science, Research and Technology (Project MeDoc, no. 08 C 7829 6).

include *grey literature*[1] and some explicitly discourage the integration of other material than Technical Reports. Moreover there is no widely available facility to search for grey literature documents and as the existing Technical Report servers offer no means of distinguishing between different kinds of documents, simply using these servers to make e.g. diploma theses and course materials available would reduce the quality of the provided service: Users searching for Technical Reports would probably find other kinds of documents not relevant for them along with what they are after.

Since many institutions participating in the German *MeDoc* project [1,2] are interested in a system for the publication of grey literature, a working group was founded to build up an *Electronic Library for Grey Literature*. Since the structure of grey literature is similar to the structure of Technical Reports, the easiest way of building such an electronic library is to enhance an existing Technical Report system. After an evaluation of the most important computer science Technical Report servers, the working group choose the *Networked Computer Science Technical Reports Library* (NCSTRL) as a basis for the grey literature library.

Although NCSTRL in its current version[2] is a very useful instrument for the electronic dissemination of and search for Technical Reports, a few limitations still prevent the widespread deployment of the system as a general tool for the electronic publication of (scientific) documents on a larger scale. Since NCSTRL was initially intended for the publication of Technical Reports, the contribution of grey literature to the collection is explicitly discouraged. Furthermore, there are still deficiencies that limit the scalability of the system: For example, all participating organizations have to be administered in a flat name space; in particular, it is not possible to divide a single organization into several, uniquely identifiable sub–organizations without inappropriately "polluting" the global name space.

This paper describes two separate enhancements to the NCSTRL–software to overcome these limitations. The first enables the integration of grey literature into the NCSTRL library, while the second allows for the introduction of multiple collections. A collection is a set of documents that is not limited to a single site or authority. Collections allow for a logical structuring of the NCSTRL library regardless of the physical structure of the underlying distributed network of servers. The two enhancements were performed by different working groups and resulted in independent modifications of the source code.

This paper is organized as follows. Section 2 describes the evaluation of the most important Technical Report server systems with respect to their suitability for the grey literature library. This evaluation was performed by various participants of the MeDoc project. Section 3 gives a brief overview of the architecture of NCSTRL. The following section discusses — in our opinion important — limitations of the current system. In section 5 we present two different approaches

---

[1] Not officially published material, as e.g. project theses, master theses and course materials.

[2] We refer to Dienst 4-1-9.

to overcome these limitations by specific enhancements of the Dienst protocol and software. The feasibility of the proposed solutions has been demonstrated in recent implementations and there are prototypes running at the universities of Stuttgart and Hamburg, respectively, in the context of the MeDoc project. We close with a summary and an outlook on future work.

2 Evaluation of Technical Report Servers

The evaluation of existing Technical Report Servers showed that NCSTRL is the most suitable system for use in the MeDoc project. There are, however, still some deficiencies.

Prior to the evaluation a catalog of evaluation criteria was developed. Then the following computer science Technical Report servers have been evaluated: Harvest Computer Science Technical Report Broker, Computation and Language E-Print Archive (CMP-LG), New Zealand Digital Library (NZDL), Ibd: Informationsdienst für Informatikberichte, Computer Science Technical Reports Archive Sites (CSTR), Wide Area Technical Report Service (WATERS), and Networked Computer Science Technical Reports Library (NCSTRL).

2.1 Evaluation Criteria

The Technical Report servers have been evaluated with respect to various criteria. The most important ones are:

- *Size of the archive:*
  There must be a critical mass of interesting documents in an archive to get people to use it and enter their documents into the archive. The size of the archive is determined by the number of documents in the archive and the number of participating institutions.
- *Bibliographic Data:*
  Very important for the quality of search results is the bibliographic data: which attributes (author, title, date of publication, classification, abstract, etc.) are provided, and what quality are the bibliographic data. The bibliographic data can be generated manually or extracted automatically from the full-text. There is a tradeoff between the work needed to generate the bibliographic data and the quality of the bibliographic data.
- *User interface:*
  Is navigation in the document database and browsing of documents supported? Is online help available? What kind of search is supported (simple search, fielded search, boolean search etc.)? How are the search results presented to the user (overview of the results, details, ranking of the hits, highlighting of search terms, format of the full-text).
- *Maintenance of the archive:*
  How much work has to be done to enter a document into the archive? Are there tools available for the maintenance of the archive?

2.2 Evaluation results

The evaluation of existing Technical Report servers showed that the different development teams had very different approaches. Some of the servers evaluated have been given up in the meantime and some of the teams joined their efforts.

The *Harvest Computer Science Technical Report Broker* was an application of the Harvest Information Discovery and Access System[3][3]. This report server used gatherers that collected files and generated citations and a broker that built the search indexes from the gatherer files. The archive was quite large, it contained references to more than 20,000 reports of about 300 institutions. The bibliographic data depended on the individual servers that provided the reports. The search engine used was Glimpse[13]. Boolean search on the bibliographic data was supported. The presentation of the search results was very limited. Only the address of the server that provided the document, the file name of the document and a list of matched lines were shown. The Harvest Computer Science Technical Report Broker doesn't exist anymore, but the Harvest Information Discovery and Access System is still frequently used although the support of this system by the developers ended with the corresponding project in 1996.

The *Computation and Language E-Print Archive* (CMP-LG)[4] is a fully automated electronic archive and distribution server for papers on computational linguistics, natural-language processing, speech processing, and related fields. It is a central archive with mirrors. The archive contains about 800 documents. There are similar archives in other disciplines (mathematics, physics). The bibliographic data supported are the author, title and abstract. The main interface to the archive is through email, but access via FTP and WWW is also available. Navigation, browsing and search in the bibliographic data (author, title and abstract) are supported. Submitted papers are preferably in LaTeX.

The *New Zealand Digital Library* (NZDL)[5][19] collects documents available in PostScript or PDF from servers, extracts the plain text and builds a full-text index. The archive contains about 40,000 computer science reports from over 300 institutions. Bibliographic data are not provided, but the search can be limited to the first page of each document to emulate search on bibliographic data. Boolean and ranked search are supported. The display of the search results shows a few lines of text that contain the search terms (highlighted) for each document found. There are links to retrieve information about the document (URL, pages, date created and retrieved, size), facsimiles of the pages, the plain text and the PostScript file.

Ibd (Informationsdienst für Informatikberichte)[6] [4] is a central archive that stores bibliographic data of computer science Technical Reports. It supports full-text search on the bibliographic data. The bibliographic data is inserted manually. Ibd is no longer supported.

---

[3] http://harvest.transarc.com/
[4] http://xxx.lanl.gov/cmp-lg/
[5] http://www.cs.waikato.ac.nz/cgi-bin/nzdlbeta/gw
[6] http://www11.informatik.tu-muenchen.de/Ibd/

Two of the more popular systems for the online publication of Technical Reports — at least among universities and other research institutions in the United States —, the *Wide Area Technical Report Service (WATERS)* and the *Distributed Interactive Extensible Network Server for Techreports (Dienst)*, finally merged to become the *Networked Computer Science Technical Reports Library (NCSTRL)* [6]. WATERS [7] was an FTP–based searchable index and repository of Technical Reports, sponsored by the National Science Foundation. Dienst [9] was developed as an ARPA–sponsored CSTR project that made searching on different fields (e.g. author, title and abstract) possible. The limitations of both systems led to the creation of NCSTRL[7]. The development of NCSTRL is controlled by the NCSTRL working group, which exists within the ARPA–funded Digital Library Forum (D–Lib Forum). NCSTRL provides a single point of access to distributed databases by distributing queries to all servers chosen by the user. About 100 participating institutions offer about 18,000 computer science Technical Reports. The bibliographic data is inserted manually, but there are tools to support the authors of documents and the administrators of NCSTRL servers in publishing documents and maintaining the archives. NCSTRL supports fielded and boolean search (and optionally full-text search) and browsing and navigation in the document archives of the participating institutions. Figure 1 shows the fielded search form of NCSTRL. The results of a search are shown as a list of documents. For each document the publishing institution, authors and title are displayed (see Figure 2). The title of each document in the result list is a link to a page that shows the abstract of the document and links to the full-text (PostScript and optionally also thumbnails and other formats).

Among the evaluated Technical Report servers NCSTRL turned out to be the system that is best suited because it offers high retrieval quality and a convenient user interface, requires only a small amount of work for the maintenance of the document archives and already contains a large number of computer science Technical Reports from computer science departments of universities in the USA and other countries.

3   Review of NCSTRL properties and structure

In order to understand the modifications and enhancements of NCSTRL presented in the next section, we will take a closer look at the original NCSTRL system. NCSTRL is a world–wide, distributed collection of computer science Technical Reports and other relevant materials based on an open–architecture, networked–based system of interoperating servers. The number of participants and the size of the individual collections are rapidly growing as the Internet becomes the basis for information dissemination and retrieval in the research community.

The NCSTRL collection provides scientists with a single access point to research results from international computer science departments and laboratories.

---

[7] For historical reasons, the protocol and software used by NCSTRL are still called Dienst.

150

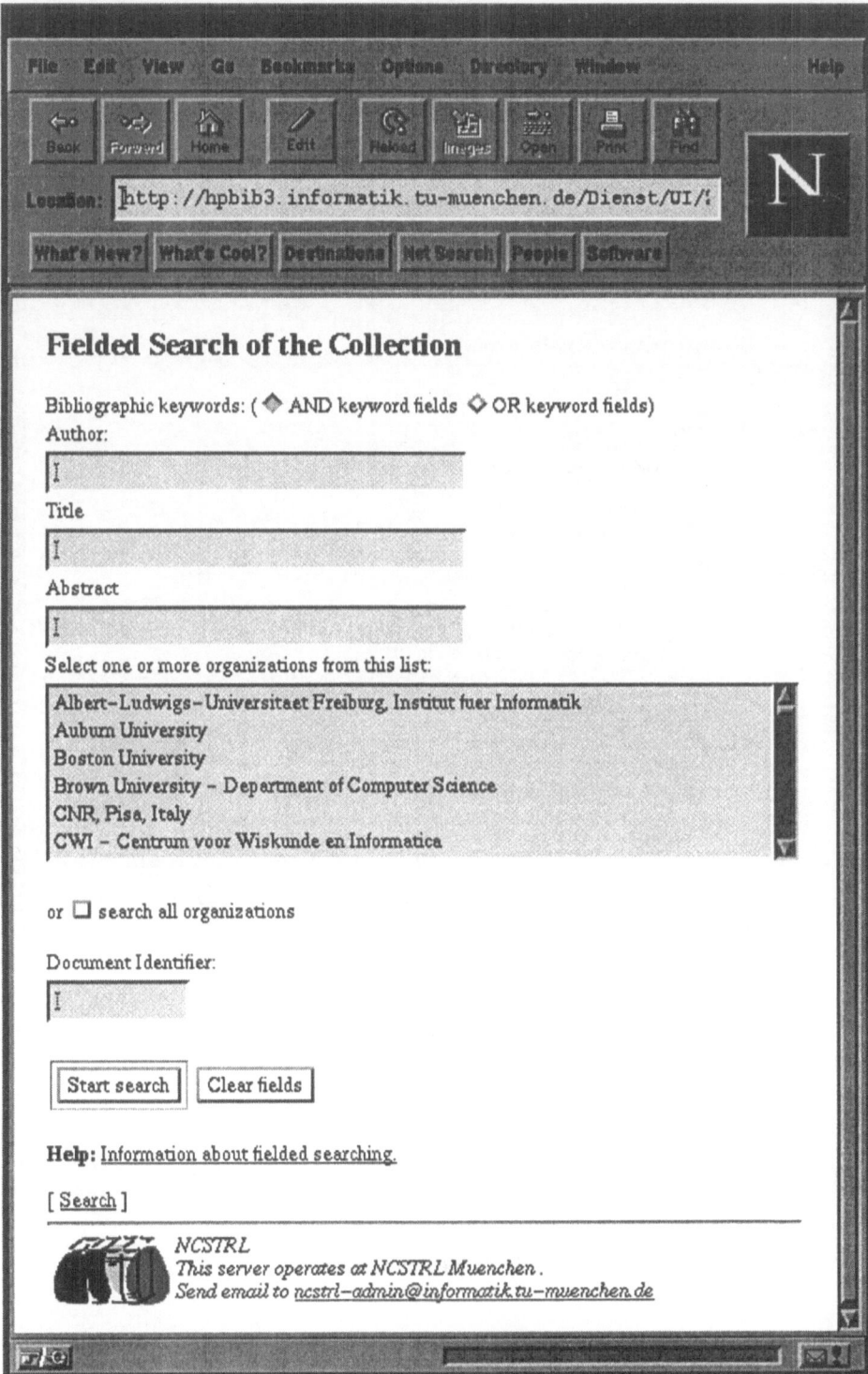

Fig. 1. Original fielded search form

[Search]

Search Results

Search fields:

- Organization:
  - ○ *GL-Site Universitaet Stuttgart*
  - ○ *Technical University of Munich*
- Documenttype = *Technical Report , Diplomarbeit , Seminararbeit , Studienarbeit*

Bibliographic keywords ("and"ed together):

- Author = *may**

Search Summary:

Organizations you selected are listed below by number of titles found.

- *(9)Technical University of Munich*
- *(2)GL-Site Universitaet Stuttgart*

Search Results:

Technical University of Munich
- ○ *Some Complexity Results for Polynomial Ideals.* Ernst W. Mayr. (TUM-I9704)
- ○ *Model Checking PA-Processes.* Richard Mayr. (TUM-I9640)
- ○ *Higher-Order Rewrite Systems and their Confluence .* Richard Mayr and Tobias Nipkow. (Sep26-1)
- ○ *Higher-Order Rewrite Systems and their Confluence .* Richard Mayr and Tobias Nipkow. (Nov4-15)
- ○ *Embedding Graphs with Bounded Treewidth into Optimal Hypercubes .* Volker Heun and Ernst W. Mayr. (Mar27-3)
- ○ *On Polynomial Ideals, Their Complexity, and Applications .* Ernst W. Mayr. (Mar27-2)
- ○ *Nested Transactions in a Logical Language for Active Rules .* Bertram Lud"ascher, Wolfgang May and Georg Lausen. (Jun20-1)
- ○ *Optimal Tree Contraction and Term Matching on the Hypercube and Related Networks .* Ernst Mayr and Ralph Werchner. (Feb1-2)
- ○ *Optimal Parallel Algorithms for Two Processor Scheduling with Tree Precedence Constraints .* Ernst Mayr and Hans Stadtherr. (Feb1-1)

GL-Site Universitaet Stuttgart
- ○ *Ein kantenbasiertes Stereoverfahren.* Christopher Mayer. (STUD-1624)
- ○ *Type-Checking and Overloading-Resolution for Hoopla.* Karsten Jung. (DIP-1386)

[Search]

 *NCSTRL*
This server operates at MeDoc RMS.
Send email to haber@informatik.tu-muenchen.de

Fig. 2. Search results

Although the repositories containing the collection and the search engines are distributed over the Internet, NCSTRL appears as a single unified (logical) collection, which is accessible by everyone through its WWW–based user interface.

In the following paragraph, an overview of the NCSTRL architecture is given. The essential services and components and the communication between them are then described in some detail.

3.1 Services

NCSTRL is based on an open architecture of interoperating (physical) *sites*. Each site runs a digital library server and provides access to the publications of one or more (logical) *authorities*, which contribute documents to the collection. Authorities are able to publish Technical Reports by themselves, logically independent from other naming authorities.

Each digital library server offers at least three services [10]:

- a repository service, that stores and provides access to documents,
- an index service realizing a distributed search facility, and
- the user interface service handling the interaction with users.

Additionally, meta servers offer a meta service that provides information about institutions taking part in NCSTRL, their indexes and repositories. The separation of the digital library server's functionality into distinct services both provides a better scalability, and enables the integration of other components. This facilitates further developments and the exchange of existing components, e.g. from conventional meta data–based index services to full-text search engines.

3.2 Regions

To support searches in a world–wide distributed network like the Internet efficiently, NCSTRL needs to minimize the response times of individual servers. In addition, a high level of fault tolerance is essential for guaranteeing a stable and reliable performance. These demands are fulfilled by the so called *region concept* illustrated in Figure 3.

Regions are arbitrarily chosen, overlapping segments of the Internet, e.g. 'NA–EAST' (North America East) or 'EU–CENTRAL' (Central Europe). The partitioning of sites in a collection to a set of regions should reflect criteria as bottlenecks in global communication bandwidth or regional concentrations of network traffic resulting from search requests to NCSTRL.

A *region* consists of one *Regional Meta Server* (RMS), at least one *Merged Index Server* (MIS) and several standard sites. The RMS holds information about the institutions (publishers) taking part in NCSTRL, the location of their indexes, their repositories and the region a site belongs to. The RMS obtains its information regularly from the *Master Meta Server* (MMS). Information about each site is maintained by manually editing the collection's *Master Meta file* (MMF) residing at the MMS. Every standard site belongs to exactly one region.

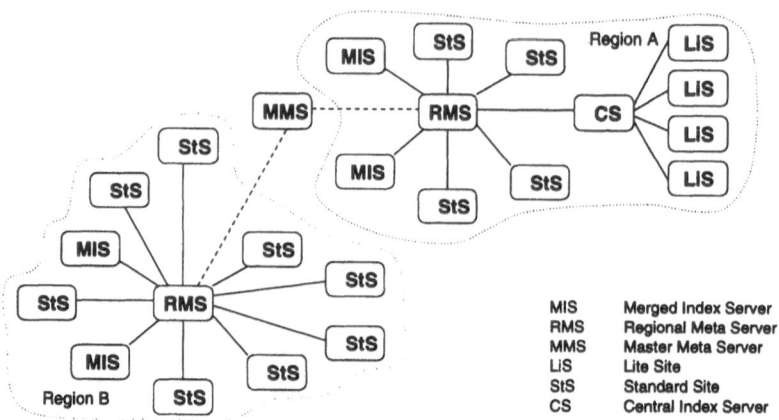

Fig. 3. Architecture of the NCSTRL system

Queries to a site within the region are sent to the site itself, while queries addressed to a site outside the region are sent to the *Merged Index Server* (MIS). The MIS acts as a mirror for the indexes of all sites outside the region. It periodically gathers new or updated bibfiles (files containing the bibliographic data of documents) from several NCSTRL sites and performs an incremental update of its index. Unfortunately, remote indexers are not able to detect withdrawn bibfiles.

In order to make the system fault tolerant in case that indexers or MIS cannot be reached, each region is supplied with a complete backup index of all the collection's authorities. For this purpose, a region may run one single remote indexer which then is called *Backup Server* (BS)[8]. Regions without a BS are nevertheless supplied with a complete backup index by the MMS. The backup index is then formed by foreign region's MISs. For a certain region, the foreign MISs appear to index only the authorities which are needed to complete the backup index. A Region may be switched down which means that it doesn't serve foreign regions. Due to this design, results of successive identical search requests may differ, even if the user interfaces used reside in the same region. Ambiguous successive search results occure because the remote indexers involved might vary. Thus, although a search result may not contain the latest reports, there will at least be a result.

Obtaining meta information A site may obtain meta information for a collection from three different sources:

- from a MMF, if it acts as the MMS for the collection. A MMF holds all of the collection's meta information about regions, publishers, repositories, indexers and remote indexers.

---

[8] Presently, one region runs a backup server which also serves as single primary indexer for the few remaining Dienst 3.5 sites.

154

- from the collection's MMS if it acts as a RMS for the collection. The MMS will recognize the RMS (by its IP–address) and supply the appropriate information for the corresponding region. In contrast to the MMS, a RMS does not distinguish different types of indexers,
- from the collection's RMS it is assigned to if it is neither the MMS nor a RMS for the collection.

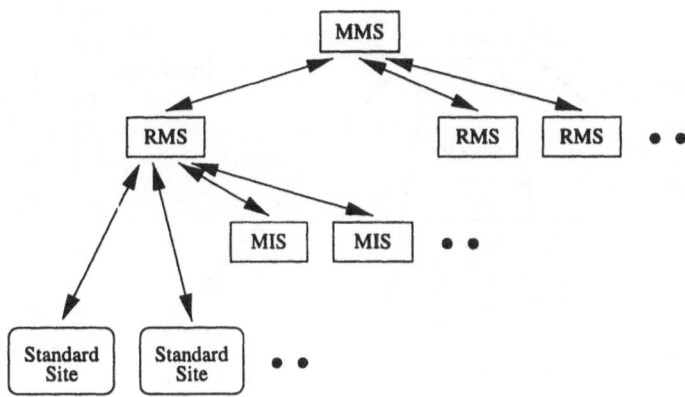

Fig. 4. Architecture of meta services in NCSTRL

3.3   Communication infrastructure

Individual NCSTRL sites interoperate via an open protocol: the Dienst protocol [15], named after one of the predecessors of NCSTRL. Using an open protocol ensures the interoperability of digital library services and facilitates the integration of other value–added services, as e.g. advanced indexing systems and information retrieval tools. Furthermore, it enables other electronic libraries, like the MeDoc system[9] [2], to interoperate with NCSTRL .

The communication flow between different NCSTRL sites is illustrated in Figure 5. Users can access the user interface service of a particular site via hypertext markup language (HTML) forms using standard WWW browsers like Netscape's Navigator or Microsoft's Internet Explorer. Requests are submitted to the user interface service via the hypertext transfer protocol (HTTP) and the common gateway interface (CGI) by the WWW browser and WWW server, respectively. The user interface service spreads the requests to the corresponding services, possibly at other sites, via TCP/IP socket–i/o in parallel. For every site selected by the user, the user interface service queries the appropriate index service, which returns a list of document references matching the query. If a user accesses one of the documents from the list of matching documents from

---

[9] http://medoc.informatik.tu-muenchen.de

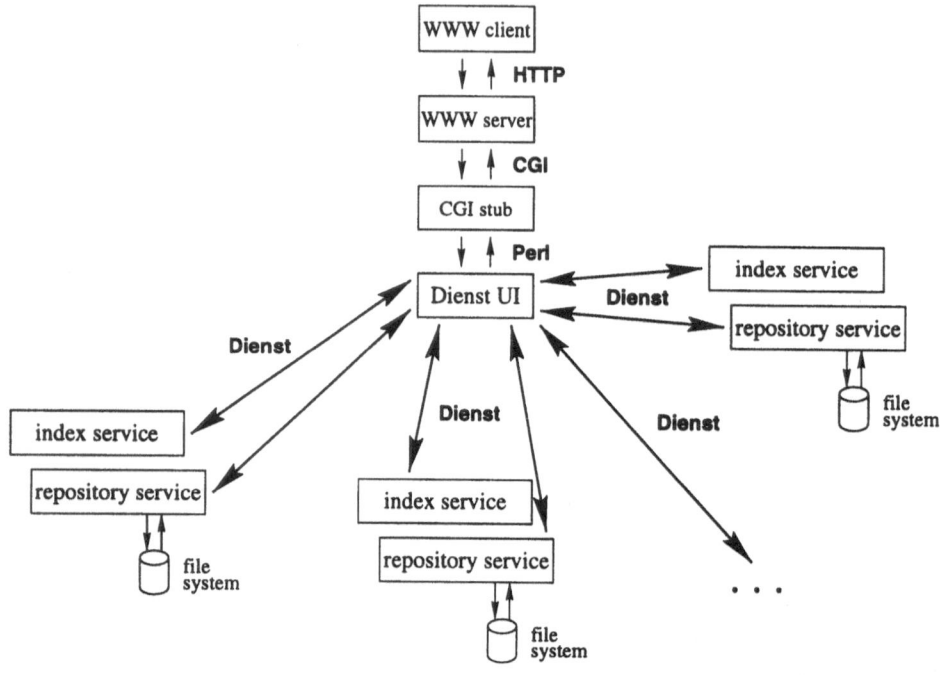

Fig. 5. The NCSTRL architecture

all sites selected, the appropriate repository–service is contacted and the document's meta data is retrieved. The meta data consists of the bibliographic record, containing e.g. the name of the author, the title, the abstract of the document, and if available links to online versions of the document.

As can be seen in Figure 5, WWW clients simply communicate via HTTP/CGI with the user interface service. Communicating with other services the user interface service uses the open Dienst protocol, which is embedded in HTTP.

3.4 NCSTRL standard and lite sites

The operation of a NCSTRL *standard site*, consisting of the Dienst servers described above, requires a certain amount of hardware and personal resources (the latter mostly for installation). In contrast, NCSTRL *lite sites* based on the architecture of WATERS, consist of a FTP repository only and thus require even less administration and resources.

An NCSTRL lite site makes document formats and bibliographic data available via a common FTP server. A dedicated Dienst server manages the authorities of lite sites and adds their bibliographic data to its index, while the actual documents remain on the FTP site. Each client intending to retrieve a document contacts – transparently for the user – the FTP server directly. Thereby lite sites can fully participate in the worldwide NCSTRL collection with their own naming authorities without supporting one of the corresponding services themselves. However, lite sites cannot offer the full functionality as provided by standard sites; e.g. page–wise browsing of documents is not supported.

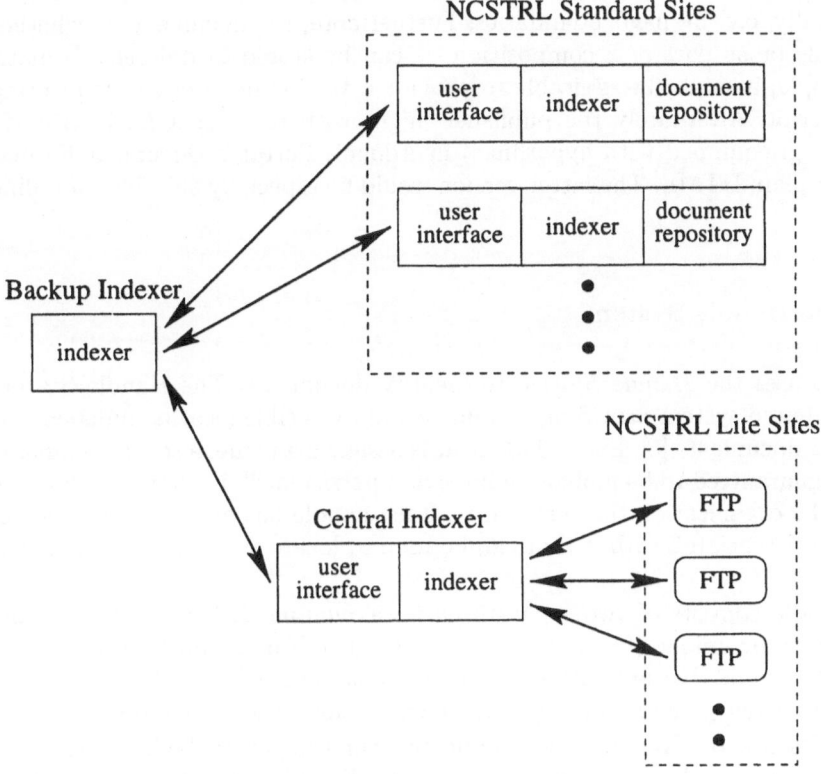

Fig. 6. Integration of lite sites in NCSTRL

3.5 The document model

One of NCSTRL's strengths — in comparison to other Technical Report servers — is its flexible and extensible document model inherited from its predecessor Dienst. The model has three essential features [10]:

 – Unique document names,
 – multiple document formats, and
 – multiple document decompositions.

One of the advantages of NCSTRL's document model as opposed to former electronic library systems is the abstraction from the names of the files associated with documents. The conventional mechanism offered by the file system is grouping files in a directory. In contrast to this, NCSTRL uses logical document identifiers, called *handles* (cf. 3.6). Multiple versions of a document — both in different formats and in different decompositions — may be associated with a handle. Thus it is possible to retrieve not only the document as a whole, but also parts of it. Parts can be understood logically, e.g. chapters and paragraphs, or physically, e.g. by page–boundaries. Furthermore, the document — whether as a whole or as part of a composition — can be stored in different formats. For example, it might be desirable to provide a version designated for printing in PostScript. Alternately the publisher might wish to present an interactive version (e.g. equipped with hyperlinks) in Adobe's Portable Document Format (PDF) or plain HTML. The latter version would be especially suitable for online reading.

3.6 The Handle System

NCSTRL uses the *Handle System* to identify documents. The Handle System is a distributed system providing a scalable and extensible location independent naming of documents [5]. Every document is assigned a name, a so called *handle*, which is guaranteed to be globally unique and persistent[10], i.e. having a lifetime beyond the organization that created it. Each handle has one or more fields of typed data associated with it that can be used to locate or access the document referred to.

A handle consists of two separate parts: a *naming authority* and a string which has to be unique (for that naming authority). Naming authorities are administrative units that are authorized to create handles. The creation of naming authorities is delegated in a hierarchy, which is referred to as the *authority tree*.

Handles are resolved by the Handle System using a scalable, distributed system of global and local handle services providing high performance and high availability. On the client side, caching services provide fast resolution of handles and minimize the necessity to access other handle services.

4 Current Limitations of NCSTRL

In general, NCSTRL has been proven to be successful: While being relatively easy to administrate and simple to use, it provides a powerful resource discovery facility for its users.

The NCSTRL collection consists of high–quality[11], relevant scientific publications from the field of computer science. Currently, however, it is not possible to distinguish documents by further means such as, e.g., their relative quality, relevance, or even the language they are written in.

---

[10] Thus handles are a kind of *Uniform Resource Names (URNs)* [18]

[11] The participants are expected to verify the quality of publications before introducing them to the NCSTRL collection.

4.1 Classification of documents according to quality and relevance

A practical example which demonstrates the need for some additional distinctions occurred recently in the context of the before mentioned German electronic library project "MeDoc": Amongst a number of computer science departments of German universities, the wish arose to use NCSTRL as a tool for the convenient electronic dissemination of documents other than Technical Reports. In addition to what NCSTRL already provides, a forum for a convenient and rapid online publication of (German) "grey literature", like project theses, master theses and dissertations was desired.

Currently, the distribution of such documents to the NCSTRL collection would contradict the policy of the NCSTRL working group at Cornell University, as the system provides no means to restrict the visibility of such documents, which may not meet the claimed standards (concerning quality and relevance) — not even for German speaking communities.

A separation of such documents from the NCSTRL collection could only be realized by using the Dienst software to build a separate, perhaps nationwide collection. However, this is not an adequate solution with the current Dienst version (4.1.9), because

- the existence of additional collections would be unknown to most NCSTRL users as there is no meta service keeping track of existing collections besides NCSTRL,
- the Dienst protocol is not prepared to access distinct collections together in one request (users would have to use multiple search interfaces instead), and
- organizations intending to use NCSTRL to contribute to multiple collections would be obligated to run multiple servers. This would increase the administrative effort and, if the standard Dienst software is used, increase the hardware requirements.

4.2 Representing organizational structures

Another limitation of the Dienst software, which is of broader significance, was also detected: The current version of Dienst provides no means to explicitly express the organizational structure of participating organizations in the NCSTRL collection, that is, in our example, the division of computer science departments into several distinct research groups. However, such organizational matters often provide important additional search criteria for electronic documents (such as "all documents of the 'Distributed Systems Group' at the Computer Science department at Hamburg University")

Although it is – in principle – possible to create sub–authorities for NCSTRL sites, such a solution is not adequate since (for compatibility reasons) the hierarchical authority tree is mapped on a flat name space. Thus every sub–authority would appear as a separate entry in the list of participating sites and in the search forms of the NCSTRL user interface. Considering the increasing number of participants, the list would soon become more confusing than it already is. Presently the list contains about 100 publishers from various countries which can only be identified by a name they have chosen for themselves.

5 Proposed NCSTRL enhancements

To overcome the shortcomings of the NCSTRL system described in the previous chapter, two enhanced versions of the Dienst protocol and software were developed independently from each other by the authors. Both versions can interoperate with each other and also preserve backwards compatibility to NCSTRL. A site may even alternate from one version to the other easily. The first enhancement was designed to use NCSTRL not only for Technical Reports, but to build an electronic library for grey literature based on NCSTRL. The second approach aims at building a full–scale integrated digital library with multiple collections.

The first enhancement comprises a special NCSTRL region which allows for the addition of non–NCSTRL authorities to a modified RMS. These additional authorities are not visible outside the special region. This solution supports searching by the newly introduced criteria document type, language and discipline. The additional authorities are dedicated to publish grey literature. As grey literature documents have other types than NCSTRL documents, the additional authorities may be searched separately by specifying the correspondent document types in the search interface.

The second approach requires extensive modifications to Dienst's meta service and user interface. It supports multiple collections and offers the entire NCSTRL functionality for all supported collections. Standard sites, possibly also acting as MMS and/or RMS, can support multiple collections. In contrast to the first approach, all supported collections can be maintained and partitioned into regions independently. The enhanced meta service and user interface group participating organizations in a hierarchy and allow accessing them by collections or countries.

5.1 A Grey Literature Library based on NCSTRL

Before adapting NCSTRL some design decisions had to be taken. The NCSTRL system is widely used and intended for the publication of high quality Technical Reports only, not for diploma theses, lab reports, etc. So an important goal was not to interfere with the existing system. Nevertheless the grey literature library is intended to integrate with the existing NCSTRL system. Therefore it is vital that grey literature other than Technical Reports (TR) is only returned to queries specifically asking for it. We decided on an architecture that will give the user the choice to extend the search to the registered NCSTRL documents only, to the registered NCSTRL documents and the "grey literature" documents at the same time or to the "grey literature" documents only.

The architecture of the grey literature library is based on the region concept of NCSTRL. A special region is build for the grey literature, the *Grey Literature Region* (GLR). People using a server within this region for searching the database may ask for grey literature and/or Technical Reports, whereas people using a site outside this region will only get Technical Reports. The GLR consists of an RMS, one MIS, registered TR sites, known outside the region, offering Technical Reports and of "grey literature sites" known only within the region, offering all kind of grey literature except Technical Reports. The registered TR sites are registered with the NCSTRL team, the grey literature sites are registered with the RMS of the GLR only. Therefore any site within the special region asking the RMS for publishers, indexes and repositories will get informed about the grey literature sites.

This approach requires changes to the RMS to support the registration of grey literature sites. There are other enhancements needed to make use and administration of the Grey Literature Library comfortable. Section 3.4 described that NCSTRL has two kinds of servers to offer Technical Reports, the standard and lite sites. Standard sites support meta data according to RFC 1807 [11]. Lite sites use a modified refer format [12,8] for their meta data. To have a uniform meta data set we decided to use the RFC 1807 for standard sites as well as for lite sites as it has the more comprehensive set of bibliographic data. This unification allows the participants to change from a lite to a standard site without too much effort. Moreover some weaknesses of the RFC 1807 format have been identified and extensions of the format to overcome these problems have been suggested and are discussed with the NCSTRL team. One such weakness concerns the distinction of different kinds of documents. We found it necessary to search for a special kind of document (Technical Report, course material, etc.). This field existed in the RFC 1807 set under the name TYPE, but it was a free text field. We standardized a set of values for that field and made it mandatory and searchable.

The integration of diploma theses, lab reports, etc. demanded another bibliographic field to be mandatory. Theses and course materials are usually written in the native language of the author. Depending on the users some languages may not be interesting at all. Therefore the field LANGUAGE has to be mandatory and searchable.

Another extension was a new field of bibliographic data regarding to the realm a document belongs to. We call this field DISCIPLINE. Inserting the discipline field allows for the integration of research realms like Mathematics, Physics, ...

The changes to the searchable attributes required the implementation of an extended and improved user interface (see Figure 7). The user interface for the maintenance of the document archives was improved to support the extensions to the bibliographic data and make the entry of documents into the archives easier.

Some institutions decided to offer their grey literature on lite sites. This decision required the existence of a lite gateway. The lite gateway regularly gets the bibliographic data of the grey literature lite sites, indexes them and answers queries to lite sites. Another task of the lite gateway is to forward document requests to the actual site. Therefore we had to implement a lite gateway to support lite sites.

Having finished all these modifications of the NCSTRL-system, we ended up with a grey literary library based on NCSTRL. But there was still no possibility

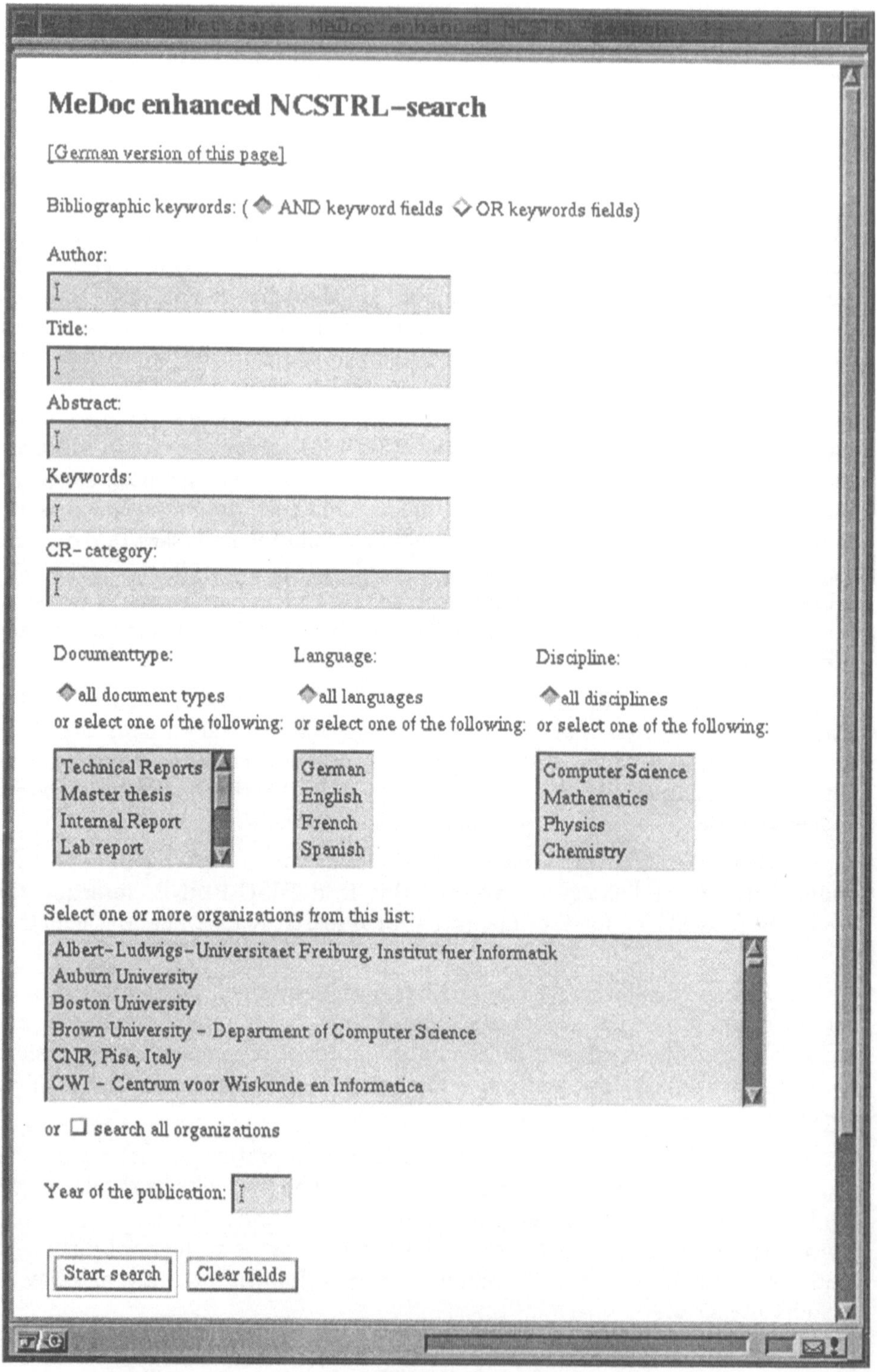

MeDoc enhanced NCSTRL–search

[German version of this page]

Bibliographic keywords: (◆ AND keyword fields ◇ OR keywords fields)

Author:

Title:

Abstract:

Keywords:

CR– category:

Documenttype: Language: Discipline:

◆ all document types   ◆ all languages   ◆ all disciplines
or select one of the following: or select one of the following: or select one of the following:

Technical Reports		German		Computer Science
Master thesis		English		Mathematics
Internal Report		French		Physics
Lab report		Spanish		Chemistry

Select one or more organizations from this list:

Albert–Ludwigs–Universitaet Freiburg, Institut fuer Informatik
Auburn University
Boston University
Brown University – Department of Computer Science
CNR, Pisa, Italy
CWI – Centrum voor Wiskunde en Informatica

or ☐ search all organizations

Year of the publication:

Start search   Clear fields

Fig. 7. Fielded search form enhanced for Grey Literature Library

to reflect the organizational structure of the participating institutions. This was realized with the help of multiple collections.

5.2 A digital library with multiple collections

In the following, an enhancement of the Dienst protocol is described, which enables the coexistence of multiple collections at a single site running an extended version of the standard Dienst software.

In order to distinguish different collections of electronic documents at a single site, an extension of the Dienst protocol is required. For this purpose, an optional argument `collection` for service requests is introduced. Logically, this argument acts as a filter which only lets information concerning the requested collection pass through. For compatibility reasons it defaults to the regular NCSTRL collection. The argument is applicable to all requests, which operate on sets of documents (e.g. search requests) as well as to all requests directed to meta servers. Additionally, the meta service supports two new requests. The first provides common meta information about the supported collections, while the second supplies meta information about participating organizations. Additionally, `organization` is introduced as a further optional argument for requests to the user interface. It serves the following purposes:

- summarizing all authorities of a single organization in different collections,
- allowing to express hierarchical organization structures,
- grouping organizations by countries, and
- supplying the URLs of the homepages from participating organizations.

Handles should be registered for organization identifiers in order to guarantee their uniqueness. Hierarchical organization structures are realized by letting organizations point to parent organizations. As the meta service might be overloaded with the entire structure of all participating organizations, the latter can be refined locally. Additional suborganizations may be added via the Dienst software's initialization files and autoconfiguration mechanism. Then this local refinement of organizations would only be visible within the respective site, of course. Suborganizations wishing to have their own document name space must have their own publishing authority and have to be known to the meta service. Organizations may be spread upon multiple sites.

Figure 8 shows the meta information flow in a possible configuration with MMS/RMS for multiple collections. The illustrated configuration fulfills the requirements of sites in Germany wishing to contribute to NCSTRL and a collection for German Computer Science papers, while using standard Dienst software.

The German CS–papers collection is referred to as 'medoc'. As it is not to be expected that the MeDoc collection will be searched as often as the NCSTRL collection, a single region ('WHOLE–WORLD') might be sufficient for this collection.

A site supporting multiple collections must obtain the meta information for each collection from the appropriate source. This may be a MMF or MMS or

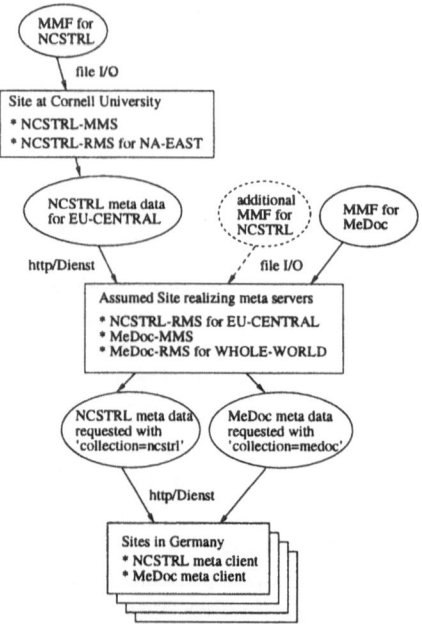

Fig. 8. Meta information flow

RMS, as described in section 3.2. As the NCSTRL collection currently does not support the newly introduced meta requests, a client of the meta service (possibly acting as a RMS) can obtain the missing meta information from an additional local MMF for the particular collection. The meta data of all supported collections is then merged in the site's working memory and all tables required by the client — eventually also acting as MMS and/or RMS for the enhanced multi–collection version — are build. When it's time to reload the meta data for one of the supported collections, first the collection's old meta data is removed from memory completely. Then, the new meta data is reloaded from either the MMS or an RMS of the collection. Subsequently, the collection's meta data is rejoined with the tables for all other supported collections.

The example configuration shown in Figure 8 assumes that one site provides the meta services needed for supporting both collections. Of course, these meta services could be distributed over distinct sites. A site may also act as a MMS and as a RMS for an arbitrary number of collections.

In the current version of NCSTRL, only sites running a MMS have knowledge about all the regions of a collection. All other sites know the region they are assigned to only. Regions can be defined independently for different collections. Regions's identifiers (e.g. 'NA–EAST') are not formulated collection specific or guaranteed to be unique among different collections. However, this ambiguity of region's identifiers causes no trouble, because the identifiers of regions are not used in the communication between sites.

The enhanced browse interface The enhanced browse interface supports browsing by (sub)–organizations possibly contributing to multiple collections. Figure 9 shows a (portion of a) possible configuration illustrating the relationship between collections, sites, organizations, authorities and documents. The configuration includes two enhanced sites, one of them split into sub–organizations.

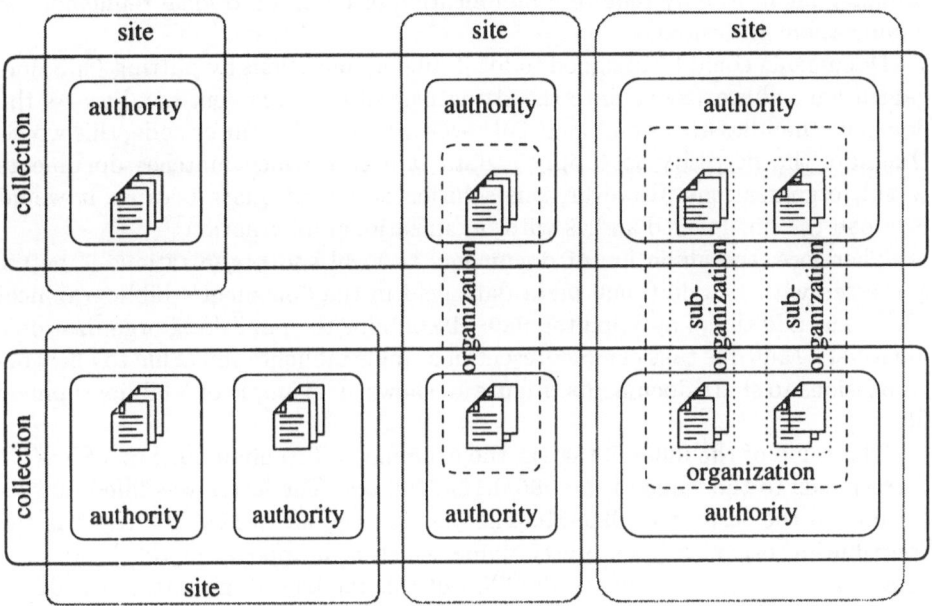

Fig. 9. Possible relationships between collections, sites, (sub–)organizations, authorities and documents

The enhanced browse interface offers various mechanisms which help to differentiate publishing organizations. It allows to

- focus queries to a certain collection, as well as to organizations residing in a certain country,
- uncover hierarchical organizational structures,
- discover the local refinement of a site's organizational structure, and to
- follow the links to the homepages of organizations.

Furthermore, this enhancement enables suborganizations to integrate lists of their own contributions into their WWW–homepages. In order to supply (sub–)organizations with a single entry point for browsing their documents, the presently distinct browse forms for browsing by year and by author are merged into one form.

The enhanced browsing interface and corresponding Dienst request can interoperate with older Dienst versions. For compatibility reasons, browsing by authorities is also supported. Information about the Dienst version used at a particular site is currently provided by meta servers together with organizational meta information. This should be omitted by incrementing the hosts's repository versions. Organizational meta information for the NCSTRL collection currently may occasionally be out of date, because it is subsequently loaded at an NCSTRL RMS. New and unknown authorities are also regarded by organization lists of the enhanced browse interface. The enhanced indexing and browsing facilities only require a modification of bibfiles if a local refinement of organizations is desired.

Documents could be assigned to local sub–organizations by putting (sub–)organization's abbreviations into the string part of the document handles. As the document handles are known as *docids* everywhere in the source code, this would eliminate the necessity to supply a data structure which matches documents to sub–organizations. However, this solution is not adequate because it would overload the document handles with organizational information[12].

Therefore, the affiliation of documents to local sub–organizations is better expressed with an additional meta data field in the document's bibliographical file[13]. The additional optional tag ORG-ID contains the publishing organization's identifiers. Multiple tags can be present in a single bibliographical file to allow organizations to share documents. Figure 10 shows an example of a bibliographical file.

The value of the ORG-ID tag (in the example "dilico.uhamburg_cs.VSYS"[14]) corresponds to the value of the ORGANIZATION tag. The latter was filled out according to the respective ORG-ID. The value of the ORGANIZATION tag[15] is the contributing organization's pretty name which also appears in the headers of browse forms. A tool automatically fills out this tag before submitting the document to the database. At the same time, the integrity of all indexed information is also checked.

Performance enhancements In order to minimize the response time for browse requests, the browse indexes supply all the information needed for building browse forms, e.g. lists of

- all organizations contributing to a certain collection,
- all organizations residing in a certain country,
- all authors contributing to a certain organization and authority,
- all documents associated with a certain author, (sub–)organization and authority,
- all years in which a certain organization and authority have published documents, and
- all documents associated with a certain year, (sub–)organization and authority.

---

[12] Thanks to Jim Davis for pointing this out.
[13] Refer to RFC 1807 [11] for the format of Dienst's bibfiles.
[14] "dilico" stands for Digital Library Contributors
[15] As Dienst presently makes no use of the ORGANIZATION tag, it just serves readers of bibliographic files.

```
BIB-VERSION:: CS-TR-v2.1
ID:: medoc.uhamburg_cs//Doc-15
ENTRY:: October 20, 1996
ORG-ID:: dilico.uhamburg_cs.VSYS
ORGANIZATION:: University of Hamburg, Computer Science Department,
               Distributed Systems Group
TITLE:: Workflow Modelling and Execution with Coloured Petri Nets
        in COSM
TYPE:: Publication
AUTHOR:: Merz, Michael
AUTHOR:: Moldt, D.
AUTHOR:: Müller, Kay
AUTHOR:: Lamersdorf, Winfried
DATE:: January 1995
PAGES::
COPYRIGHT:: You are granted permission for the non-commercial
           reproduction, ...
LANGUAGE:: English
NOTES:: In: Workshop on Applications of Petri Nets to Protocols,
        Proceedings 16th International Conference on Application
        and Theory of Petri Nets, 1995
ABSTRACT:: Modern distributed organisations use data communication
           increasingly fast, globaly and at decreasing costs. ...
END:: medoc.uhamburg_cs//Doc-15
```

Fig. 10. A document's bibliographical file

The current Dienst version calculates a lot of this information at request time. For example, browsing by year is currently realized by accessing an optional year string contained in the document handles. By including the value of the DATE tag in the browse indexes, it is no longer required for handles to contain a year string. Furthermore, this allows to list documents in proper temporal sequence (during a particular year).

The enhanced browse indexes speed up browse requests perceptibly while only slightly slowing down the indexing of the database[16]. Due to the ability of Dienst's indexers to compress items to hex-codes, the demand for working memory does not rise significantly.

An implementation specific problem should also be mentioned: The current Dienst version supports different search engines[17], but does not separate the creation of indexes for searching and for browsing. Therefore, the source code files concerning different search engines currently duplicate the code for building

---

[16] Larger databases than presently available at the University of Hamburg are needed for meaningful performance measurements of the indexing and browsing enhancements.

[17] Presently a built-in Perl search engine and the WAIS search engine[17,14] are supported.

browse indexes. Thus, the building of the advanced browse indexes has to be integrated into the source code files concerning all supported search engines. In order to facilitate the support of additional search engines or modifications to browse indexes, the separation of source code managing the building of search indexes and browse indexes is suggested.

Further enhancements The bibliographic file in Figure 10 includes an author ('Müller, Kay'), whose family name contains an ISO 8859-1 formated German umlaut ('ü'). Unfortunately, Dienst currently does not have any rules for national character sets. The problems resulting from this omission are:

- Keywords in incoming requests to the user interface may be in varying formats, because individual keyboards and platforms differ.
- Forms produced by the user interface should be enabled to display special characters.
- Browse indexes should use HTML coded special characters in order to avoid unnecessary conversions and support a fast output.
- Some search engines (e.g. Glimpse) are not capable of dealing correctly with HTML special characters.
- The format used in bibfiles should be chosen with regard to readability. On the other hand, by using the same format as for the search engines, slowing down the indexing operation by character translations could be prevented.

The formats used in bibfiles and for supplying the search engine should be defined in Dienst's configuration files. An automatic translation between the diverse representations could then be implemented. Keywords contained in incoming requests have to be checked for all formats which may be produced by users on any platform. Some users might wish to rewrite special characters (e.g. "ue" for "ü") because they use keyboards which cannot generate language specific special characters. Rewritten special characters could also be supported as an additional incoming format, but it has to be considered, that — especially for the German language — it is not always possible to uniquely identify a rewritten character (e.g. "virtuell" should be left unconverted).

As a further enhancement, the optional argument `author` is supported for browse requests. Thus authors are enabled to integrate lists of their own publications into their WWW–homepages. The circumstance, that Kay married meanwhile and as a consequence thereof changed his family name to "Müller–Jones", leads us to the necessity, that the `author` argument should be applicable multiple times on browse requests.

6 Conclusion and Outlook

NCSTRL is a relatively simple, yet powerful tool for the convenient dissemination of and search for electronic publications. Although originally intended for online–publishing of Technical Reports only, the NCSTRL system can —

in principle — also be utilized for the electronic publication of other kinds of documents.

However, the current versions of the underlying Dienst protocol and software have a few, yet not unimportant, shortcomings preventing the employment of NCSTRL as a general tool for the electronic publication of (scientific) documents on a larger scale. On the one hand, it is not possible to group related documents together in separate collections, e.g. as a means for the online–publishing of grey literature from German universities. The decision of about 10 computer science departments in Germany to build up Grey Literature sites shows that there is a need for such a system. Furthermore, the participating organizations appear to be relatively undifferentiated and no means exist to express the organizational structure of participants in the NCSTRL collection, e.g. the division of computer science departments into several research groups.

In this paper, two approaches to overcome the above mentioned deficiencies are described. Both solutions will be submitted to the NCSTRL working group and will -- hopefully — be integrated with future NCSTRL releases.

The first adaption utilizing a special RMS is already fully implemented and is presently operated at the University of Stuttgart[18]. After an initial phase it will move to the University of Leipzig. This approach offers an immediate solution for the most urgent problems of organizations wishing to use NCSTRL for the publication of grey literature documents. These organizations can contribute to a special region and "hide" their grey literature documents from other NCSTRL regions. An extended search interface enables separate searching for these documents. As the necessary changes to the source code are limited to only two subsystems, it is possible to integrate this solution into future Dienst releases with little effort.

The second approach is more comprehensive and partially still in progress. As it requires extensive modifications to the source code, it can only survive on a long term, if it will be integrated in an official future Dienst release. This approach offers a number of specific solutions solving the above mentioned deficiencies and further improving the usability of the system. First, an extension of the Dienst protocol enables sites to handle multiple collections. Second, the enhanced browse interface allows users to orientate and navigate in the list of participating organizations. Third, an enhancement of NCSTRL provides a refinement of participating organizations, which is only visible within the respective site. Furthermore, the creation and utilization of dedicated browse indexes improves the performance of the whole system significantly. Last, but not least, a better support for national character sets is suggested. The described enhancements of the Dienst protocol and software are essentially implemented at the University of Hamburg[19]. The present prototype version implements the enhanced meta service capable of multiple collections and all functionality for the enhanced indexing and browsing. Backwards–compatibility to standard NCSTRL sites, i.e. sites running Dienst version 4.0, is achieved in the described manner.

---

[18] http://medoc.informatik.uni-stuttgart.de:1111/Dienst/htdocs/Welcome.html

[19] http://medoc.informatik.uni-hamburg.de/

The authors of the second approach will now focus on the modification of the search interface. It is intended that the search interface will also group participating organizations like the browse interface already does. Besides this, the implementation and utilization of an enhanced meta request for authorities is considered. An additional new version of this request could also supply the items document type, language and discipline which are introduced by the first solution. The implemented new meta request for collections already supports these items. Comprehensive and useful lists of values for the items "document type" and "subject" are described in [16]. If a site having some information about the locations of documents matching these criteria would exist, it could spread search requests more precisely. Thus a reduction of network traffic could be achieved in the future. The modification or adaptation of search engines to support these items will not be the subject of this approach, because it is already covered by the first solution. Once these enhancements are fully implemented and integrated into a future NCSTRL release, an additional NCSTRL master meta file occasionally being out of date would no longer be required.

Some further enhancements of the NCSTRL system are planned at the University of Hamburg. We currently develop a Java–based administration tool, which will replace (and significantly improve in respect of user friendliness) the current command–line tools and automate the introduction of new documents to a collection to a great extend. We also consider implementing a new version of the meta service. Its performance could be improved significantly by using the Handle System to manage the meta data. As arbitrary data can be associated with a handle, all kinds of meta information can be stored together with a handle. Currently, handles are already registered for authorities and documents. Thus the authority tree roots could be used as handles for collections. Furthermore, handles could also be registered for regions, sites, indexers and repositories. The handles of documents could contain a list of all document formats available and even replicate the whole bibfile. This would allow faster remote indexing (with less network traffic).

References

1. A. Barth et al. The MeDoc Digital Library Project: Its Goals and Major Achievements, in this volume.
2. D. Boles et al. The MeDoc System – A Digital Publication and Reference Service for Computer Science, in this volume.
3. M. Bowman, P. Danzig, D. Hardy, U. Manber, M. Schwartz, and D. Wessels. The Harvest Information Discovery and Access System, 1996. Accessible via the WWW under the URL http://harvest.transarc.com/
4. A. Brüggemann-Klein. Ibd: Der Informationsdienst für Informatikberichte. Technical report, Universität Freiburg, 1993. Accessible via the WWW under the URL http://www11.informatik.tu-muenchen.de/Ibd/ibd.ps
5. Corporation for National Research Initiatives. *The Handle System*, 1996. Available via the WWW under the URL http://www.handle.net/overview.html

6. J. Davis. Creating a networked computer science report library. *D-Lib Magazine*, September 1995. Available via the WWW under the URL http://www.dlib.org/dlib/september95/09davis.html

7. J. French, E. Fox, K. Maly, and A. Selman. Wide area technical report service: Technical reports online. *Communications of the ACM*, 38(4):45, April 1995.

8. B. W. Kernighan and M. E. Lesk. UNIX document preparation. In J. Nievergelt, G. Coray, J.-D. Nicoud, and A. C. Shaw, editors, *Document Preparation Systems: A Collection of Survey Articles*, pages 1–20. Elsevier North-Holland, Inc., New York, NY, USA, 1982.

9. C. Lagoze and J. Davis. Dienst: An architecture for distributed document libraries. *Communications of the ACM*, 38(4):47, April 1995.

10. C. Lagoze, E. Shaw, J. Davis, and D. Krafft. Dienst: Implementation reference manual. Technical Report TR95-1514, Department of Computer Science, Cornell University, May 1995. Available via the WWW under the URL http://cs-tr.cs.cornell.edu/Dienst/UI/2.0/Describe/ncstrl.cornell4?abstract=

11. R. Lasher and D. Cohen. A format for bibliographic records. RFC 1807, Network Working Group, June 1995. http://ds.internic.net/rfc/rfc1807.txt

12. M. E. Lesk. Some applications of inverted indexes on the unix system. In *UNIX Programmer's Manual*, volume 2b. Bell Laboratories, Murray Hill, NJ, 1978.

13. U. Manber and S. Wu. Glimpse: A tool to search through entire file systems. Technical Report TR 93-34, Department of Computer Science, University of Arizona, October 1993. ftp://ftp.cs.arizona.edu/glimpse/glimpse.ps.Z

14. H. Muelner. WAIS and information retrieval on the Internet. *J.UCS: Journal of Universal Computer Science*, 1(4), April 1995.Accessible via the WWW under the URL http://www.iicm.edu/jucs_1_4/wais_and_information_retrieval.

15. NCSTRL working group. *Dienst protocol version 4.0*, 1995. http://www.ncstrl.org/Dienst/htdocs/Info/protocol4.html

16. M.L. Nelson, K. Maly, and S.N.T. Shen. Buckets, clusters and dienst. Technical report, Old Dominion University, May 1997. Accessible via the WWW: http://lite.ncstrl.org:3803/Dienst/UI/2.0/Describe/ncstrl.odu_cs%2fTR_97_30

17. U. Pfeifer, N. Fuhr, and T. Huynh. Searching structured documents with the enhanced retrieval functionality of freeWAIS-sf and SFgate. *Computer Networks and ISDN Systems*, 27(6):1027–1036, April 1995. Accessible via the WWW under the URL http://www.igd.fhg.de/www/www95/papers/47/fwsf/fwsf.html

18. K. Sollins and L. Masinter. Functional requirements for uniform resource names. RFC 1737, Network Working Group, December 1994. Accessible via the WWW under the URL http://ds.internic.net/rfc/rfc1737.txt

19. I.H. Witten, C.G. Nevill-Manning, and S.J. Cunningham. Building a Digital Library for Computer Science Research: Technical Issues. In *Proceedings of the 19th Australasian Computer Science Conference*, 1996.

Digital Publishing for Conference Proceedings on CD-ROM

Dieter W. Fellner

Department of Computer Science, University of Bonn, Germany
fellner@graphics.cs.uni-bonn.de

Abstract. This contribution discusses the support of the editorial work for a scientific conference by electronic publishing technology from the electronic submission of conference papers to the production of the printed conference proceedings including a CD-ROM.

The paper is based on the experiences gathered and lessons learned while organizing the international workshop MVD'95 and, more recently, EUROGRAPHICS'97, a highly visible international conference on Computer Graphics.

The experiences and lessons learned might be valuable to a general audience and not only to those organizing a scientific event in the near future (i.e., programme chairs and publishers).

1 Introduction

EUROGRAPHICS'97 is the first conference in its series to fully exploit the power of electronic documents and computer networks. This year, the submission of papers, the delivery of papers and attached multimedia material to the international Programme Committee (PC) members and to the reviewers as well as their online access, the feedback to the authors, and the delivery of the final documents (with the accompanying multimedia data) has been (almost) exclusively carried out electronically.

This report briefly describes the architecture behind the work of the program committee from the first call for papers to the production of the printed proceedings and the CD-ROM holding the technical papers, State-of-The-Art Reports (STAR's) and tutorials.

A first test of the concept presented has been carried out during the organization of the international workshop *Modeling – Virtual Worlds – Distributed Graphics '95 (MVD'95)* [4] which took place near Bonn, Germany, in November 1995.

EUROGRAPHICS'97 is the first conference in its series to fully exploit the power of electronic documents and computer networks. For this conference,

- the submission of papers
- the delivery of papers and attached multimedia material to the PC members and to the reviewers as well as their online access
- the feedback to the authors and
- the delivery of the final documents (with the accompanying multimedia data) has been (almost) exclusively carried out electronically.

2 Submission

The Call-for-Papers invited electronic submissions and printed copies, with the preference clearly given to the electronic route. Authors were asked to submit their paper as a gzip-ed postcript file by FTP to Budapest, Hungary, the location of the conference venue. In order to be prepared for almost all authors submitting their paper in the very last minute, a backup FTP server has been set up at the University of Bonn, Germany.

To everybody's surprise authors started well before the deadline – January 17, 1997 – to transfer their submissions to Budapest. The transfer itself worked smoothly in most cases. The only significant problems have been reported from colleagues in Austria, France, and Israel. From these countries authors simply couldn't transfer their papers to any of the two ftp sites.

A short test revealed the fact that the Internet connection from all of these countries to Budapest as well as to Bonn were routed through Paris, France, where the lack of bandwidth made ftp connections simply impossible. Even a command to list the contents of a directory would eventually timeout without listing a single file!

As a quick solution authors were asked to gzip and uuencode their submissions and send them by email. This worked without problems.[1]

The lesson learned is that email is currently more reliable in delivering submissions. It might take a little while but, compared with FTP in some countries, it worked at the speed of light. The additional benefit of this approach is the fact that the mail system will buffer unexpected peaks caused by too many authors submitting at the very last minute.

Of course, life would be much too easy, if all mailers were properly supporting the MIME protocol. As long as this isn't the case, the best option is to use a MIME compliant mailer at the receiving side and to ask authors either for MIME attachments or for gzip-ed and uuencoded material.

In summary, electronic submission has been widely accepted by the authors. This is supported by the fact that from 112 submitted papers only 14 arrived in printed form only. Two authors provided both, electronic and printed, because they felt that the printed reproduction of the images is relevant for the reviewing process.

Comparing this to the list of finally acccepted papers, it turns out that only one paper-only submission has been accepted (of course, acceptance was *only* based on quality) for the conference. Interestingly, the authors of this contribution had no problem to deliver the final version in electronic form. They didn't even need a revision cycle to fully match the desired format (see below).

---

[1] Due to this last minute action all emails went to the PC chair's mailbox filling it up very quickly with many megabytes of postcript data. It should be observed, that a separate user/mail-id for conference purposes only – not just an email alias – enables the person in charge to continue his/her normal business life. Something which is not true otherwise.

3 Reviewing

Online access to *all* electronically submitted papers has been provided with a
Hyperwave [7, 8] server, a multimedia web server with lots of handy features
supporting the maintenance and access control to a web information base. Access control for the registered user is based on the membership to one or more
(hierarchical) groups, inheriting access permissions. PC members had access to
all submissions whereas reviewers were granted access on a need-to-know basis
only.

With 33 PC members and approx. 160 reviewers the management of the
access control is only one issue to be resolved. The real time-consuming task, at
least for conventional web servers, is the creation of the 160+ index pages for
each individual reviewer. We could not have managed this without the features
of Hyperwave which

1. handles groups of web pages very well. In our case PDF files with attached
   multimedia material like TIFF images, MPEG clips, ... were collected in
   so-called *collections* which can also contain other collections.
2. dynamically creates the index page for each collection, taking care of individual access rights.

These two functions are the key to an efficient management of an online
submission/conference server. Due to the automatic and dynamic creation of
index pages for each collection, there is no need for manually creating or, even
worse, maintaining the 'inner nodes' of this 'web' (which is really a directed
acyclic graph). Not a single explicit hyperlink has been created during the whole
operation.

When a user accesses a specific collection, its content (i.e., the documents
grouped by it) is individually checked for proper access permission. Only those
documents which the user is allowed to access will be included in the list. Thus,
all PC members and reviewers would access the submission server at the same
entry point but each reviewer would see a different page (assuming that no two
reviewers had an identical list of papers to review) holding a different set of
submissions to review. Only PC members would see the full list of electronically
submitted papers.

Uploading of submitted papers to the Hyperwave server and control of access
permissions has, for the reviewing, been done with dedicated Hyperwave clients.
In the meanwhile, as for the online presenation of the final papers, STAR's and
tutorials, uploading is done with standard web clients like NetScape or Interent
Explorer. Thus, the typical data flow would consist of Postscript files arriving
by email which are then stored locally and converted to PDF (by the Adobe
Distiller). The resulting PDF files were checked for completeness and consistency
and uploaded to the web server.

After the submission deadline, papers were assigned to PC members by sending lists of submission ID's (could be URL's) to the individual PC member asking him/her to organize the reviewing for the particular list.
The benefit for the PC chair is obvious:

- papers don't have to be sent by standard mail which reduces the cost of shipping
- papers arrive at the speed of the Internet which is definitely faster than even courier mail
- additional 'copies' can be distributed without extra effort or cost

However, it must be observed that the cost of reproducing the submissions is now shifted to the group of PC members and reviewers as they have to actively *pull* the papers from the server and print them locally – in contrast to *pushing* the hardcopies onto their desk. Despite the significant data reduction resulting from the conversion from Postscript to PDF the time for loading and printing, especially at the PC member's site, can easily become significant.

With the current speed of the Internet the lesson learned for the distribution of the papers is that PC members, due to the typically high number of papers they manage, should have the option to receive printed copies. For reviewers the distribution by electronic means (pull) seems to be acceptable as the number of papers is typically low.

4   Production of Hardcopy and CD-ROM Proceedings

For a number of years now the conference proceedings for the annual event have been published as issue Number 3 of the journal *Computer Graphics Forum*. Being one issue of a journal there was an obvious desire to make the conference proceedings fully blend in with the regular issues. Further, the conversion process from Postscript to PDF can be significantly improved *and* automated if an appropriate style or template can be offered to the authors.

Experience from EUROGRAPHICS '97 tells us that the majority of authors use LaTeX for the typesetting process: only two of the finally accepted papers were compiled with a different system (one in Framemaker, one in Word). Thus, the time to adapt the LaTeX style of the *Computer Graphics Forum* to provide the necessary support for the conference proceedings, tutorials, and STAR's was well invested [5].

Actually, it was the only feasible way, to enforce the use of Adobe's Type 1 fonts which are absolutely necessary to achieve a good quality for the electronic versions.

The issue of Type 1 fonts is closely related to the decision for PDF as the main format. Currently, the only alternatives to produce electronic documents at high quality and at feasible cost are HTML and PDF. Considering HTML's limitations with regard to presentation of mathematical expressions there was no alternative to PDF.

In summer of 1996, the reluctance among many colleagues to use PDF as the main format was largely based on either the unfamiliarity with the functionality of PDF or on the assumption that PDF viewers would not be readily available to the PC members, the reviewers, or the end users of the electronic version of the conference proceedings. Fortunately, PDF viewers and plug-ins for web clients matured and became commonly available on many platforms within a short period of time. As a result, no problems related to the choice of PDF have been reported during the reviewing process.

The production of PDF documents can be achieved in many ways. Almost all office packages directly support PDF as a native output format. In the Microsoft Windows world, PDF files can generally be produced from any application by printing to a virtual printing device which does the conversion to PDF. Adobe also provides the *Distiller*, a tool which converts Postscript files into PDF. In the public domain, conversion from Postscript to PDF can also be done with *ghostscript*.

Although any reasonably well-behaving Postscript file can be converted to PDF, this does not necessarily produce an acceptable quality. The primary reason being, that many document processing systems use raster fonts at a given resolution (from 180 dpi upwards). Of course, printing the resulting PDF file will produce the same result on paper than the original Postscript file. However, the displayed quality for online reading – and this is an essential functionality – is not acceptable. With current technology, Postscript files store raster fonts as medium to high resolution pixel arrays. This representation cannot be changed easily in the conversion from Postscript to PDF which forces the PDF viewer to downsample these pixel arrays (to approx. 72 dpi) on the fly, producing unreadable text (except for large zoom factors).

The solution to the problem is to inform the PDF viewer about the nature of each font. Instead of handling pixel arrays – which could represent anything, not just a character of a specific font – the PDF viewer has all relevant information on the character to be displayed and can, in case of the geometrically defined Type 1 fonts, optimize an anti-aliased bitmap for speedy and high-quality display.

Realizing that Type 1 fonts are very well supported by all PDF viewers the remaining task was to produce postcript files (almost) exclusively making use of such fonts. For packages like Framemaker or Word this can be achieved by simply selecting an appropriate font from the font selection menu. For LaTeX, the style mentioned above had to be augmented by another style called dfAdobe.sty [6] which wasn't too difficult at all as LaTeX2e now comes with a rich set of functionality to control the font selection. This substyle (called package according to LaTeX2e) redefines the font selection for font families serif (rm), sans serif (ss) and teletype (tt). It also redefines most of the characters from the math alphabet, thus automatically producing very readable results at the end of the conversion pipeline (LaTeX – Postscript – PDF).

Additionally, it should be noted that the choice for PDF as the 'backbone' for electronic conference proceedings also provides an integrated *fulltext search* facility over *all* documents in an archive or on a CD. Of course, cross-document fulltext searching is a feature of Adobe's viewer whereas the creation of the fulltext index is done by a separate package, called Adobe *Distiller*.

As a side effect of having a consistent format for the regular issues and for the conference issue the two-column format significantly reduced the amount of pages used for the proceedings. Considering the hassle of each editor to have authors observe the given page limit, this fact should not be ignored.

Problems Experienced

As already mentioned, out of 38 finally accepted papers 2 papers were not produced with LaTeX. The authors approximated the LaTeX layout as closely as they could but, still, some finishing touches like the copyright notice at the first page had to added by the editor.

If low-level hacking, i.e., directly editing the Postscript file, is not an option, editors need a tool providing comfortable access at the document level. *Re:Mark*,[2] for example, is a plug-in to Adobe Acrobat [1] which is designed for exactly the task of electronically editing a PDF document. Missing text parts can be entered as attachments which can also be made 'permanent' by making the attachments an integral part of the document. Having added the missing bits and pieces to the header page of one paper, the attachments can be stored and added to other papers in one single step.

From the remaining 36 papers, 3 authors were not able to configure their LaTeX/dvips environment in order to produce a Postscript file of the desired quality. In these three cases the LaTeX sources together with the included Postscript images were sent to the PC chair who ran the final production run. After some investigation it turned out that not the LaTeX class/package/style was the problem but the configuration of the dvips tool, converting the dvi-file into Postscript. Instead of storing Type 1 font references in the Postscript file these configurations would replace the font references by raster definitions of the according Type 1 fonts.

The lesson learned from this problem is that conference organizers also need to provide a dedicated configuration file for dvips (psfonts.map) to warrant proper font definitions in the resulting Postscript file.

Roughly 50% of the authors needed one revision cycle which, in most cases, only consisted of including the package dfAdobe and re-running LaTeX. The other 50% submitted a final version exactly matching the specification given in the guidelines for authors.

Reflecting the discussion with the authors, editors are well advised to make the templates or LaTeX styles already available well *before* the initial submission deadline. Even if some details are missing from the style files at this stage, it's fair to assume that the style would not change too radically. Layout decisions on the number of columns, for example, affect the way authors place their images in the text. More importantly, the page limit for submissions can only be defined together with a given layout.

Summary

Altogether, the experience with our approach of following the electronic route for many aspects of the PC/editor work is very promising.

- Electronic submission, based on email, is a reliable vehicle. With increasing support of full MIME compliance much of the work to extract the original data sent by the authors will disappear.
- Online access to all submissions is a real added value to PC members as they get a better feeling on the overall quality of papers.
- Complexity of the online server management with regard to access rights is very high and must not be underestimated. However, new web server concepts are available, almost completely eliminating this time-consuming task.
- *Push* versus *Pull*: slow Internet connections and many papers to load from the server can easily take too much of the time PC members are willing to spend on the event. Whoever is supposed to review a larger number of papers should have the option to have the papers delivered in printed form.
- Placing the papers on an online server is an important milestone for the production of a CD-ROM. It serves as a testbed how well submissions could be converted into suitable formats and how easily and at which quality they can be retrieved and displayed with the suggested tools.
  It can also serve as a marketing instrument in case it is not clear if a CD-ROM should be produced at all.
- The time to create a LaTeX/LaTeX2e style which takes care of the layout and specifically supports each stage in the conversion pipeline up to the the final destination format is very well invested.
  Phrasing it differently, high quality proceedings with a uniform layout for the printed and for the electronic version cannot be produced otherwise.
- With regard to document format PDF is currently the best choice. It can easily be converted from Postscript which can be produced by everybody having access to a computer. It maintains the presentation and, if care has been taken of the font selection in the production of the input Postscript file, it will produce high quality output on all PDF viewers. PDF viewers do support fulltext searching across large collections of files. Finally, the support for PDF is growing quite rapidly, especially in the field of professional publishing.
- Authors were very cooperative in the production of the CD-ROM. This is documented by the significant amount of additional multimedia material provided, ranging from true-color images, animated GIF's, MPEG and quicktime movies, VRML scenes, to interactive simulations based on Java applets.

Acknowledgement

Without the experiences from the MEDOC project [3, 9] and without the skills and support from the members of the Graphics Group at the University of Bonn we would not have been able to follow the electronic route. Special thanks go to Michael Brown and Steve Scott of Blackwell Publishers and to Frank Kretschmer and Andreas Kusserow of the Graphics Group at the University of Bonn for their help in the production of the printed conference proceedings and the CD-ROM.

References

1. ADOBE SYSTEMS INC.: Adobe Acrobat. http://www.adobe.com/acrobat.
2. AMBIA CORP.: Re:mark. http://www.ambia.com/.
3. BART A. ET AL: *The MeDoc Digital Library Project: Its Goals and Major Achievements.* in this LNCS volume.
4. FELLNER D. W. (Ed.): *Modeling – Virtual Worlds – Distributed Graphics.* infix, Sankt Augustin, 1995.
5. FELLNER D. W.: LATEX / LATEX2e support for consistent layout of printed and electronic conference proceedings, state-of-the-art reports (STAR's), and tutorials (eg97.sty). available from http://www.graphics.uni-bonn.de/EG/EG97proc/, 1997.
6. FELLNER D. W.: LATEX / LATEX2e support for Type 1 fonts (dfadobe.sty). available from http://www.graphics.uni-bonn.de/EG/EG97proc/, 1997.
7. HYPERWAVE TEAM: Hyperwave online. http://www.hyperwave.com.
8. MAURER H. (Ed.): *Hyper-G/now Hyperwave – The Next Generation Web Solution.* Addison-Wesley, Harlow, England, 1996.
9. MEDOC PROJECT-TEAM: MeDoc. http://medoc.informatik.tu-muenchen.de/.

Books and Journals in MeDoc - Experiences on Bringing Publications Online

U. Schwab

Springer-Verlag Berlin Heidelberg, Tiergartenstr. 17, 69121 Heidelberg
Mail: schwab@springer.de

Abstract: This paper offers an overview of the experiences and problems encountered on converting books and journals existing in different electronic source formats into fully functional online-versions either in HTML or in PDF. The article focuses on the organisational point of view rather than explaining specific techniques and programmes for the conversion. It describes pros and cons of specific output formats as well as the wanted and achieved functionality of the derived online contents.

1. Introduction

One of the majour aims of the MeDoc-project is to offer a 'critical mass' of electronic publications of high quality (books and journals from renown publishers next to technical reports and conference proceedings) over the Internet.

At present, 60 books and 22 journals from twelve German publishers as well as from the IEEE and ACM are offered via the MeDoc service. License agreements had been signed for 80 books and 24 journals, 194 books and journals had been on the inquiry lists. Not all of the books defined in the lists could be offered. Reasons for this will be given later on.

While electronic journals become more and more common, complete electronic versions of printed books were not to be found on the Internet at the beginning of MeDoc and are still. MeDoc is considered to be one of the largest collection of electronic books of approved quality.

In the project 14 publishers agreed to grant licences of their respective printed books to be offered online. But only in one case a complete electronic version could be offered for instant online publishing (i .e. in HTML or PDF format) from the publisher as the data usually was not available in these formats.

There was clear concencus in the project description, that in terms of creating a critical mass of information no book should be created from the scratch. Therefore electronic source material of the books had to be collected and converted into the appropriate target formats. This article describes the typical workflow of the conversion, the common problems and conclusions of the experiences made.

The process of the conversions was organized by the author of this article by means of contacting the respective persons, maintaining online-list of running conversions, to inform about the wanted functionality of the electronic book (checklists), establishing synergy effects for pilot users with same source/target-data etc.)

2. Workflow of conversion

Usually a number of persons were involved in the collection and conversion of the source material as well as the surveying of the resulting version, namely the author, the publisher, representatives of the MeDoc project and the converters.

It turned out therefore to be necessary to control the conversion process from the beginning (contacting the publisher for receiving the sources) to the end (acknowledging the result of the conversion and importing the electronic book into the MeDoc fulltext storage). The process of the conversions was organized by the author of this article by means of contacting the respective persons, keeping up-to-date an online-list of running conversions, giving information on wanted functionality of the electronic book (checklists), developing synergy effects for pilot users with comparable source/target-data etc.)

One of the first results of this work was to develop a typical workflow for the conversion and the online publishing of the progress made to synergize the ongoing work. A usual workflow is printed below in short:

1. A book is considered relevant for MeDoc (list of pilot users, recommendations by MeDoc participants), publisher and author were informed and agreed on conversion and online publication of the respective book, publisher/author give information on availability of source material and desired target format
2. Acquisition of pilot users (in some cases the author) for the conversion, contact between person doing the conversion („converter") and publisher/author
3. Transfer of source material - involving the author into the conversion process was very desirable
4. Converter gives an offer for the conversion (costs and duration of conversion, added-value over printed version etc.) - if accepted, offer will be sent to project office - contract is worked out (if conversion is paid for by own funds of the pilot user institution, no contract is necessary), when contract is signed by the project and the pilot user institution: report to BMBF (first payment „Mittelentsperrung")
5. Converter informs MeDoc and publisher/author, when prototype of conversion is available („secret" URL), at least four weeks prior to finishing date. MeDoc checks quality and functionality of prototype according to the checklists (see below) - feedback and request for changes from MeDoc and publisher/author
6. If conversion is accepted, description of file structure, report of conversion as well as target data has to be sent to the project office on an appropriate medium (CD-ROM, Disk, DAT) (as agreed in the conversion contract), when conversion is approved, report to BMBF for final payment and closure of contract

7. Report to OFFIS ('Zentrale Beratung MeDoc-Server'), downloading of the target data, enriching book data according to data model by means of meta information, transfer to dedicated MeDoc-Server, making accessible through MeDoc (importing to fulltext store, referencing via provider agent and broker)

Some remarks on these points:

1. Choice of books to be made available in MeDoc was made in two steps (so called stage 1 and stage 2) - the books for stage 1 were derived from a most wanted list collected at the very beginning of the project (autumn 1995) whereas books for stage 2 had been added to the list and to the respective licence agreement enclosures one year later.

2. As the project went on, some pilot user institutions built up knowledge for specific source or target formats. Synergy effects were quite visible after the second or third conversion of a comparable type, not only in technical details but also concerning the experiences whom to contact, becoming familiar with the workflow and the like. Over the months some pilot user institutions gathered experiences by doing a couple of conversion, while other institutions were not engaged in conversions at all. The most desirable option was to have the conversion done by the author. Most likely she or he had the best understanding of the structure and content of the book and was very demanding concerning the quality of the online version.

3. Receiving the electronic version of a respective printed book turned out to be more difficult than presumed. Very often the publishing company did not archive the data that came from the author and therefore could not offer an electronic version of the book to be converted. In same cases, the data could be delivered from the type setter - but in the majority of cases, a complete and accurate electronic version could only be obtained from the autor. This was especially true when the data consists of a variety of files in different formats only the author was able to reconstruct. But even in those cases where the autor was involved, it was sometimes difficult to decide whether the version available was the final release of the manuscript and in complete accordance with the printed version. For comparison the printed version of the book was a bare necessity for the further conversion process. Sometimes even the data transfer from the author/publisher to the converter was not easy: Not every author/publisher was able to offer the material on a ftp-server for download or could upload to a ftp-server at the converters institution. Disks were not the right transport medium for large volumes. The variety of high storage media (DAT, CD-ROM, MOD, Syquest Cartridges, Iomega ZIP-disks etc.) sometimes caused problems.

4. Especially at the beginning, estimation of cost and duration of the conversion was not easy, as no experience was available on what is desirable and how much could be done automatically by conversion tools. Costs for a complete conversion range from 1. 500 DM to 10. 000 DM. The conclusion of a contract was the rule. Only in a couple of cases the conversion was paid for by institutional funds. The project

funds granted by the BMBF for conversions had to be increased, as the complexity and costs turned out to be higher than presumed.

5. In most cases postprocessing - partly to a large extend - was necessary as the prototype required improvement in layout and functionality. The sooner the deficiencies were made known to the converter, the easier it was to correct them automatically and to safe manual work in the wrong direction. Feedback from authors and publishers ranges from showing hardly any interest to detailed suggestions for improvement.

6. A description of file structure and file name conventions was necessary to assign single files to logical units (e. g. chapters, samples etc.) for database access. Especially the report of the conversion experiences is a most valuable source for other converters and of course the publishers. Only when all the required data and information was delivered, the contract was closed.

3. Books not offered in MeDoc

A couple of books had been ranked high in the most-wanted lists, but nevertheless are not available in MeDoc. Reasons for this were:

Sources were not available	the complete and accurate electronic version could not be provided from neither author or publisher
no contact to author	electronic version would have been only available from the author - but we could not get in contact with him/her (especially difficult with foreign authors
Waiting for next edition of printed book	a revised edition was planned from the publisher - no outdated information should be offered in MeDoc
Structure too complex For HTML or PDF	some books (e. g. encyclopedia) turned out to be very complex in structure. Therefore a structured search should be available (e. g. data stored in SGML) which was not feasible with the chosen storage formats

Sources only convertible With enormous efforts	for some source formats even rudimentary conversion tools simply were not available on the market (e. g. Ventura Publisher). Conversion would have to be done manually or via an intermediate format with less chance to maintain any structural information
Author and/or publisher did Not agree with publication of the online-version	in a couple of cases the author and/or the publisher feared a negative influence on the print market for the respective book. Some authors agreed to offer their book online only with appropriate additional information (e. g. multimedial add-ons) which they could not provide at the moment. Therefore no online version was offered at all
Publisher is not the Copyright-owner	e. g. with translations

4. Statistics and information on source and target formats

4.1 Source formats

The source material was to be found in a variety of formats, often incomplete and/or mixed with data in other formats. This applies not only for the textual material but even more for the graphic files.

21 of the books were offered in word processing formats - Word (Macintosh, Windows, DOS) and Word Perfect).

29 of the books were offered in TeX and LaTex with a variety of macro packages and third party tools used.

The rest of the material was offered in miscellaneous formats, e. g. Framemaker, PostScript, Ventura Publisher, Pagemaker or ASCII).

As for the graphics nearly all known formats were offered, often two or more different ones in a single book. In some cases, the graphics were contained in the respective text document, in other cases graphics were delivered separately. Twice nearly all of the figures had to be scanned as there was no electronic version available at all.

A very important factor for the efficiency of the converting process had been the quality of the source material. The more structure included the more automation was possible. Often we found hardly any structure at all, even when the originally used programme did offer automatic enumeration, table of contents etc. Enriching these flat information prior to the conversion normally was less time consuming than enriching the output information.

4.2 Target formats

The MeDoc project defined HTML 3.2 and PDF 1.1 as the basis output formats. 25 books are offered in PDF, 38 books are offered in HTML. Normally the output format was the choice of the publisher granting the license.

Pros for the conversion into HTML were the general suitability for online publishing and the high distribution being an approved international standard, as well as its readability onscreen. Negative aspects are the necessity to display formulae as graphics and the missing layout control.

Pros for PDF were seen in the preservation of the layout (corporate identity), the possibility to prohibit the printing of the document and having no problems with the inclusion of formulaes and complex tables. Cons are by far longer download times due to larger file size as well as using a still proprietary product with the need to use special viewers as an addition to the browser.

As a rule PDF turned out to be converted into easier as there was nearly always the possibility to use PostScript as intermediate format. Therefore in some cases, the choice of the output format was influenced by the source material and the problems of converting it into HTML.

5 Conclusions

At the beginning of the project (Sep. 1995) there was little experience what it means to bring a printed book online with a certain functionality. This was clearly seen, when on the one hand the converting institutions had problems estimating the time and costs of a planned conversion and often exceeding both, on the other hand the participants had problems of exactly defining what the desired functionality and layout of the online book should be.

Problems occured due to the distribution of the project partners. Achieving synergetic work and passing on experience between all participants was not easy but vital to build up knowledge. To transfer the know-how to other institutions a workshop had been organized together with the Deutscher Boersenverein. Also an electronic book, covering the whole conversion experiences including the more technical details is published by MeDoc.

From the technical point of view we have learned, that there are very few programmes available which work at least to some extend reliable and decrease the need for manual conversion. A couple of things which adds value to the electronic version could not be done automatically (for example setting non-structured links).

The speed and accuracy of the conversion was highly dependable not only on the source format but also on the quality of the source material concerning structural information and use of automatism. Guidelines for authors for how to use their writing tools appropriately should be collected and made accessible to ensure easier conversion in the future. Publishers should continue to offer and enhance macro packages and style sheets for word processor programmes. Authors have to be convinced of using these new possibilities more often for the benefits of all.

Appendix: Checklists for layout and functionality of the books

Due to the nearly complete lack of electronic versions of printed books online or even offline it was not easy to define exactly, how an electronic book should look like and what functionality is desired. The supposed users of these books as well as the publishers had to collect their first thoughts and define their wishes and often made - as it seemed - their first experiences as the first conversions went on. Two checklists (for HTML and PDF respectively) were created and updated as new user feedback was available.

HTML Checklist:

content:	complete, all pictures, footnotes, appendices etc. included; comparison with printed version
segmentation:	segmentation functionally solved; as a rule one HTML-file per sub-chapter; small sub-chapters should be combined, large sub-chapters should be splitted navigation: all navigational links active and correct; usual functionality: buttons for back, forward, table of contents, index, up (one hierarchy-level up); navigation bar on top and bottom of each HTML-page
links:	all links active and correct (by random sample, preferably automatically by means of link-checker-programmes); every reasonable information linked (e. g. see chapter, see figure, links to bibliography, index etc.); only relative links used
table of contents:	very large tocs should be splitted into different HTML-files, alternatively: one toc with first-level hierarchy information, respective tocs for each chapter; clear presentation of chapter-hierarchies (indent sub-chapter information)
bibliography:	use of external links (e-mail of author, URL of primary source); possible: backlinks from the bibliography into the appropriate chapter
index:	how are two or more occurences of one index entry solved; target of index entry link is named by page number, by (sub-)chapter or both; large index should be splitted into separate HTML-files (e.g. A-E, F-J etc.); even with only one index-file, navigation by first letter is advisable (letter-bar at top of the page)
footnotes:	realized at the bottom of the same HTML-page (smaller font) or as a link into a separate footnode-file
heading:	choice of headings (h1 to h6) reasonable and consistent for respective chapters and sub-chapters

figures and images:	quality versus size (resolution) of file; captions for every figure according to print version; figures in GIF/JPEG only (possible: links to separate files for other formats or resolutions, optional use of thumbnails)
welcome page (index.html):	should consist of book cover and short explanation of the contents, links to publishers homepage, information about author (e-mail-link) etc.; welcome page should link to table of contents file.
sample-pages:	for each book a sample should be offered, usually consisting of welcome page, table of contents, index, bibliography and first chapter, accessible for free
title-tags:	title-tag should consist of name and numeration of the (sub-)chapter - this will be the retrieved information given in the hit-list when searching for documents
filenames:	Sensibility of upper and lower case and consistency of the respective links (Windows/DOS is case insensitive - UNIX as operating system on the dedicated MeDoc-server is not); use expressive filenames for GIF- and HTML-files wherever possible

PDF-Checklist (additional information)

navigation (bookmarks):	navigation should be offered via PDF-bookmarks; for each PDF-file bookmark entries should consist of sub-chapters of the file, links to previous and next chapter, table of contents, index and bibliography; bookmarks should be presented automatically when PDF-file is opened
links:	each link shown versus intuitive use (show only links that are not apparent, show no links at all to not affect the layout); choice of link-layout (box, underline, color) by third party-tools or Acrobat Exchange 3.0
index:	Very large index files should be splitted by means of bookmark information (A-E, F-J etc.)
fonts and graphics:	embedded font readable on screen - quality of embedded formulaes and figures
sample-pages:	if the whole book consists of only one PDF-file, a second file for the sample-information has to be offered
miscellaneous:	PDF-Files should be saved with internet optimization (byteserving) - only available with Acrobat Distiller 3 - for faster delivery; thumbnails usually need not to be offered; reasonable choice of startup magnification (e.g. fit page vs. fit width)

Experiences in Document Conversions During the MeDoc Project

Hubert Feyrer[1] hubert.feyrer@rz.fh-regensburg.de

Fachbereich Informatik/Mathematik, Fachhochschule Regensburg, Prüfeningerstr. 58,
D-93053 Regensburg, Germany

Abstract. This paper summarizes the experiences made in converting printed books from various text file formats into electronic formats for use in the MeDoc library. Starting with an overiew of the source formats and conversion tools the problems arising with them are discussed and technical guidelines are given for the conversion process.

1 Introduction

Building an electronic library of books related to the field of computer science was one objective of the MeDoc project [7]. The majority of these books were converted from existing printed original books into electronic documents which could be used over the Web. Essential conditions set for this task were

- the MeDoc objectives specification as layed down in [5],
- the time available (less than two years for more than 50 books),
- the involvement of many publishers, authors, libraries and institutions,
- the use of HTML and PDF as distribution formats.

Responsible for the management and the surveying of all conversion activities were M. Breu (FAST. e.V) and U.Schwab (Springer Verlag). The author of this paper has converted several of the books for the MeDoc library and monitored a group of students who converted additional books. Members of many other institutions have also participated in the conversion activities.

In general the conversion process started from the text and image source files supplied by the publishers or by the authors. So the text processors involved ranged from archaic to rather advanced systems. Up to now there is no straightforward, automatic way to convert any of these text formats into the target formats HTML or PDF. Even if there are conversion tools, problems arise from their relative immaturity.

This paper reports about the experiences stemming from our conversion activities and gives recommendations for the use of the various conversion techniques and tools.

2 Document Formats and Conversion Tools

Electronic document formats can be devided into three groups

- author formats,
- reader formats and
- intermediate formats.

Author formats are used in the process of writing books and articles while reader formats are used to distribute electronic documents to the end users. During the conversion process additional intermediate formats may be necessary, especially, if there is no direct conversion path from the author format to a reader format. Table 1 lists some popular formats of these types.

Name	Category	representation	More information
FrameMaker	Source	binary	http://www.adobe.com/
LaTeX	Source	ascii	http://www.dante.de/
WinWord	Source	binary	http://www.microsoft.com/
DVI	intermediate	binary	http://www.dante.de/
MIF	intermediate	binary	http://www.adobe.com/
PostScript	intermediate	ascii	http://www.adobe.com
RTF	intermediate	ascii	http://www.microsoft.com/
HTML	reader	ascii	http://www.w3.org/
PDF	reader	ascii/binary	http://www.adobe.com/

Table 1. Popular document formats

Author formats

Today numerous different author formats are in use, a fact which contributes considerable complexity to the task of converting documents from author into reader formats. Each text processor uses its own proprietary format and by now there are few serious attemps to reduce this variety.

Reader formats

The reader formats used in the MeDoc project were HTML and PDF. HTML documents include document structure information but their presentation layout depends on the target platform. PDF documents include no structure information but the original layout is preserved by the viewers on any platform. General aspects of these two reader formats, for instance their layout capabilties, their use for indexed search or their security aspects are discussed in [6]. Therefore our discussion of reader formats in the next section will be limited to conversion aspects.

Conversion tools

Table 2 lists document manipulation tools used in the conversion process together with their scope of use and a reference URL. Most of them are independent utilities. Some, PDFwriter and Word Internet Assistant for example, are integrated into text processors. Other utilities for examples graphic tools, screen capture tools, conversion tools for graphic formats or viewers are also needed but not contained in this list.

Tool Name	Inputformat → Outputformat Where to get
Adobe Distiller	PostScript → PDF http://www.adobe.com/prodindex/acrobat/main.html
Adobe Exchange	PDF → PDF http://www.adobe.com/prodindex/acrobat/main.html
Adobe PDFwriter	any author format→ PDF http://www.adobe.com/prodindex/acrobat/main.html
dvips	DVI → PostScript http://www.radicaleye.com/dvips.html
frame2html	Native FrameMaker, MIF → HTML ftp://ftp.nta.no/pub/fm2html/fm2html.v.0.8.9a.tar.Z
FrontPage	HTML, ASCII, RTF, Word → HTML http://www.microsoft.com/frontpage/
Ghostscript	PostScript → TIFF, PDF, ... http://www.cs.wisc.edu/ ghost/
HotDog Pro	HTML, ASCII → HTML http://www.sausage.com/store/indexST.htm
latex2html	TEX, LATEX→ HTML http://www-dsed.llnl.gov/files/programs/unix/latex2html/
rtf2html	RTF → HTML http://www.sunpack.com/RTF/latest/
TEX	TEX, LATEX→ DVI ftp://ftp.tug.org/tex/
WebWorks HTML Lite	Native FrameMaker, MIF → HTML http://www.frame.com/
Word Internet Assistant	ASCII, Word, RTF, ...→ HTML http://www.microsoft.com/word/internet/

Table 2. Document manipulation utilities

3 Guidelines for Document Conversion

The following sections identify keypoints which need attention during the conversion process and give hints how to solve arising problems.

3.1 Fonts

Choosing font size
For HTML documents the readers can choose the font size as an option of the HTML browsers, but this has two serious drawbacks:

- The size of images and particularly of formula which are represented by images is not changed according to the new font size and

- Frame sizes are usually specified in relation to the window size, and by changing the font size a text may become to large for the frame containing it.

To avoid these problems it is important for HTML conversions to select explicitly a font size suitable for most reader platforms. Tables should be used instead of f rames because they can adapt their size to their contents.

PDF viewers on the other hand allow any zoom factors. So the font size in the electronic document may be the same as for the printed book and can be adjusted arbitrarily by zooming on the reader platform.

Replacing TeX pixel fonts
When converting TeX-documents into PDF (via DVI and PostScript), the original pixel-fonts of the TeXconfiguration should be replaced by PostScript fonts. This improves highly the readability of the electronic document on the screen, reduces its size and makes it independant of the resolution of the output device.

Embedding fonts into PDF documents
Embedding fonts into PDF documents is a recommendable option of Distiller which garantuees exact correspondence to the original irrespective of the fonts available on the reader system. Even if the font embedding option is not used, PDF viewers simulate the original font with special serif or sans serif Multiple Master fonts. This font substitution does not cause documents to reformat since the width and height of the original characters is retained.

3.2 Colors

HTML browsers use default colors for background and text if there are no explicit color specifications in the document. This might affect the legibility of tables with borders, horizonztal rules and other objects. So for HTML documents it is recommendable to embed explicit color specifications for text and background.

Since the layout of PDF documents corresponds exactly to the original on all reader platforms, no additional considerations concerning color are necessary for their conversion.

3.3 Images

Adjusting color depth and resolution
The pixel resolution of modern displays is 72 dots per inch, much less than for typical printed images and drawings. Reducing the resolution of images to that amount reduces their memory and bandwidth requirements considerable. A similar argument is valid for color depth if it is not needed for an image. While automatic reduction of resolution is an an option of Distiller for conversion into PDF, in all other cases standard graphics tools must be used.

Adjusting image size
When adjusting the size of images, antialiasing techniques should be used to

preserve image quality as much as possible. Large images should be embedded as small thumbnails into the text and linked to a high resolution version which can be loaded when required.

In HTML documents an ALT-parameter in the IMG-tag should generate a substitute textual description for browsers with disabled image loading option.

3.4 Document segmentation

For HTML documents it is a standard technique to generate separate files for each subsection. So only those parts of a document are downloaded which are actually of interest and the need for scrolling through long documents is reduced.

For PDF files segmentation is not necesary since they can be optimized to support byte serving, a technique by which web-servers deliver any page out of a PDF document.

3.5 Links

Some important aspects of links in documents are the following:

- When following a link to a new page in most cases the navigation bar should be visible on that page when it is entered. Since latex2html produces links of the form "xxx#yyy" to the first heading of a page these should be modified to "xxx"
- While references like "see chapter xxx" or "see figure xxx" can be used as anchors for links to these objects, in a reference of type "see page xxx" the page number should be replaced by a symbolic icon if the page numbers in the electronic document do not exist or do not correspond to the printed original text. Similarly links to page numbers in the document index must be replaced by symbolic icons, by section or heading numbers.
- It should be checked carefully that all links in a document are valid.

3.6 Table of Contents, Index and References

- For HTML documents long tables of content should be splitted to facilitate navigation. It is a good choice to put the main headings into a top level page, while the tables of content for each chapter are put into linearly linked pages on a second level.
- Similarly a large index in HTML documents should be splitted. The top level index page may contain a character jump bar leading to the headwords of the index pages on the second level.
- For PDF documents the Catalog utility can generate a full text index thus avoiding the necessity of a separate index with headwords in many cases.
- References to other books, journals or articles should be equipped with URLs to web-servers, where they can be downloaded, or with the Email address of the author. It is also possible to insert backlinks from the reference section to the document sections where the references are cited. The hyperref-macros used for LaTeX-to-PDF conversions produce these backlinks automatically.

4 Conclusion

This paper can only summarize the most striking technical points of the conversion process. More detailed information can be found in [8] where the reports on all conversions performed during the MeDoc-project are collected.

But in addition to that the conversions are strongly influenced by decisions out of this scope, for example the choice of the author and reader formats, the availability and completeness of the source files or the cooperation between the publisher, the author and the conversion team.

The most important lesson learned however is, that authors should take into account, that the final product eventually will be delivered not only in printed form but also as an electronic document, before they are writing down the first lines of text.

References

1. Adobe Systems Inc.: PostScript language tutorial and cookbook (the blue book), Addison-Wesley, Reading, MA, 1985.
2. Adobe Systems Inc.: PostScript language reference manual (the red book), 2nd ed, Addison-Wesley, Reading, MA, 1990.
3. Adobe Systems Inc.: PostScript Language Program Design (the green book), Addison-Wesley, Reading, MA, 1988.
4. Brüggemann-Klein: Präsentation auf dem MeDoc - Verlegertreffen anlässlich der Frankfurter Buchmesse, TU München,
   http://medoc.informatik.tu-muenchen.de/deutsch/organisation/projektbibliothek/folien/brueggem.ps
5. Brüggemann-Klein, ed.: Projekt MeDoc - Pflichtenheft,
   http://www11.informatik.tu-muenchen.de/proj/Medoc1/Pflichtenheft/
6. Brüggemann-Klein: Elektronisches Publizieren: Formate und Konvertierungen, Workshop Digitale Bibliotheken, Aachen, 1997
7. Breu, Brüggemann-Klein, Endres: Elektronische Informations- und Publikationsdienste für die Informatik - Ergebnisse des Projekts MeDoc, Jahrestagung der Gesellschaft für Informatik in Aachen, 1997
8. Collection of all conversion reports of the MeDoc project.
   http://medoc.springer.de/konvertierungen/konvertierungsberichte/
9. Knuth, Donald E.: "The TeX Book", Addison-Wesley, Reading, MA, 1986.
10. Microsoft Product Support Services: "Rich Text Format (RTF) Specification", Microsoft Corp., 1994,
    http://night.primate.wisc.edu:70/0/software/RTF/RTF-Spec-1.3.ps
11. Tim Bienz, Richard Cohn, James R. Meehan: "Portable Document Format Reference Manual, Version 1.2", Adobe Systems Incorporated, 1996,
    http://www.adobe.com/supportservice/devrelations/PDFS/TN/PDFSPEC.PDF

Digital Books in MeDoc - A First Analysis of Usage Patterns

Michael Breu (breu@fast.de)[1]

Research Institute for Applied Software Technology (FAST e.V.), Munich

Abstract. The MeDoc digital library service has been offering on-line access to over 40 books for more than 10 months. With this project first long-term data is available to give a first insight into how electronic on-line books are used. The data were collected in two ways: Readers were questioned how the electronic books offered by the MeDoc electronic library service are used. In addition, the usage of the digital library service was monitored through network facilities and evaluated. This paper gives the most significant results of both evaluations.

1 Introduction and Motivation

Digital libraries on the Internet make scientific information available at the desktops of students and scientists. A number of digital library projects (see e.g. [9, 8, 7, 12, 4, 10]) have been launched, but the collection of field test experiences is just starting (e.g. [5]).

The MeDoc digital library has been operating since March 1996 and a library system that manages library access is working since November 1996. Since then, the inventory of the library had grown to over 40 books and 6 on-line journals as of October 1997. One of the major goals of the project was to understand how the results of the project were received by the end user. To this end, a two-tiered approach was pursued:

On one hand qualitative data was collected in a survey in order to evaluate the subjective reception of the service. The project has conducted a series of surveys to determine users expectations of the library [3] and whether these expectations were met [6]. During June 1997 a final survey was conducted to find out how the on-line books were used and to get direct feedback on the presentation of each book.

On the other hand, usage was monitored by the system to verify some of the subjective data and evaluate the quantitative usage of the service. One goal of usage monitoring was to measure acceptance of the services and its features in order to tune these services further. Another goal was to forecast the future usage development of the library services.

The following contribution therefore has three parts: first we give a short overview of the inventory structure of the MeDoc library, then we present the results of the user survey. In the third part we show what is monitored and what conclusions can be drawn so far.

2   The Structure of the Library

The projects goal was to have more than 50 computer science books and 25 journals on-line by the end of 1997. Up to Oct. 1997 there were already 40 books and 7 journals available with continuous extensions. For details on the overall project and on technical implementation see [1] and [2]. The books and journals are available via standard WWW mechanisms (i.e. via the http-protocol), but users need to aqcuire a licence (i.e. an access right) to read a book. To this end the participating institutions acquire a number of licences and lend them out to their users. Licences are *personal licences,* i.e. a license is assigned to a user for a specified time (e.g. 4 months) before it can be returned and lent to another person. License management is fully automated (see [11]).

The books are either presented in HTML or PDF format. Quite an effort was taken to give these books at least some basic added values like a table of contents and an index with links to the respective pages. Some books have significant added value like movies or Java programs. For historical reasons two early available books were available in Postscript and plain PDF format without links[1].

Before aqcuiring a licence the user can browse through a sample of the book. The sample typically contains the title page, the table of contents, the index and the first chapter of the book. The complete digital book contains the complete document and a full text search mechanism. Books are either presented in HTML-format together with GIF's or in PDF-format and may have supplements such as movies or Java-programs.

3   The Books Survey

The intention of the survey (furtheron referred to as *books survey*) was to find out how each of the electronic books was received. I.e. we asked how people came to know about the availability of a book, how the electronic edition was handled, and how the value of the electronic edition as compared to the paper edition was assessed.

3.1   Method of Data Collection and Data Analysis

The survey was carried out through a WWW form. The first section of the questionnaire contained ten questions regarding the book and the second section contained two questions regarding the institution and the role of respondents who filled out the form. We decided to keep the questionnaire short, and to ask generalized questions on different areas concerning the presentation of each book and also general handling. For each question we left possibilities to give detailed remarks.

---

[1] These documents are denoted as trivial conversions in the following statistics

Since we wanted to get comments on each book users had to fill out questionnaires for each individual book. But the structure of all questionnaires was identical. This fact was considered during statistical analysis.

The target group for this survey were all readers of the electronic books. The survey was announced through the standard MeDoc E-mail-list and posted on the WWW server. In addition a reminder email was sent to each person who requested a license for a book. At one university the questionnaire was announced to students during a lecture where one book was recommended as basic literature. The data collection was anonymous. The following results are based on the return of 178 questionnaires.

The number of replies per books is quite unequal, therefore a statistical analysis for each individual book is not allways sensible. Instead the following analysis was mainly done relative to the presentation format. Figure 1 shows the shares of the book formats of the returned questionnaires.

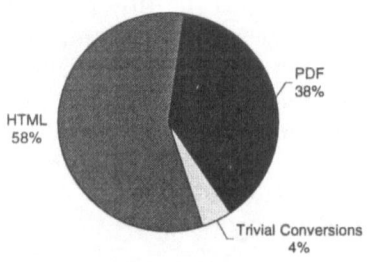

Fig. 1. Returned questionnaires per format

For each questionnaire the Internet domain of the respondent was recorded. The distribution is presented in figure 2.

There is some correlation between both diagrams, because most of the questionnaires returned from the above mentioned university, were mainly concerning one specific book, whereas from other schools there was nearly an equal distribution over all online-books.

Of the replies 64% came from universities, 29% from technical colleges (Fachhochschulen), the rest from the library of a participating research institute.

The distribution of the occupation of respondents was as follows: 26 questionnaires were returned by professors, 61 by research assistants, 35 by undergraduate students, 52 by graduate students, and 2 from library staff.

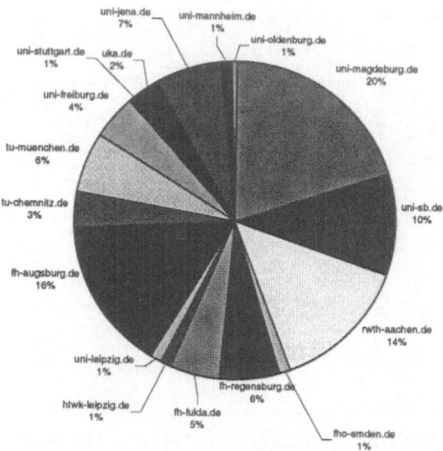

Fig. 2. Returned questionnaires per Internet domain

3.2 Results of the Books Survey

Knowledge about the MeDoc library: There are different ways to find a book in the MeDoc library, either through direct announcement through the MeDoc E-mail list, on the WWW server or through on-site information by local supervisors. Alternatively the book can be found through a MeDoc library search. In some cases the electronic edition of a book was recommended as a basic information source by a lecturer. Since the samples are freely available, the books can also be found through WWW search engines.

As presented in figure 3 most of the respondents learned of the availability through direct announcement of the MeDoc service either via E-mails or via local activities of the MeDoc supervisors. Alternative entry path was a search through the MeDoc library. Only in one lecture, the electronic edition of a book was announced. Nearly all replies with "announcement in lecture" came for this book. The "other" replies were mainly from MeDoc project participants that tested the MeDoc library inventory. Word of mouth propaganda and web surfing played a neglectable role.

Samples: For each book offered through the MeDoc service there is an additional sample freely available. Typically it contains the table of contents, the index, and the first chapter. For books with multi-media extensions, the sample also contains extra multimedia elements (e.g. movies).

Quite often the sample was not read. Instead a license was immediately acquired. This stands in contrast to observations from usage monotoring (see 4.2) which shows that approximately 75% of the sessions at the MeDoc servers are accessing sample documents. Most remarks of what was missing in the sample suggested that the first chapter of some books were not informative enough to base a decision upon. In addition it was proposed to add information about

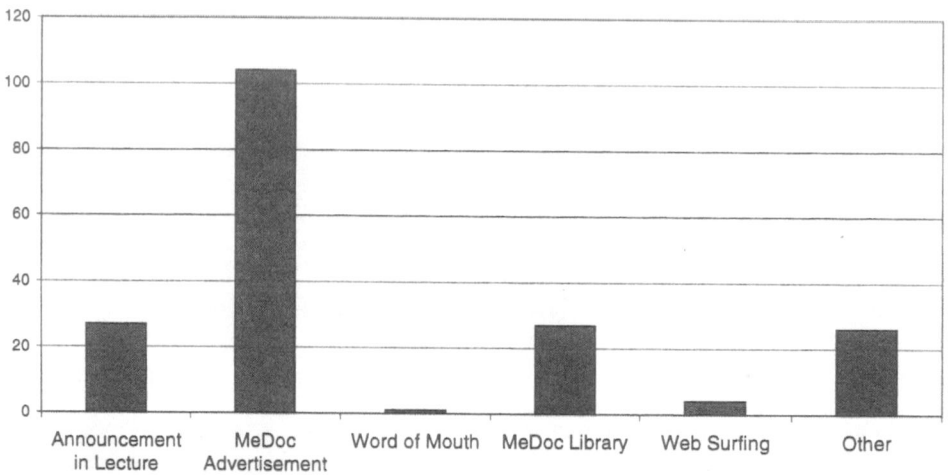

Fig. 3. Question 1.1: How did you learn about this electronic book? (*multiple answers possible*)

pricing of the full license and the paper edition and about the required tools to read the book.

Main reason to acquire a license for the electronic edition: Figure 4 shows that (for the time being) the driving force for using the MeDoc library is mainly curiosity or general interest. Most respondents had a general interest in the subject area. Quite a few also had an interest just for the electronic edition or acquired it for curiosity. About a quarter used the electronic edition to fulfill concrete information needs.

Successful Usage of the Electronic Edition: Were the information needs better or faster fulfilled by using the electronic edition compared to the paper edition? Of all respondents 57% said that their information needs were at least partially better or faster met. A more thorough analysis shows that there is a significant dependency on formats: Books in HTML fulfilled the information needs much better, compared to books in PDF (see fig 5).

Main Way of Access: For most of the books in the MeDoc library there are different ways to find the relevant information: through the table of contents, index, full text search, or flipping through pages. Figure 6 shows how the electronic editions were mainly used. The main entry point was through the table of contents, while the alternative entry point was the index of the book. Quite a few respondents also said that they flipped through the pages to find relevant information. This result also coincides with an analysis of the log-files (section 4.2) which also revealed the same usage patterns.

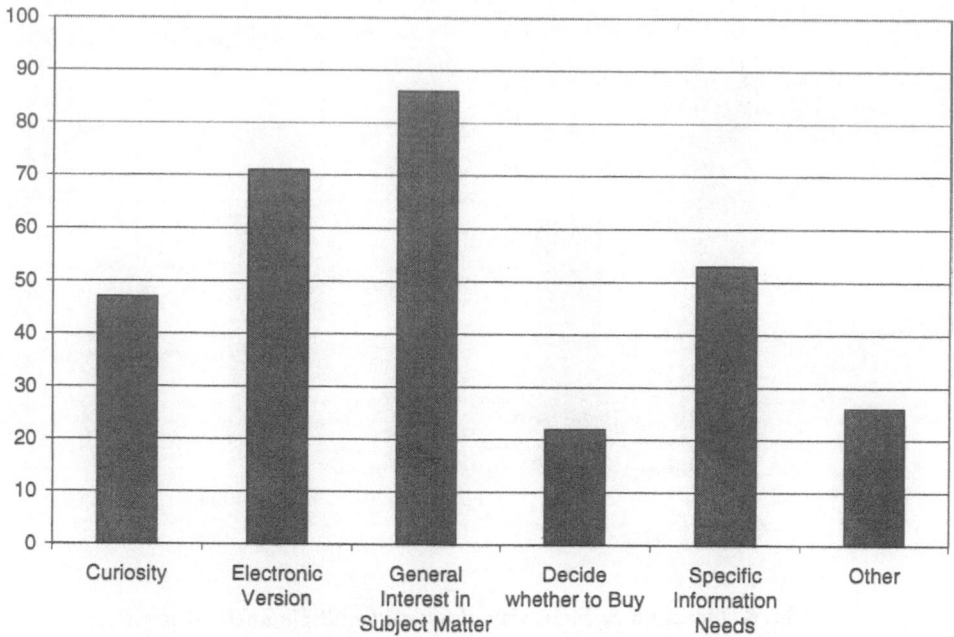

Fig. 4. Question 3: Main reason to acquire a license

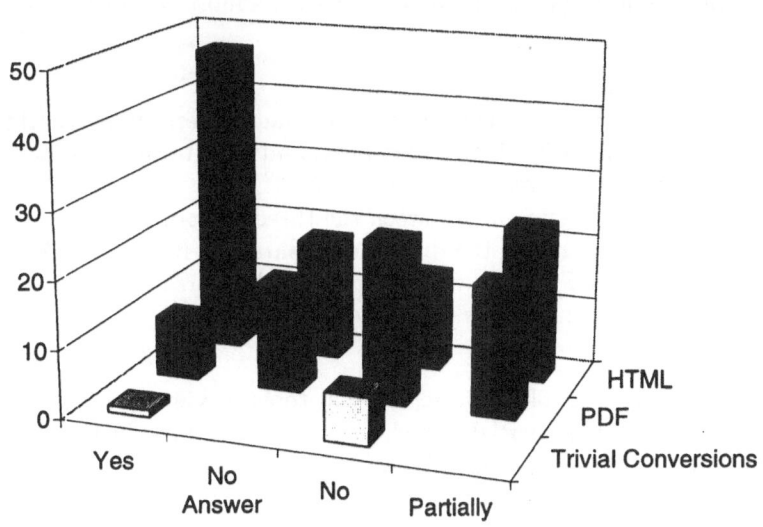

Fig. 5. Question 4: Successful usage of electronic edition

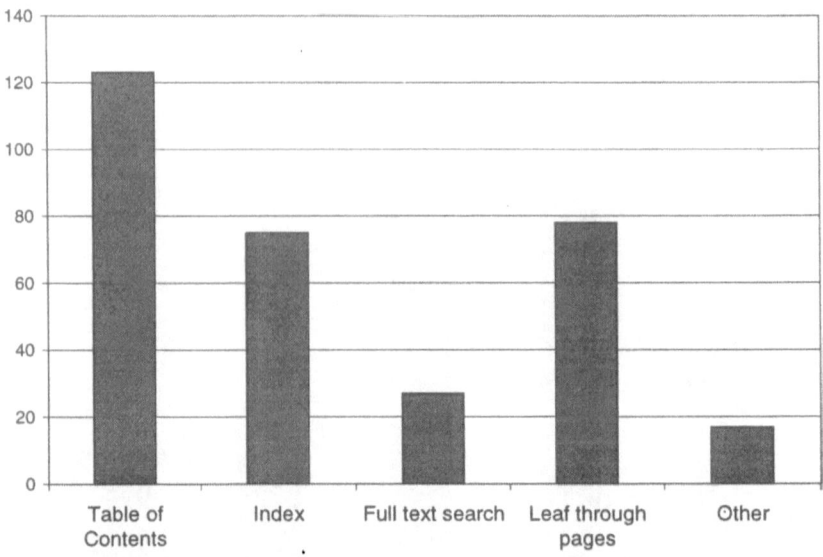

Fig. 6. Question 5: Main way of access (*multiple answers possible*)

There was no significant difference between books in HTML and PDF format. Surprisingly, full text search was not a main option for finding relevant information. Since not all books offered this service, a more thorough analysis is needed.

Presentation of the books: The respondents had to determine whether the book is aesthetically pleasing, clearly presented, and easy to use. The scale was from 1 (very good) up to 5 (very bad or very poor)[2].

The numbers didn't vary much between the three categories, but there were clear differences when analyzing the different formats (see fig. 7). HTML-Books were rated the best. PDF books were rated slightly worse. Not surprisingly, trivial straight forward conversions were rated rather poorly.

Required Tools Some books required special tools to view the full contents. This is the case for books in PDF which need a special plug-in for Netscape, and also for one mathematical "handbook" which requires a movie player and supports the mathematic formula package Maple.

The results show that in general the required tools were already installed. Some tools were installed extra in order to use the full functionality of the book. For PDF-books a significant number of users had to install the PDF reader. From the remarks of some respondents it could be deducted that not all users

---

[2] Please note that this means: The smaller the columns in fig. 7 the better the rating.

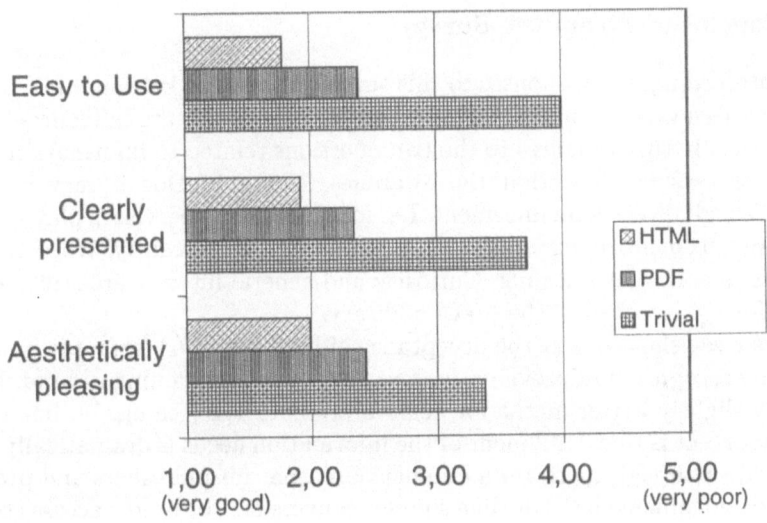

Fig. 7. Question 6: Please rate the appearance of this book on a scale of 1 (very good) to 5 (very bad)?

were able to install the PDF plug-in correctly. Therefore following WWW-links in the PDF viewer sometimes didn't work.

Importance of Printing Licenses: With two exceptions the books in the MeDoc library are offered as "browse only" licenses. Therefore, we asked the readers which of the following two statements holds for them:

- The electronic version supplements a printed book. I do not need an extra printing license.
- I would acquire an extra printing license.

35% said they are willing to acquire an extra printing license, while 21% said they are not. But the majority of 44% "no answers" shows that there is still considerable uncertainty about this topic.

Incentive to Buy the Paper Edition: We always thought it probable that the availability of the electronic version would positively influence the traditional paper book market. Indeed there are examples of complete books on the WWW that are intended as incentives for buying a paper edition.

15% of the respondents already bought or planned to buy the book. 43% said that they only wanted to use the electronic edition. Here too, a large share of 42% "no answers" shows that there is still considerable uncertainty.

3.3   Conclusions from the Survey

When interpreting the responses to this survey, one has to keep in mind that the MeDoc service was still in its startup phase and the result are influenced by this fact. Especially the responses to the two questions related to information spread and access reasons show that the awareness of the MeDoc library inventory comes through direct announcement. I.e. local MeDoc supervisors play a crucial role. Announcements in lectures can raise awareness significantly. Word of mouth propaganda is not far-reaching. Curiosity and general interest are still the main driving forces for entering the MeDoc library.

The survey showed that the acceptance of books in PDF-format is quite low, as already recognized in previous surveys [3, 6], but it is gaining ground. HTML gets only slightly better marks for general presentation (see fig. 7), but what is more important is that fulfillment of the information needs is dramatically better (see fig. 5). Although there are a number of reasons for publishers and providers to provide documents in PDF (like simpler conversions, or better access control), this still seems to be unacceptable for users.

The problem of providing extra printing licenses for the electronic editions is still unsolved. A considerable percentage of respondents said that they would like to acquire an extra printing license. But we have not (yet) asked for acceptable prices. With the current price models proposed by the publishers, a printing license for a full book is considerably more expensive than buying the book in a book shop. We would have to provide and charge for the printing of single pages, which is both a technical and an organizational problem. This seems to be a field where more thorough investigation is needed.

This survey can only be the starting point of a continuous feedback channel about the quality of the MeDoc service and its inventory. Regular evaluation of feedback will help finding out deficiencies and tuning opportunities for smoother presentation of new books.

4   Usage Monitoring

Digital books offered on the Internet allow more precise on-line observation and evaluation of their use. Accesses to HTML pages can be analysed in order to understand how electronic books are read.

4.1   Monitoring Concepts

The basic input for monitoring are the standard logfiles of the web servers. In the logfile each request to a document component (e.g. an html-file or a gif-image) is logged together with further information such as the requesting host, and a time stamp. There are numerous statistic logfile analysis packages available. Their dominant goal is to measure the throughput through a WWW server in hits or megabytes in order to facilitate tuning the performance of WWW servers in general, however they do not give adequate answers on how books are used; for instance: how often is a book consulted? Is it more used as a dictionary, i.e. just to look-up a certain concept, or is it used more as a teaching book, read page by page? Are there typical usage patterns?

To answer these questions we have to analyze all accesses to the pages of an electronic book during one use of a book as a single unit. In the following sections we call this unit a session. In order to reconstruct such sessions from a logfile, we approximate a session from the logfile by at least three HTML pages from the same client host, with no more than 20 minutes of delay between two subsequent accesses. All evaluations below are based on this definition of a session.

It has to be said that there are problems in extracting session based information from a logfile. First, a host does not always identify a unique user. There can be several parallel sessions from the same host or via the same proxy server. Also local caching of documents may not result in a correct logging of accesses. However, manual checks have shown that both problems are not relevant for the time being, but need to be reconsidered if the number of parallel sessions increases.

4.2   Usage of the MeDoc Library

The overall development of the usage of the libary is shown in fig. 8. Between July 1996 until October 1997 there were 3276 sessions with licensed books, 5067 sessions with samples, and 982 sessions on books of which the full-text was worldwide free without restriction.

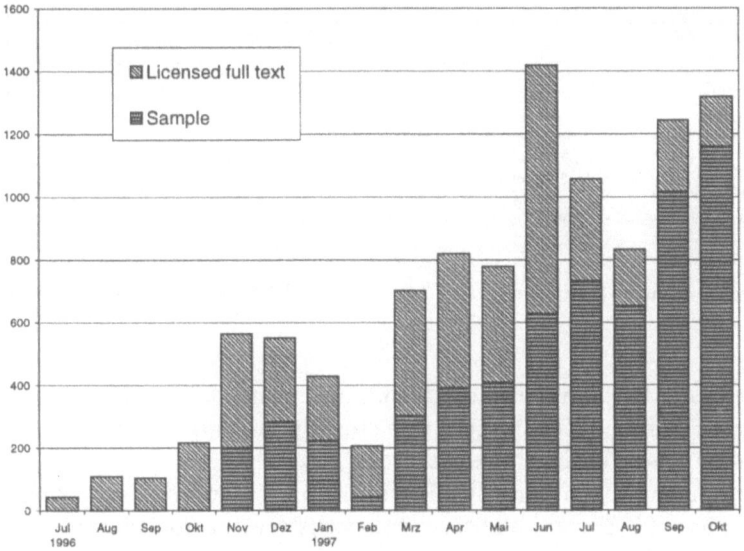

Fig. 8. Development of accesses to all on-line books over time

Since this development was strongly influenced by the gradual extension of the inventory, we restrict the following analysis on two books that are available since November 97. Both books are monographies, addressing master students and scientists, not so much students in lower semesters. For both books samples with table of contents, index and the first chapter are available. In order to respect confidentiality of usage information required by the respective publishers, we do not give details on each book individually.

In the period from November 1996 to October 1997 there where 1351 sessions related to these two books; 892 sessions reading the sample and 459 sessions reading the licensed books.

We also have monitored the license requests. For technical reasons we only can give figures up to mid of July. Up to then 134 licenses were requested and 355 licensed accesses took place. I.e. there were not only readers that read it once but revisited the books several times.

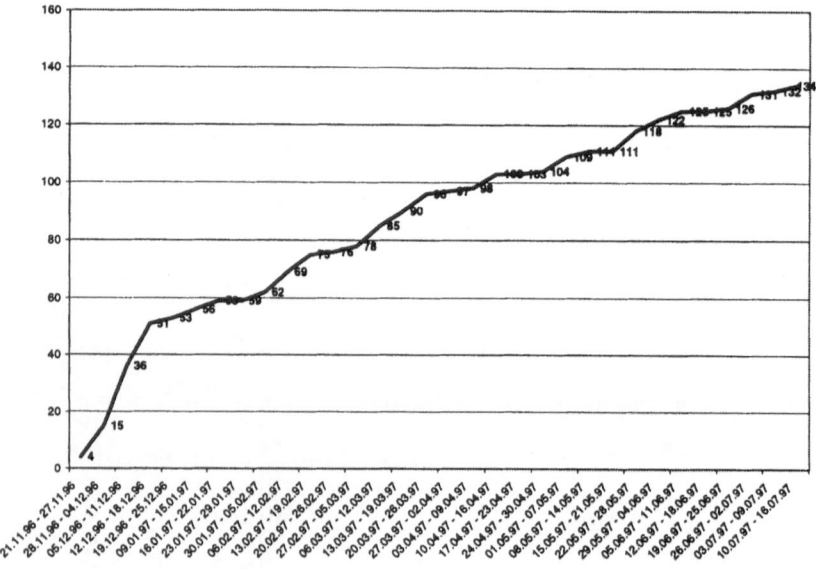

Fig. 9. Development of licence requests for Bibel and Raasch over time (per week)

Figure 9 shows that after some starting effect and quite a long Christmas holiday period the request of licences was steadily growing. I.e. per week there were about 4 to 5 new license requests.

The development of the number of accesses to samples and licensed full text is shown in figure 10). It can be observed that there was a considerable start-up effect at the end of November and beginning of December. After that the access to the licensed fulltext was decreasing to 20 to 25 sessions per month. However until October it was growing up steadily to 40 to 50 sessions per month. The exceptionally high access rate in June was caused by the survey which is discussed in Chapter 3.

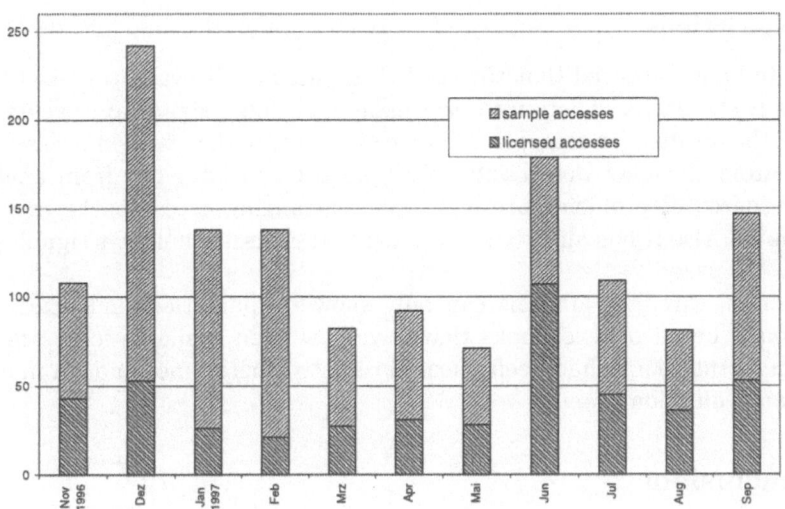

Fig. 10. Distribution of sessions for two books over time

A possible explanation could be that in the start when the service was announced, quite a number of people accessed the samples to obtain information about the books. This behaviour was then replaced by a more pragmatic use of the (digital) library. The reader looks up a specific book and takes it out (i.e. recalls a license) in order to read it or to consult it on his/her desktop. Presumably, it is exactly the same behavior that is expected in a traditional library.

First figures on the sessions themselves are available. On average in a session 10 HTML pages were accessed for the licensed version and 6 HTML pages for the sample version. An average session lasted about 7 minutes for the licensed version, and about 4 minutes for the sample version. The longest session lasted more than 1 hour.

A closer look on at distribution shows that there are quite a number of short term sessions. An initial analysis of the visited pages of each session shows that there are three patterns of sessions

- The majority of readers jump immediatly from the table of contents to a specific topic, read some pages there and then leave the book.
- Some readers jump from the table of contents to the index and from there into one or two pages and then leave.
- A minority of readers reads a complete chapter or even two in a stretch.

Not surprisingly, this shows that on-line books are used more like reference books rather than study books that are consulted for a longer time. Further investigation is needed to give a more precise analysis of these patterns and their distributions.

4.3 Restrictions

It needs to be emphasized that the statistical base of this evaluation is still not stable as it should be. There were too many additional significant events that influence the results. For example, a source of errors are the maintenance sessions or visits from so-called web-robots which we tried to filter out from analysis. Another source of problems are effects of rearranging access paths to books and samples. Also it has already been noted that semester holidays significantly influence the usage.

Therefore, this first analysis can only show up potential tendencies. This evaluation is based on two books that have now been available for 12 month. Although further books had been released recently, there is not enough material to base an evaluation upon.

5 Conclusions

This initial analysis of the usage shows that the MeDoc library is developing well. The number of readers and the number of accesses are slowly but steadily increasing. The main contact points to the library are still local information events to mobilize the end users. Therefore it is important to keep them informed and to establish local multipliers at each participating institution such as local supervisors, announcements in lectures. Samples also play an important role in making the library inventory well known to potential users.

Of course, the attractiveness of the library strongly depends on the attractiveness of its inventory. Therefore it is important to furnish the library with well presented books. To get a starting nucleus for the library, available paper books were converted into electronic versions. Now we know what added value for electronic books is important. Therefore authors can now prepare their work to make them available online and use the new possibilities of electronic media.

Acknowledgments

I want to thank Ms. Anja Brau for her support and patience in producing the statistics and charts for this document and Ms. Hasangi Nandasena for her careful proofreading of the document.

References

1. A. Barth et al.: The MeDoc Digital Library Project: Its Goals and Major Achievements, *in this book*

2. D. Boles et al.: The MeDoc System - a Digital Publication and Reference Service for Computer Science, *in this book*

3. A. Brüggemann-Klein, C. Haber, K. Junge: Auswertung der Umfrage zu Nutzer-wünschen (in German), MeDoc-Report,[3]

4. J. Dijkstra: Decomate: Delivery of Copyrighted Material to the End User, *in this book*.

5. C. Lloyd: Decomate: a new digital library project on delivery of copyright materials in electronic form User Study[4]

6. U. Hauptfleisch: Nutzung des MeDoc-Angebots: Eine Umfrage zur Nutzung elektronischer Volltextdokumente der MeDoc-Bibliothek - Stufe 0.5 (in German), [5]

7. H. Maurer: Multimedia Repositories and the LIBERATION Project[6]

8. M. Röscheisen, M. Baldonado, K. Chang, L. Gravano, S. Ketchpel: The Standord InfoBus and Its Service Layers, *in this book*.

9. B. Schatz, W. Mischo, T. Cole, J. Hardin, A. Bishop, H. Chen: Federating Diverse Collections of Scientific Literature, IEEE Computer, May 96

10. U. Steinmann, D. Shearer: Reusing Multi-Media Components: A Catalogue Implementation, submitted for the EMMSEC'7 conference, Florence

11. R. Weber, A. Endres: Cost Models and Accounting in MeDoc, *in this book*

12. I. Witten, S. Cunningham, and M. Apperley: The New Zealand Digital Library Project, D-Lib Magazine, November 1996[7]

---

[3] http://www11.informatik.tu-muenchen.de/local/proj/Medoc1/Umfrage/-Umfrage10.96/index.htm

[4] http://www.lse.ac.uk/decomate/docs/71.htm, 15.7.1997

[5] http://medoc.informatik.tu-muenchen.de/deutsch/organisation/projektbibliothek/-folien/medoc_umfr0.5.html

[6] http://www.lib-online.com/liberation/multirep.htm;internal, 15.7.1997

[7] http://www.dlib.org/dlib/november96/newzealand/11witten.html

Use of MeDoc Offerings in Technical Education

Andreas Spillner

Hochschule Bremen

Abstract. This report describes the task of the MeDoc-Project pilot users. The activities include the use and evaluation of services provided in order to feed back experience to the developers. The pilot users come from a wide range of universities and technical colleges thus providing a varied response about its usefulness. The experience gained from the introduction and use of the services at Hochschule Bremen are described together with lessons learned from dealing with various methods for stimulating the interest of the students in the services. The integration of the services in the teaching is also discussed.

1 Introduction

The main goal of the MeDoc-Project is to provide access to computer science literature as fulltext documents via internet. The project involves a core group concerned with the central project activities and several pilot users tasked with evaluation and feedback activities. The central project activities include: selecting, developing and evaluating appropriate tools and formats needed to support the electronic publishing process, and designing and evaluating advanced information resource discovery and retrieval tools for heterogenous and distributed information sources.

There are more than twenty pilot users from universities and technical colleges (Fachhochschulen) actively involved in the MeDoc-Project. Every pilot user has its specific background which together covers a wide range of different faculties including all aspects of computer science (hardware, software, theory, and application). At the Hochschule Bremen the study of computer science includes technical aspects; hardware and applications forming the main parts.

The pilot users are tasked with the use of services, tools and prototypes offered in order to provide real response to the developers. The pilot users independently evaluate the tools and materials selected or developed by the core group. If many students and teachers are using the services many reactions and hints about the usefulness of the services can be collected. However, in order to use the facilities, the students and teachers must know about the services. Therefore, promotion of the MeDoc-Project is another key activity of the pilot users.

The Hochschule Bremen is one of the pilot users and this paper describes our task in the MeDoc-Project. The other pilot users have different tasks which are not discussed here.

2   Introduction of the MeDoc-Project

The first activity of a pilot user in the initial phase of the project was to define and set up the local infrastructure. There was a standard homepage for the pilot users offered by the Fachhochschule Regensburg. There were no problems adapting this page to the requirements of the Hochschule Bremen.

We started very early to promote the project. We presented the MeDoc-Services in our lessons and in special talks (eg. [1]). There were tutorials for the students and for the teachers, the tutorials for the students being held nearly twice per semester. However, the response was not very good - few of the students were interested in the MeDoc-Services.

We started too early with the advertisement of the MeDoc-Project. At this time only a few publications were available via net, and so the attraction of the MeDoc offering was poor. A demonstration of the MeDoc-Library in our lectures would have been a better approach to introduce the students to the facilities on offer.

After no increase of use the next step was to change the style of the MeDoc homepage of the Hochschule Bremen [2]. The idea was to increase the attraction of the user interface. We used colours and animated pictures. This was possible because the visitors of the page are our local users (mainly students) and it does not take a lot of time to transfer the animated pictures via internet. The style of the page was unconventional in order to gain the interest of the students.

After announcing the new pages to all MeDoc participants, we got both positive and negative reactions. There were enquiries about further animated pictures from different pilot-users and there was critique concerning the relation between the pictures and the semantic contents of the links.

The next activity to promote the project was to place the MeDoc posters in the computer rooms of the faculty. We had the idea of giving every student in the faculty a flyer with information about the MeDoc-Project [3]. We didn't use the MeDoc flyer with the information about the architecture of the project and other project details, instead we produced a specific flyer for students. The flyer describes how to use the services. It was presented as a dialogue between two students. One student is searching for information and asks the second student for help. His answer is to get the information through the internet, not using one of the searching machines but using the MeDoc-Services. The actual use of MeDoc - step by step - is documented in the flyer. Four different ways to get information from the MeDoc-System are described (looking for information in electronic books and journals, and the use of the CompuScience database from FIZ Karlsruhe).

The flyer has a north german touch (the names of the both students are specific for the northern part of Germany). It was also used by the pilot users in Emden, Hamburg and Rostock.

We got further reactions after the distribution of the flyer. There were requests for books which are not on our list of licensed books and many students are interested in the journals *c't* and *iX*. Some students remarked that the use is complicated, because it is not very easy to browse through many different books.

The user has to get a password for each book which takes time. Also, if there is no licence ordered by the Hochschule for a particular book, it can take several days before the student can start reading. However, the MeDoc-Services were used by the students.

2.1 Involving MeDoc-Services in teaching

¿From the beginning, we had the idea of integrating the MeDoc-Services into our teaching. At the Hochschule Bremen, the students have to work on a project over a period of two semesters with a total of eight hours of work per week. The first part of the project took place in the summer semester 96 and the second took place in the summer semester 97. We (myself together with my colleague Prof. Dr. J. Lübcke) are the teachers of the project RuPios (which stands for "Recherchieren und Publizieren in online-Systemen - researching and publishing in online systems").

In the summer semester 96, the students worked with the MeDoc-Services, but at this time only a few books and journals were available. The main task in the RuPios-Project was to evaluate the database selection of the project TP2 (tool platform). Three database systems were under review; BRS, Fulcrum and PLWeb. The main part was the evaluation of PLWeb. The students had to use the PLWeb database and had to fill out a questionnaire. There was a cooperation with the Offis in Oldenburg. After the semester, the students criticised the task, because they wanted to develop some software rather than just using and evaluating other tools.

In the second semester of the RuPios-Project, five working groups were established. The groups worked at the following subjects:

- Installation and use of a Windows-NT-Communication server
  The server is used for WWW and FTP. All reports and other documents which are produced from the RuPios-Project are archived on this server. The students administrate and maintain the server.
- Installation and use of mailing lists
  A mailing list for the project was installed and all actual information was published through this mechanism. Detailed descriptions of the installation of a new mailing list and subscription to an existing list were written.
- Prototype of an SQL-Server and a Java-Interface
  A SQL-Server was developed and a time-table for the students for each semester was offered.
- Installation and use of the communication server
  The journal c't offered a free version of a communication server especially for use in schools. The students in this working group evaluated the server and wrote a report of their experiences.
- Prototype of an archive for master theses
  Each faculty has the problem archiving master degrees theses. A prototype of an archive was also developed in RuPios. The results of the RuPios-Project are published on the internet (in german, see [4]).

Other student projects are using the experience of the RuPios-Project. They make use of the intranet and internet to communicate and to offer their documents to the project participants and to other people interested in this work.

The facilities of the MeDoc-Service were also integrated in our normal lectures. For example, in the lecture "software engineering" the students had to perform different tasks using the MeDoc-Library. Each student group had a definite topic (eg. prototyping, data dictionary, McCabe-metric, reviews). The students had to obtain information about the respective topics (with support through the teachers). As a starting point the MeDoc-Library was to be used. Short talks on the topics were held by the students and written reports produced.

Not all teams had found the desired information in the MeDoc-Library and they had to look in the "non digital" library or to search in the internet. The experiences of the students dealing with the MeDoc-Services were varied. Disillusion rose if the search was unsuccessful. One major benefit with the service is the possibility of searching through a whole document. Parts of a book or a journal dealing with a special topic can be found even if not listed in the table of contents or in the index.

A further big advantage of the MeDoc-Project is the easy way of working with literature. A walk into the "normal" library necessitates a change of the workflow. If the literature search could be done directly from a workstation, the search would be quicker and could be done more frequently. Electronic books and journals are never lent out (in the sense of a "normal" library) and the electronic library is not subject to opening-times. However, for both kinds of libraries, the crucial criterion for use is the quantity and quality of the books and journals available. Within the MeDoc-Project it was not required to build up an electronic library which is comparable to other libraries w.r.t. the number of books and journals.

Another activity of our faculty has also been initiated through MeDoc. There are a lot of documents produced by students, teachers, and committees of the faculty. The idea is to archive all these documents in a database and to use it via internet and intranet. A first prototype is installed (see [5]).

2.2 Promotion of the MeDoc-Project in Bremen

After presenting the MeDoc-Project in the faculty, we decided to inform the people in the Hochschule and in Bremen. A report of the project was published in the magazine of the Hochschule [6].

The next step was the presentation of the MeDoc-Project in the newspapers. First we had a small article in "Die Welt" (May, 5, 1997). After presenting the project in the "Weser Kurier" (June, 5, 1997), which has a large circulation in the city, we received a lot of reactions. Some colleagues of other faculties asked for a presentation of the project services. The audience was very interested in the MeDoc-Services and they got a lot of hints for their further work.

Also people beyond the Hochschule are interested in the project and have asked for more information. These people are working at different companies in Bremen for example hospitals or aerospace companies. The companies are planning to install an intranet to provide information to their staff. They are very interested in the different possibilities of the MeDoc-Servies and in the technical details of the project.

The interest of the companies conforms with the notion that the MeDoc-Project is a pilot-project for all aspects of information transfer via intranet and internet and not only a pilot-project for use within the universities and technical colleges.

3 Lessons Learned

It takes a lot of time to transfer a printed book or journal in digital form for use on the net. For this reason, the quantity of books and journals were insufficient in the MeDoc-Library at the beginning and even now at the end of the project. The first use of the MeDoc-Library was a little bit frustrating for the students, because only a few books and journals are available. We started too early with the promotion of the services. It is very difficult to persuade a student to visit the library a second or third time after frustrating him the first time.

The books and journals in the library are *standard* books and books discussing special aspects in computer science. When a student is searching for some information in the MeDoc-Library, he cannot be sure to find the desired information because the service includes too many aspects of computer science areas. Taking into account our experiences, we believe that a library offering books and journals concerning specific aspects (eg. database systems or software engineering) would be more acceptable for students because the use of the library will be more effective. If there is a limitation to one aspect the critical mass of books and journals is easier to reach. It is very important to have sufficient offers in a library. If a person is looking for information to this special topic he or she can be sure to find some useful information in the MeDoc-Library and the person will visit MeDoc again.

A further criticism was the complicated procedure to get a licence for a book or a journal. If a student was interested in a book, it was very difficult to get a licence (next day), and the licences had to be ordered by the Hochschule. "Why not getting an *identification card* for the whole library - to look in all books and journals?" the students often asked. The ease of use is a very important aspect and needs further investigation.

Promotion is always needed and takes a lot of time and work. Also, good services, like the MeDoc-Services, are not self running projects. It was a very good idea to involve pilot users in the project to do this task and to pick up the experiences. The mixture of universities and technical colleges in the pilot users group provided an opportunity to gather a wide range of experiences.

4 Conclusions

Since resources are extremely limited at the technical colleges, services like MeDoc are needed for the improvement of the infrastructure. However, despite the obvious improvement, many activities have to be carried out for the introduction of the service and for the promotion of its use by students and teachers.

At the Hochschule Bremen, we pursued several approaches to create an interest in the MeDoc-Services. These approaches have been successful in varying degrees. The best and easiest method may be to force the students to use the services by giving them tasks within their courses that require the use of the services. However, such a forced use can lead to a rejection which surely is not in the interest of the project.

References

1. MeDoc-Presentation (Power Point slides)
   http://www.iia.hs-bremen.de/dokumente/vortraege/3/index.htm
2. MeDoc-Homepage Hochschule Bremen
   http://www.iia.hs-bremen.de/medoc/
3. MeDoc-Flyer (Corel Draw 6.0 file)
   http://www.iia.hs-bremen.de/medoc/public/falt.zip
4. RuPios - Recherchieren und Publizieren in online-Systemen
   http://www.learnnet.hs-bremen.de/Projekte
5. Documents of the Faculty of Electronic Engineering
   http://www.fbe.hs-bremen.de/scripts/dok_suche.idc
6. Umbruch (No. 02/96, pp 24-25), Magazine of the Hochschule Bremen
   http://www.iia.hs-bremen.de/dokumente/vortraege/5/umbruch.htm

Prof. Dr. Andreas Spillner
Hochschule Bremen
Faculty of Electronic Engineering
Department of Computer Science
Neustadtswall 30
D - 28199 Bremen
Germany

Tel.: ++49 421 5905 -467 / -412 (FAX)
spillner@informatik.hs-bremen.de
http://www.fbe.hs-bremen.de/spillner/

The Stanford InfoBus and Its Service Layers: Augmenting the Internet with Higher-Level Information Management Protocols

Martin Röscheisen, Michelle Baldonado, Kevin Chang,
Luis Gravano, Steven Ketchpel, Andreas Paepcke

Stanford Digital Libraries Project
Computer Science Department
Stanford University, CA 94305

Abstract. The Stanford InfoBus is a prototype infrastructure developed as part of the Stanford Digital Libraries Project to extend the current Internet protocols with a suite of higher-level information management protocols. This paper surveys the five service layers provided by the Stanford InfoBus: protocols for managing items and collections (DLIOP), metadata (SMA), search (STARTS), payment (UPAI), and rights and obligations (FIRM).

1 Introduction

The Stanford Digital Libraries project is one of the six participants in the 4-year, $24 million U.S. "Digital Library Initiative," started in 1994 and supported by NSF, DARPA, and NASA together with a set of industrial partners. Rather than addressing issues related to a specific content collection, the Stanford project focuses on developing a set of service protocols by which different information resources and services can be "glued" together. This set of service protocols is referred to collectively as the "Stanford InfoBus." The InfoBus is a prototype infrastructure that is designed to provide a bottom-up way of extending the current Internet protocols with a suite of higher-level information management protocols that the Internet currently lacks.

In this paper, we survey the design of the Stanford InfoBus and its five service layers: protocols for managing items and collections (DLIOP), metadata (SMA), search (STARTS), payment (UPAI), and rights and obligations (FIRM).

Also part of the Stanford project but not the focus of this paper is work that leverages the InfoBus middleware to experiment with novel user interfaces (DLITE [5], Sense-Maker [2]) and services (GlOSS [6], SCAM [11], Fab [10], InterBib [9]).

2 The Stanford InfoBus Architecture

The Stanford InfoBus is an architecture that gives clients uniform access to distributed, heterogeneous information resources and services. A collection or a service is "on" the InfoBus if it either uses one of the InfoBus protocols natively or if there exists an *InfoBus proxy* for this service.

InfoBus proxies are wrappers that can be operated either by a service itself or by some other service provider (e.g., a "digital library"). This flexibility makes it possible to enrich the information infrastructure and to achieve interoperability in a bottom-up

214

way: It is not "imposed" (top-down) that services directly follow the InfoBus protocols; any third party can "plug" its favorite services into the InfoBus. For example,
InfoBus clients can easily make use of the power of standard Web search engines such
as Digital's AltaVista as soon as someone implements an InfoBus wrapper to
AltaVista and publishes its availability. However, it is not required that this wrapper
necessarily be run by Digital itself; it can be autonomously maintained by third parties
(with the use of proper rights management).

Note that it is of course usually advantageous for a service provider to be also directly
the operator of a corresponding InfoBus proxy. This allows them to make sure that the
proxy implementation exploits the service's native features in the best possible way
(making the service "look good" in the uniform InfoBus world); it allows them to
guarantee quality of service, etc. In other words, there is a built-in incentive (a social
push) for proxies to be moved out further to the sources–thus effectively leading to
the adoption of the InfoBus protocols without the necessity to formally standardize on
them.

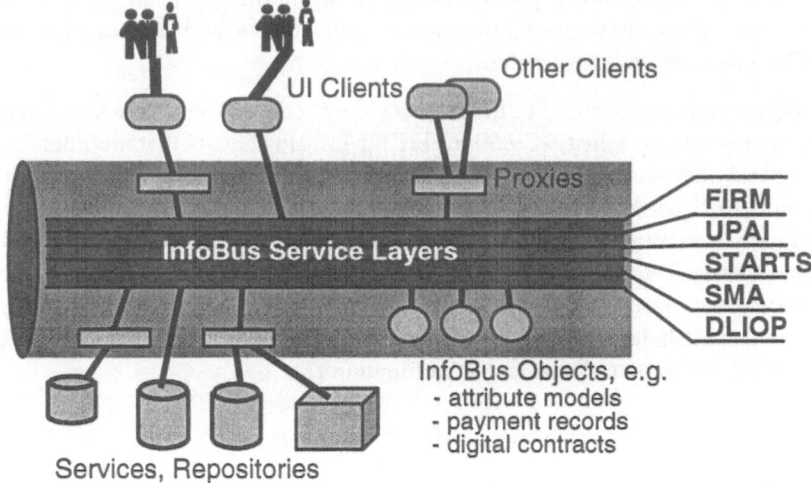

Fig. 1. The Stanford InfoBus and Its Service Layers: Clients and services
access InfoBus services either directly or via InfoBus-compliant proxies.
The InfoBus provides services for managing items and collections (DLIOP),
metadata (SMA), search (STARTS), payment (UPAI), and rights and obligations (FIRM).

The Stanford InfoBus is designed to make it easy to provide such wrappers for an
increasing number of clients and services. Ideally, clients and services would freely
interact, simply by plugging themselves into 'the system', just as hardware devices
can be plugged into a bus. We therefore call our vision the *InfoBus*. (Cf. Figure 1.)

Clients use InfoBus resources to accomplish complex tasks such as writing papers,
publishing newsletters, and tracking the development of industrial product lines.
Information resources include information repositories such as online catalogs, stock
feeds, census data, newspapers, and so on. Resources also include services that oper-

ate on information such as document translation, document summarization, remote indexing, and payment services and copyright clearance.

At an implementation level, the architecture of the InfoBus clearly melds well with technologies such as CORBA and DCOM that support object-oriented design in a distributed environment (although there is no reason why one could not implement the InfoBus protocols, say, on top of HTTP–in fact, our specifications are independent of any such implementation choices).

In our testbed, we have experimented with the use of CORBA as a prototyping environment for developing the InfoBus. Specifically, we have used the CORBA implementation of one of our industrial partners: Xerox PARC's ILU system. Each participating entity (clients, information resources, documents, attribute models, contracts, etc.) is then either directly implemented as an object, or an object is created to act as a *proxy* to the entity. These objects can be placed on any machine on the network and can be accessed remotely from anywhere. The CORBA infrastructure makes it possible to implement proxies on different platforms and in different languages. In our case, we have used a mixture of Python, Java, and C++ to implement the various objects of the infrastructure.

InfoBus proxies communicate with the services they represent via the native service access protocols such as telnet, Z39.50, or HTTP. InfoBus clients that are interacting with the proxies do not need to be aware of these differences; they can simply use protocol calls to access the proxies. Examples of services that we have linked up to the InfoBus by wrapping them with proxy objects include Knight-Ridder's Dialog Information Service, Web search engines, automatic document summarizers, bibliography maintenance tools, OCR services, and others. InfoBus services also take care of any remaining translation tasks (e.g. translation of queries). More detail about the InfoBus and its implementation can also be found in [1].

3 DLIOP: Managing Items and Collections

The Digital Library Interoperability Protocol (DLIOP) is a protocol layer that provides basic services for managing *items* (e.g. documents) and *collections* in a networked environment. It allows InfoBus clients to communicate with information repositories, and to request and receive information asynchronously from InfoBus proxies. Proxies obtain this information natively from the information services they represent. Cf. Figure 2 for an example of a simple arrangement.

DLIOP combines advantages of stateless protocols such as HTTP (e.g., optimization for short-lived resource usage) with the advantages of session-based protocols such as Z39.50 (e.g. interaction efficiencies for multiple, related interactions). The protocol provides a testbed for experimenting with dynamic resource reallocation to achieve load balancing. It allows documents and computation to be moved among machines while interactions between clients and services are in progress. Furthermore, DLIOP enables experimentation with different caching strategies in contexts where clients sometimes request follow-up information quickly and at other times only after several days have elapsed.

The DLIOP protocol specifies methods invoked among two basic kinds of components: *Clients* and *collections* of *items*. "Clients" are any kind of application programs that want to access an information collection. "Items" are the most general form of an InfoBus information object; subclasses of items include documents, services, attribute models, rights, contracts, etc. "Collections" are objects (in the sense of object-oriented programming) that manage a set of items.

The basic goal of DLIOP is to provide a flexible transport mechanism by which collections of items at the server end can be made available at the client side without the overhead of having a client request each item individually across the network whenever an item is needed. DLIOP facilitates the interaction between a client and an external service proxy by managing the way in which proxies to external services can return collections of items to an InfoBus client in response to a service request (e.g. a search query). In this section, we outline key aspects of the DLIOP service layer.

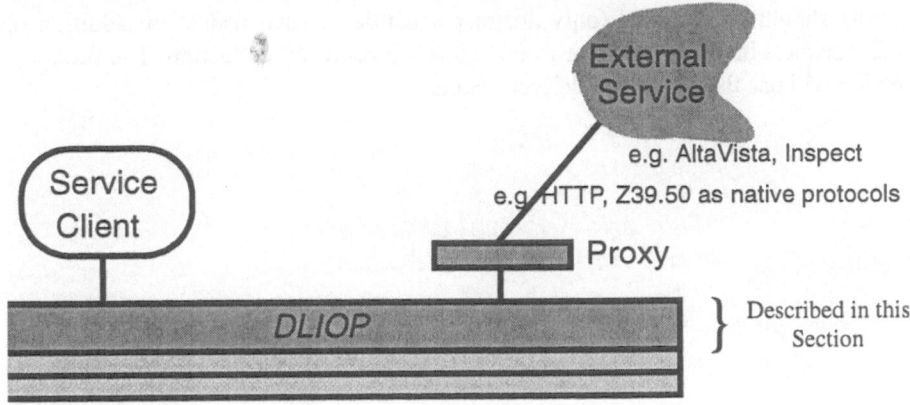

Fig. 2. The DLIOP Service Layer

3.1 Collections of Items

Collections are container objects with a simple interface. It includes methods such as `GetTotalItems()`, which returns the number of items in the collection, or `AddItems()`, which inserts new items into a collection if possible. An important subclass of collections is *constrainable collections*. Constrainable collections can be asked to produce a result collection that contains a subset of the items that they currently hold.

We use such constrainable collections to implement InfoBus proxies to information repositories: While behaving like a true collection to clients, such collections can be "virtual" in that they do not necessarily need to hold all of the items of a repository directly, but they only materialize them on an as-needed basis. When such a collection receives a constrain request, it issues a query to the external information source, and retrieves result information from it. This information from the native source will usually not be available in the InfoBus item format, but the proxy will make it available via this uniform interface. In Figure 3, the proxy representing the external service is thus implemented as a special kind of collection object, a constrainable collection which is a collection that may be queried.

3.2 Basic Search Interaction

Figure 3 shows an example of a basic search interaction. The client wishes to search over some external service for which a constrainable collection object acts as a proxy. Note that while the steps in the figure are numbered for reference, most of them occur asynchronously. Arrows in Figure 3 represent method calls.

As a first step, the client creates a local collection object for holding the results. Then the client issues a query to the constrainable collection that acts as the external service's proxy. The query contains information on which objects are desired (authors must contain the word 'Smith'). It also contains instructions on how many results should be returned as soon as they become available (10), and on which parts of those results should be included (only abstract and title of each result). In addition, the query request includes a pointer to the client's local result collection. The proxy collection will use this pointer to deliver results.

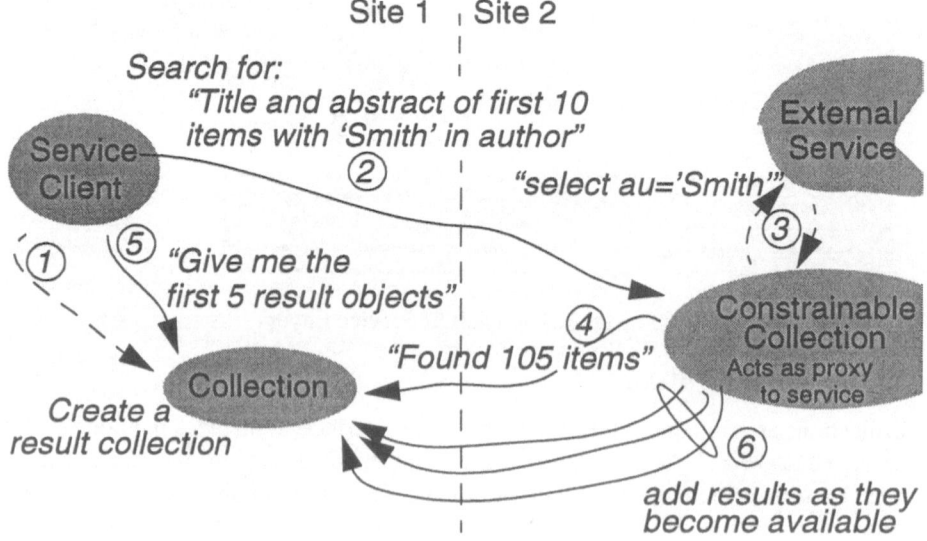

Fig. 3. DLIOP: A Basic Search Interaction

Once the query has been delivered, the client is free to perform other work while the query is processed: the query call to the proxy collection is asynchronous. Alternatively, the client may immediately ask its local result collection for the total number of results, and/or for some or all of the result objects. These calls could block until the required information is actually available.

Meanwhile, the proxy collection delivers the query to the external service by whatever means are appropriate: e.g. HTTP, Z39.50, a telnet connection, or its local file system. As soon as the proxy collection knows how many hits to expect, it notifies the client's result collection. In (possibly) multiple calls to the client's collection object, the proxy collection subsequently delivers results. Each call (step 6) to the client's collection delivers some number of title/abstract values as lists, each list being the desired (title/abstract) excerpt from one result. The client collection creates a local object for each result, filling its title and abstract properties with the corresponding values. It is up to the proxy collection to decide whether to wait for all 10 results to arrive from the external service before delivering them to the client's result collection, or whether to collect a few and deliver them as early as possible.

At some point, the client will have received and examined the initial 10 results from its original request. Whenever the service client requests more results from its local result collection than are currently scheduled to arrive there, the result collection contacts the proxy collection at the server side for more of the hits. These are then delivered just like the original results. Notice that in order to do this, the proxy collection needs to let the client's result collection know the proxy collection's object ID. This is done as one of the parameters in each of the (partial) result deliveries.

3.3 Load Balancing at the Server Side

Sometimes it may be desirable to free the object that acts as proxy to the external service from handling new requests at the same time it is processing a pending request. Figure 4 shows how this requirement can be accommodated.

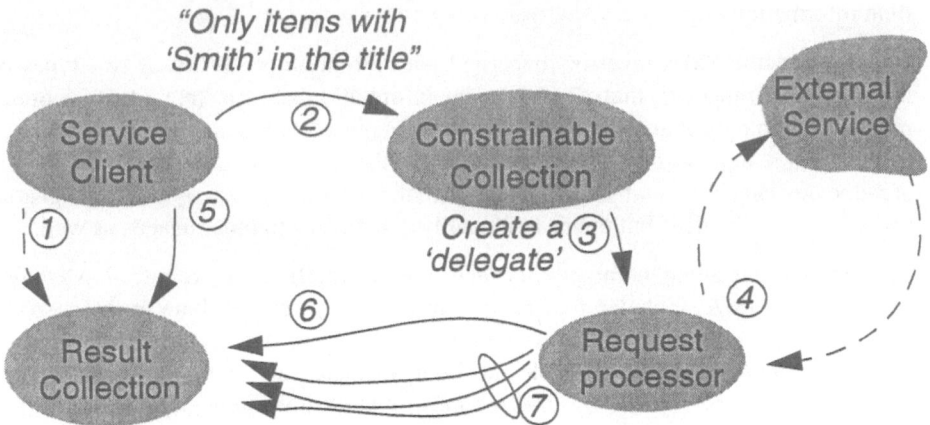

Fig. 4. DLIOP: A Search Interaction with Server-side Off-Loading
(Interactions 1, 2, 4, 5, 6, and 7 are as in Figure 3)

Instead of interacting with the external service itself, the constrainable collection immediately creates a 'delegate' object which takes over the remaining processing of the query request. It then returns to accepting more requests. Note that the request processor object created as the delegate may reside on a machine other than the one running the constrainable collection. The client is unaware of the origin of calls in steps 6 and 7.

The DLIOP allows server-side objects to perform load balancing even while results are being delivered to the client. This is easy because the OID of the proxy collection is passed to the client's result collection every time a set of results are delivered.

Before delegating further work to a new object, the proxy collection can issue a call to the client's result collection, adding an empty set of results, and specifying a new OID as the target for future requests for additional result hits.

3.4 Implementation Status

A CORBA-based implementation was completed early in the project and has since then provided the foundation for many other protocols and services. DLIOP has also been used to interoperate with collections developed by other DLI digital library projects.

4 SMA: Managing Metadata

The Stanford Digital Library Metadata Architecture (SMA) defines a service layer for the uniform exchange and management of the metadata necessary for finding InfoBus services, for querying these services, and for interpreting the structured results returned by these services. Before this architecture was put in place, each InfoBus service handled metadata in its own ad hoc way. This led to incompatibilities at the user level (a query constructor might ask a user to fill in an "author" field, while a result analysis tool might refer to an author as a "creator") and at the infrastructure level (query constructors and query translators must communicate with each other about field information).

In particular, the SMA layer is concerned with the interoperability of two types of metadata: (1) metadata that describes the information objects (e.g., textual documents) available through search services, and (2) metadata that describes the services themselves. A more in-depth characterization of the metadata needs addressed by this architecture can be found in [3]. Note that the following descriptions are geared towards search services but the design readily generalizes to other usages as well.

To facilitate metadata compatibility and interoperability, the Stanford Metadata Architecture (SMA) includes four basic component classes: attribute model proxies, attribute model translators, metadata facilities for search proxies, and metadata repositories. *Attribute model proxies* elevate both attribute sets and the attributes they define to first-class objects. By this, we mean that attribute sets and attributes have computational representations through which they can describe themselves and interact with other components of the architecture. They also allow relationships among attributes to be captured. *Attribute model translators* map attributes and attribute values from one attribute model to another (where possible). *Metadata facilities* for search proxies provide structured descriptions both of the collections to which the search proxies provide access and of the search capabilities of the proxies. Finally, *metadata repositories* accumulate selected metadata from local instances of the other three component classes in order to facilitate global metadata queries and local metadata caching.

4.1 Attribute Model Proxies

Structured descriptions of resources and services are built out of *attributes* and *attribute values*. One level of aggregation beyond the individual attribute is the *attribute model*–a self-contained collection of attributes. Well-known attribute models include the USMARC set of bibliographic attributes (referred to as "fields" in the USMARC community), the Dublin Core set of attributes, and so on.

In our metadata architecture, we reify both attributes and their encompassing attribute models as first-class objects. Attributes are instances of class `AttributeItem`. *Attribute model proxies* are implemented as InfoBus collections. Attribute model proxies represent real world attribute models, just as search proxies represent real world search services.

An `AttributeItem`'s properties include the following: model name, attribute name, aliases usable for queries, value type, documentation, various other information used by query translators, and so on.

The model name and attribute name are both strings that serve to identify the `AttributeItem` uniquely. As an example, an attribute might have the model name "Dublin Core" and the attribute name "Title." The model name is repeated in all items to make them self-contained. This is important when the items are passed around the system to components other than the "home" attribute model proxy. When examining an `AttributeItem`, a client can always determine to which attribute model it belongs.

The attribute value type information in an `AttributeItem` dictates the data type that can be contained in fields described by the `AttributeItem`. We use the interface definition language (IDL) that is part of our CORBA implementation to specify these types. It is up to each search service proxy to ensure that the values it returns conform to these type specifications. If the external service that the proxy represents natively returns a different type, then the proxy is expected to transform the value into the specified type before returning it.

Attribute model proxies make attribute models first-class objects in our computational environment. They allow us to store and search over attribute-specific information that is independent of the capabilities possessed by any particular search proxy. Since an attribute model proxy is a collection, it is accessible via the same interface as all other search service proxies. In other words, the attribute model proxy has a search method that responds to a query by returning the appropriate subset of the included `AttributeItem`. Furthermore, attribute model proxies record what relationships hold among the included attributes. We currently record "is_a" and "part_of" relationships. This is important for some services, such as sophisticated user interface services, that require *structured* attribute models.

4.2 Attribute Model Translators

In heterogeneous environments, many different attribute models co-exist. This inevitably leads to mismatches when InfoBus components that support different attribute models attempt to communicate with each other. For example, consider a bibliographic database proxy and a client of that proxy. The bibliographic database proxy might support only the Dublin Core attribute model, while the client might support only the USMARC bibliographic data attribute model. In order for this client and this proxy to communicate with each other, they must be able to translate from USMARC attributes to Dublin Core attributes and vice versa. In other words, they require intermediate *attribute model translators*. Attribute model translators serve to mediate among the different metadata conventions that are represented by the attribute model proxies. These translation services, available via remote method calls, translate attributes and their values from one attribute model into attributes from a second attribute model.

Translation services do more than map source attributes onto target attributes. They must also convert each attribute value from the data type specified for the source attribute into the data type specified for the target attribute. This conversion can be quite complex. For example, one attribute model might call for authors to be represented as lists of records, where each record contains fields for first name, last name, and author address. Another model might call for just a comma-separated string of authors in last-name plus initials format. When translating among these values, some information may again be lost if, for example, the address is simply discarded.

4.3 Metadata Facilities for Search Proxies

The *metadata facility* that we attach to each search service proxy is responsible for exporting metadata about the proxy as a whole, as well as for exporting metadata about the collections to which it provides access. Collection metadata includes descriptions of the collection, declarations as to what attribute models are supported, information about the collection's query facilities, and the statistical information necessary for resource discovery services like GlOSS [6] to predict the collection's relevance for a particular query. Clients can use the information to determine how best to access the collection maintained by the search service (i.e., what capabilities the search service supports).

We have decided to make the interface for accessing the metadata facility of search service proxies very simple in order to encourage proxy writers to provide this information. Search service proxy metadata is accessed via the getMetadata() method, which returns two metadata objects. Alternatively, each proxy may opt to "push" these metadata objects to its clients. The first metadata object contains the general service information, and it is based heavily on the metadata objects defined by STARTS (cf. Section 5). The general service information includes human-readable information about the collection, as well as information that is used by our query translation facility.

4.4 Metadata Repositories

Metadata repositories are local, possibly replicated databases that cache information from selected attribute model proxies, attribute model translators, metadata facilities for search proxies, and other InfoBus services in order to produce one-stop-shopping locations for locally valuable metadata. We allow for metadata repositories to pull metadata from the various facilities, as well as for the facilities to push their metadata to one or more repositories directly. The intent is for these repositories to be a local resource for finding answers to metadata-related questions and for finding specialized metadata resources.

4.5 Implementation Status

We have implemented prototype instances of all four component classes of our meta-data architecture: several attribute model proxies, two attribute model translators, a metadata repository, and a metadata facility for a search proxy. Our attribute model proxies include implementations of proxies for Z39.50's Bib-1, Dublin Core, Refer, BibTeX, GILS, and a subset of USMARC. We can, for example, search over our USMARC proxy for all attributes containing the word Title in their description. This returns five entries, including attributes for Title Statement, Varying Form of Title, and Main Entry -- Uniform Title. This information will be used in our user interface to help users select proper attributes for search.

5 STARTS: Managing Search

The Stanford Protocol Proposal for Internet Retrieval and Search (STARTS) is an emerging protocol for Internet retrieval and search. In this section, we give a brief survey of the STARTS service layer; further information can be found in [7].

5.1 Objective

Users have many document sources available, both within their organizations and on the Internet (e.g., the CS-TR sources, an emerging library of Computer Science Technical Reports; cf. http://www.ncstrl.org/). The source contents are often hidden behind search interfaces and models that vary from source to source. Even individual organizations use search engines from different vendors to index their internal document collections. These organizations can benefit from *metasearchers*, which are services that provide unified query interfaces to multiple search engines. These give users the illusion of a single combined document source.

The goal of STARTS is to facilitate the main three tasks that a metasearcher performs:

- Choosing the best sources to evaluate a query

- Evaluating the query at these sources

- Merging the query results from these sources

Also, as will become clear after the discussion below, STARTS makes it easier to build InfoBus proxies to external services.

5.2 Problems Addressed and Approach

Building metasearchers is currently a hard task because different search engines are largely incompatible and do not allow for interoperability. In effect, a metasearcher faces the following three problems:

- *The source-metadata problem:* A metasearcher might have thousands of sources available for querying. It then becomes crucial that the metasearcher just contact potentially useful sources. So, the metasearcher needs information about the sources' contents to choose the best sources for a given query.

- *The query-language problem:* A metasearcher submits queries over multiple sources. But the interfaces and capabilities of these sources may vary dramatically. Thus, the metasearcher has to translate the original query to adjust to each source's syntax and capabilities.

- *The rank-merging problem:* Most commercial sources rank documents according to how "similar" the documents and a given query are. Merging query results from different sources is hard, since a metasearcher might have little or no information on how the document ranks are computed at the sources.

In order to address the source-metadata problem, STARTS defines the information that sources should export about themselves. This information includes automatically generated content summaries to assist in choosing the best sources for a query. It also includes a description of the query capabilities available at the sources, since the STARTS query language has several optional parts that sources might decide not to support.

To address the query-language problem, STARTS defines a simple query language that sources should support. This language is based on a simple subset of Z39.50. A STARTS query contains two (optional) components: a Boolean expression that defines the documents that qualify in the answer to the query, and a ranking expression that associates a score with these documents and ranks them accordingly. STARTS also defines a suggested set of *fields* (e.g., author, title), and a suggested set of *modifiers* (e.g., thesaurus, stemming) that should be available for searching at the sources. If sources follow these suggestions, then query translation becomes greatly facilitated.

Finally, to address the rank-merging problem, STARTS requires that sources return some statistics together with the results for a given query. This way, a metasearcher can ignore the scores that the sources compute for the documents, and compute its own scores from these statistics without having to retrieve the documents in the query results. The metasearcher then ranks the documents using the new scores. Statistics returned include the number of times that each of the query keywords occur in the documents in the query results, for example.

5.3 Discussion

Although STARTS intends to make the search-engine world more uniform, it leaves many aspects of the protocol open. As a notable example, STARTS does not specify how sources should answer queries. Instead, it just specifies a query syntax, with many options and significant room for future extensions.

A key goal in the STARTS specification is to keep the protocol requirements low and easy to implement. For example, the content summaries that sources should export are easily computable from the standard inverted-file indexes that search engines use to answer queries efficiently.

Throughout the STARTS specification, there are ways of extending the protocol with new, unforeseen features. For example, a new set of search fields may be defined in the future for some specific domain. A source may then support this new field set by simply specifying the set name in the source's metadata.

The goal of STARTS is to facilitate searching over *text* sources. No attempt is made to cover non-textual information, for example. As a result, the STARTS specification is much simpler and focused than what it would have been otherwise.

STARTS could have adopted a "least common denominator" approach. However, many interesting interactions would have been impossible under such a solution. Alternatively, STARTS could have incorporated the sophisticated features that the search engines provide, but that also would have challenged interoperability, and would have driven us away from simplicity. Consequently, we had to walk a very fine line, trying to find a solution that would be expressible enough, but not too complicated or impossible to quickly implemented by the search engine vendors.

5.4 Implementation Status

STARTS has been developed in a unique way. It is not a standard, but a group effort involving more than a dozen companies and organizations. The Stanford Digital Libraries Project coordinated search engine vendors and other key players to informally design a protocol that would allow searching and retrieval of information from distributed and heterogeneous sources. The key participants in this effort are Infoseek, Fulcrum, PLS, Verity, WAIS, Microsoft Network, Excite, GILS, Harvest, Hewlett-Packard Laboratories, and Netscape.

The STARTS specification is completed. A reference implementation of the protocol has been built at Cornell University by Carl Lagoze. Also, the Z39.50 community is designing ZDSR, a profile of their Z39.50-1995 standard based on STARTS.

6 UPAI: Managing Payment

The Universal Payment Application Interface (UPAI) protocol is the Stanford InfoBus layer that provides services related to payment. UPAI, described in detail in [8], makes it easy to have client applications (such as a merchant's online storefront or a user's browser) that include payment transactions without requiring the client itself to know the details of about a specific payment mechanisms.

6.1 Objective

A number of vendors have offered solutions for secure, digital payments over the Internet. First Virtual's system and e-cash from DigiCash are examples of early payment systems. These and others payment mechanisms all share a few basic conceptual states and transactions; yet they differ greatly in protocol content, format, and order of execution. UPAI steps in at this point, and provides conceptual unification of the different mechanisms as well as ways by which these concepts can be mapped into the native protocols.

A traditional application developer who want" to support both the First Virtual and the DigiCash payment mechanism would add the logics for both protocols to his or her application–as well as a mechanism to select the protocol to use for a particular transaction. As new payment systems gain users, such an application developer would have to add new sets of subroutines to legacy applications.

In contrast, UPAI permits existing applications to remain unchanged. New kinds of payment systems are supported by simply adding new proxies. The existing applications would be able to communicate with any new payment protocol since newly introduced objects would respect the pre-defined interface of the application as specified by UPAI.

6.2 Architecture

Figure 5 depicts key components of the UPAI service layer. The rectangle at the bottom of the figure represents the native payment mechanism protocol. Notice that the application code (both the browser on the customer's side and the storefront on the merchant's side) never makes direct calls on the native protocols. Instead, they always make the UPAI defined calls through intermediate objects. First, the *Payment Control Record*, represented by the central square labelled PCR, encapsulates all of the necessary information about one payment, such as the source and destination account (represented by `AccountHandles`), and the amount. `AccountHandles` are proxies that translate from UPAI calls such as `StartTransfer` to the corresponding native calls of the payment mechanism, perhaps generating an e-mail message of a particular format or invoking a UNIX command.

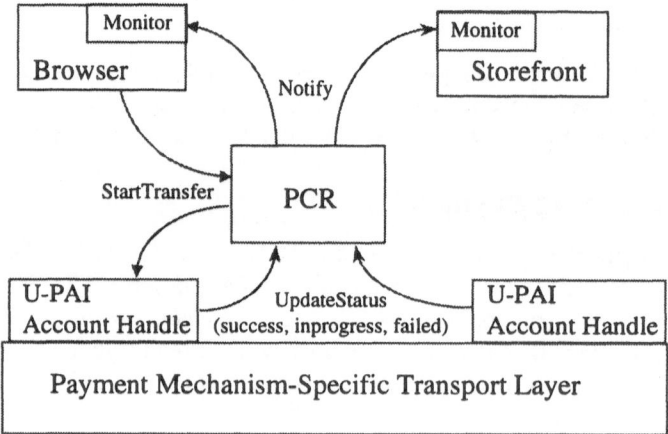

Fig. 5. The UPAI Service Layer: Components.

Just as calls from the application code to the payment mechanism code are mediated by UPAI proxies, so the return values generated by the native payment mechanism protocol are converted by proxies into appropriate UPAI responses. The status updates are composed of two pieces: a *major status* taking one of three values (`Complete`, `InProgress`, or `Failed`); and a *minor status* (which may be of any type). The `PaymentControlRecord` collects this status information, and rebroadcasts it to each of the *Monitor* objects. Monitor objects have basic interfaces defined by UPAI, but may be subclassed to add additional functionality. The monitor objects are integrated into the user or merchant's application. They register an interest in tracking the status of the transaction, and receive all updates. If a failure is reported, the user application may, for example, select a different payment mechanism and try again.

6.3 Discussion

UPAI has been designed to be efficient for simple cases and easy to use. For instance, a standard payment is a common operation, and may be done with a single call in the interface to StartTransfer. (Of course, the PCR must be first created with the requisite control information.) This simplicity is in contrast to the complexity of the native payment mechanisms, which often require multiple calls to the operating system for a single payment. Note that UPAI does not provide an *operational* efficiency gain–the proxies still make whatever calls are dictated by the native payment mechanism protocol. UPAI instead provides a gain in *implementation* efficiency; it simplifies the coding process for the application developers. The proxy itself could be developed by the payment system provider or a third party.

The UPAI protocol is by its nature adaptable to new payment mechanisms. As described above, the applications need not be aware of the particular details of any specific payment mechanism. They merely make calls to the UPAI proxies which are identical regardless of the underlying native system. Moreover, the limited set of feasible return values also disguises the underlying details of the native system. Therefore, a browser implemented for a (hypothetical) "CyberBucks" system knows that it should expect the goods that it has ordered if the StartTransfer invocation on the CyberBucks AccountHandle proxy results in a Complete status update. On the other hand, payment mechanism-specific information may also be conveyed in the "minor" status field, if the application's Monitor object was designed with awareness of CyberBucks. For instance, if the MajorStatus is Failure, and the MinorStatus reports that the public key server is temporarily unavailable, the Monitor object may reinitiate the transfer after an appropriate delay.

The UPAI protocol's scope is limited to only the operational aspects of payment. It does not, for example, provide any primitives related to the user interface for wallet management. If desired, a higher level protocol could be built on top of UPAI to interact with the user to set spending limits and provide expense reporting.

The UPAI protocol is also designed as an asynchronous protocol. Callbacks are used to convey return values, while the methods themselves return as soon as they are invoked. Although this introduces some additional complications in process management, it provides a number of benefits. If a payment system is unavailable (or if it is simply taking longer than expected), the user can recover quickly, returning to an application task, making a second payment, or aborting the initial payment and selecting a different mechanism.

6.4 Implementation Status

A prototype implementation of UPAI has been completed. UPAI is used as part of the Stanford Digital Library testbed to deal with the fulfillment processing for payment obligations that are part of digital contracts defined by the InfoBus FIRM rights management service layer. Proxies for the First Virtual and DigiCash protocols were developed for an earlier version of the UPAI protocol.

7 FIRM: Managing Rights, Obligations, and Contracts

The Stanford Framework for Interoperable Rights Management (FIRM) defines a rights management service layer on top of existing Internet protocols, supporting a host of usages including, but not limited to, digital contracting, privacy negotiations, and network security.

In this section, we give a basic survey; further detail can be found in [12]. We briefly highlight FIRM's object reifications and its transaction model, and the architecture that enables such a design.

7.1 FIRM's Object Reifications

In FIRM, "form designers" develop standard digital contract forms that are then made available as the "stationery" that anyone can easily take, customize, and instantiate into computational contract objects. These "smart contracts," also called "commpacts," articulate and enforce the terms and conditions of a given rights relationship (subscriptions, site licenses, etc.). Commpacts are first-class control objects that are managed independently of the objects they control (by "commpact manager" services), accommodating a wide variety of transaction scenarios. The following is a summary of the some of the major object reifications in FIRM.

Epers (also: e-person): An epers is a software agent that is the persistent digital representation of (a role of) a person with a structured request interface. When acting online, users are identified by a (possibly opaque) handle to their e-person, allowing any communication partners to get back this structured representation and negotiate access conditions in detail—only in some cases involving the user (e.g. when certain interactions are not covered by the default preferences that a user set up for his or her e-person). One person can have more than one epers. A Unix account can be seen as a current form of a limited version of an e-person.

Home Provider: A home provider is the service that provides an "online home" for persons in the form of an e-person. Current online services and ISPs can be home providers, although in principle people with a permanently connected machine can also run their own home provider.

Commpact (also: smart contract): A commpact is the computational object that is the digital representation of an agreement between two or more parties, be it a legal contract or a more light-weight "communication pact" (e.g. one related to privacy). Commpacts are "smart contracts" in that they have a structured (FIRM) interface, code that implements behavior, state (e.g. the validity status, the number of times a right was exercised, etc.), and a set of textual descriptions. In other words, commpacts represent a mixture of informal textual descriptions and implementation code (where the fact that both have the same semantics is the responsibility of the designer of the underlying commpact form). Commpacts are effectively a network-centric form of an authorization monitor. They authorize actions, enforce prerequisites ("student status required"), and provide a way to live up to obligations (e.g. initiate a payment transfer when fulfilling an obligation). The piece of text by which we generally know legal contracts is just the result of one of the many methods that can be called on commpact objects–but there are also others, including negotiation methods (e.g. 'terminate'), structural messages ('get me the set of promise objects'), and, last but not least, authorization interactions ('exercise this right').

Commpact Manager: A commpact manager is the service that keeps, manages, and interprets commpact objects that have been assigned to it. Commpact managers can be co-located with clients (e.g. for usage control, for the mobile case), servers (conventional access control), or trusted third parties (e.g. rights clearing houses); the protocol remains the same in each case. Every epers has a default commpact manager.

Commpact Form: A commpact form is the basic "template" of a commpact. Commpact forms are much like a standard rental agreements in that they have been carefully designed by someone once, but then they are readily available as "stationery" to everyone else; general users can just "take" such a form, customize it, fill in some parameters (such as the actual price offered, etc.), and then declare it an offer. Commpact forms are assumed to be designed by what we call a "commpact forms designer." They are made accessible through "commpact forms providers."

Commpact Forms Provider: A forms provider is the service that actually operates an online server that carries a collection of commpact forms—such that people can search or browse for the ones that they are interested in.

7.2 A Network-Centric Architecture for Managing Control Objects

FIRM is architecturally based on a "network-centric" design in which control information is encapsulated in first-class (relationship) objects ("commpacts") that can live in principle anywhere on the network and that stand in a $m{:}n$-relation with the objects and services that they control. Cryptographic means are then used to determine which control objects are eligible to control which other objects, and, vice versa, which objects may be controlled by which control objects. Note that the fact that control and controlled objects are independently managed does of course not exclude the possibility that in some cases commpact managers and content servers are realized in the same address space on one and the same machine (reflecting a traditional access control model).

In other words, rather than attaching control information to controlled information, we have first-class control objects that *designate* the objects that they control (using a constraint). In this way, we keep independent two dimensions that are orthogonal: the question of which controls apply and the question of which objects control is applied to. Note that, among other things, this gives us the flexibility of being able to independently deliver and modify objects of each of the types (e.g. providing a pay-per-view contract in addition to a subscription contract for one and the same online article; making available a new article under a previous subscription contract, etc.).

7.3 FIRM's Transaction Model

FIRM closely follows contract law principles in defining the structure and behavior of its objects. A FIRM interface specification is available in CORBA's Interface Definition Language (although nothing in FIRM intrinsically relies on the availability of a CORBA distributed object infrastructure).

The FIRM transaction protocol has been designed to have the following characteristics:

- *Simple cases are simple in the FIRM protocol.* In particular, a typical specialization of a simple case turns out to be essentially the same as standard HTTP authorization. In fact, due to the flexibility of the architecture, FIRM is likely to be faster than this in many cases.

- *Complex cases are uniformly possible.* The main point is then that the FIRM protocol uniformly extends to cases that are not possible in existing protocols (e.g. negotiating new relationships). It accommodates sophisticated negotiation and control behavior, although the number of message exchanges will of course scale with the complexity of what is trying to be accomplished.

7.4 Implementation Status

FIRM has been prototyped in a system called "RManage." RManage augments services such as Web servers with plug-ins that allow these services to make use of the FIRM infrastructure. RManage also provides implementations of the e-person and commpact objects that FIRM assumes. Furthermore, RManage can be used either with a plain Web browser or integrated into DLITE [5], an interface viewer developed as part of the Stanford Digital Libraries project.

RManage enables services to make available information governed by (FIRM-compatible) digital contracts. The sample contracts currently used include various forms of subscriptions, site licenses, and pay-per-view contracts, each with different forms of search rights, approval rights, notification obligations, and payment obligations. These digital contracts are "smart contracts" in that they integrate behavior related to what the contract is about (authorization, payment, privacy protection, etc.). For example, RManage provides fulfillment processing for a whole range of payment obligations by making use of the UPAI payment application interface (see the previous section), also prototyped as part of the Stanford project, that provides an abstraction layer to integrate native payment protocols from a variety of providers such as First Virtual, DigiCash, VISA, etc.

FIRM provides the necessary "glue" for managing rights and obligations. FIRM's language is at the rights level only, that is, it does not talk about issues such as fulfillment processing. For example, if we have an online purchase transaction, then FIRM would posit a payment obligation with attributes describing the amount to be paid, the terms and conditions in case of non-payment, etc., and with methods that allow relevant participants to declare this obligation to be fulfilled, etc. But the actual (domain-specific) way in which such a payment obligation will be fulfilled is not part of the FIRM specification; it is an issue of the specific fulfillment implementation.

8 Conclusion

We have outlined the architecture of the Stanford InfoBus and its five service layers for managing items and collections (DLIOP), metadata (SMA), search (STARTS), payment (UPAI), and rights management (FIRM). The Stanford "Infobus" extends the current Internet protocols with a suite of higher-level information management protocols that define the technical concepts for a sophisticated future information infrastructure.

Acknowledgments

Scott Hassan developed significant parts of the underlying testbed infrastructure of the project, whose principal investigators are Hector Garcia-Molina, Terry Winograd, and Daphne Koller. Other contributors include Marko Balabanovic, Steve Cousins, Arturo Crespo, Rebecca Wesley, Frankie James, Larry Page, Vicky Reich, Mehran Sahami, Tom Schirmer, Narayanan Shivakumar, and Alan Steremberg.

9 References

1. Paepcke, A., S. Cousins, H. Garcia-Molina, S. Ketchpel, M. Röscheisen, and T. Winograd (1996). Towards Interoperability in Digital Libraries. *IEEE Computer,* 29 (5).
2. Baldonado, M. (1997). SenseMaker: An Information-Exploration Interface Supporting the Contextual Evolution of a User's Interest. *Computer-Human Interaction Conference CHI'97,* Atlanta.
3. Baldonado, M., K. Chang, L. Gravano, and A. Paepcke (1997). The Stanford Digital Library Metadata Architecture. *International Journal of Digital Libraries,* 1(2).
4. Chang, C.-C., K., H. Garcia-Molina, and Andreas Paepcke (1996). Boolean Query Mapping Across Heterogeneous Information Sources. *IEEE Transactions on Knowledge and Data Engineering,* 8(4):515-521, August.
5. Cousins, S., A. Paepcke, T. Winograd, E.A. Bier, and K. Pier (1997). The Digital Library Integrated Task Environment (DLITE). *Proceedings of DL'97.*
6. Gravano, L., K. Chen-Chuan Chang, H. Garcia-Molina, and A. Paepcke (1996). STARTS: Stanford Protocol Proposal for Internet Retrieval and Search. Accessible at http://www-db.stanford.edu/~gravano/starts.html
7. Gravano, L., K. Chen-Chuan Chang, H. Garcia-Molina, and A. Paepcke (1997). STARTS: Stanford Proposal for Internet Meta-Searching. *Proceedings of SIGMOD'97.*
8. Ketchpel, S., *et al.* (1996). U-PAI: The Stanford Universal Payment Application Interface, Stanford Digital Libraries Project. In *USENIX 96--Electronic Commerce.*
9. Paepcke, A. (1996). InterBib. Cf. http://www-db.stanford.edu/~testbed/.
10. Balabanovic, M. and Y. Shoham (1997). Combining Content-Based and Collaborative Recommendation. *Communications of the ACM,* 40(3), March.
11. Shivakumar, N., and Hector Garcia-Molina (1995). SCAM: A Copy Detection Mechanism for Digital Documents. *Proceedings of DL'95.*
12. Röscheisen, M. (1997). *A Network-Centric Design for Relationship-based Rights Management.* Ph.D. Dissertation, Computer Science Department, Stanford University.

Objectives, Results and Conclusions of the European DECOMATE Project: Delivery of Copyright Material to End Users

Joost Dijkstra

Tilburg University, POBOX 90153, 5000 LE Tilburg, The Netherlands

Abstract: This short article describes the objectives, overall results and main observations and conclusions of the Decomate project that was carried out between March 1995 and February 1997 by coordinator Tilburg University (the Netherlands), Universitat Autonoma de Barcelona (Spain) and the London School of Economics (United Kingdom) in the framework of the Telematics for Libraries programme under execution of DGXIII of the European Commission in Luxembourg.

1. Project objectives

The goal of Decomate is to provide end-users access - through the library - to copyright materials distributed by commercial publishers in electronic form. In order to achieve this general goal the following subgoals have been set.
- The project should integrate a number of existing technologies and ongoing developments in order to create a new and modern type of library service.
- It should provide a demonstrator of electronic distribution of published documents, involving publishers, libraries and end-users.
- The technical approach should be based on open, generic solutions which are as independent as possible from the specific technical environment of the Decomate partners to ensure a maximum level of transferability to other libraries in the European Community; to demonstrate this aspect the generic system will be implemented in the technical environment of each partner.
- Attention should be paid to the copyright issue, which should be also a contribution to mutual understanding and future cooperation between libraries and publishers.
- The Decomate software will be based on a pilot system already under development; it should be expanded and generalised, resulting in a generic system which can handle various types of documents and document formats, and which can be implemented in a variety of technical infrastructures.
- The system will be the subject of intensive user studies in order to study the usefulness and effects of electronic document distribution, especially of mainstream, copyright materials.

With these goals in mind, the specific objectives of the project were:

(1) To create and demonstrate solutions for distribution of scientific publications in electronic form to end-users. These solutions are to be based on, bilateral, licensing agreements between publishers and libraries, and on a generic software application which provides the necessary functionality for coping with a variety of document types, formats and technical infrastructures.
(2) To develop a generic, transferable system for electronic document distribution. The system will include an end-user application which will allow access to bibliographic and document databases. This application will link bibliographic records to electronic documents and provide document browsing, viewing and delivery functions. The system is also to include a monitor function for user authorization, usage registration, management information and reporting.
(3) To develop the system as a set of generic modules, providing the functionality in a way which is as independent as possible of specific document formats, bibliographic databases, document servers and system environments.
(4) To demonstrate the transferability of the software solution by implementing the Decomate system within the technical infrastructure of the participating libraries.
(5) To set up a document distribution service to end-users in the participating libraries in order to study the usefulness and effects of electronic distribution of mainstream, copyright materials.
(6) To disseminate the results of the project as widely as possible, finishing with an international conference on the Decomate project.

2. Overall project results

The project succeeded in its main goal to set up an electronic document delivery system to provide end-users access through the library to copyright electronic material delivered by commercial publishers in electronic form. The generic software of the Decomate system has been implemented and integrated at the three sites and local customization has been pursued at all sites. The system is running as an experimental system since October 1996 at all sites as a testbed for the user studies.

The main characteristic of the system, -and only variation to the original plan- , is the WWW application through which end-users have access to both the bibliographical database and the full text documents. The project succeeded in implementing a system that uses both the standard Z39.50 protocol to access the bibliographical databases as well as the de-facto standard http protocol to retrieve electronic documents in a WWW environment. Both worlds come together in the Decomate server of the system.

In theory (and in practice as a demonstrator) the system allows the storage and display of multiple document formats as long as an external viewer application is available that allows the system to display the particular document format. The external viewer will be launched by the Decomate software as soon as a request for a document is encountered that requires a particular viewer. In practice, all project partners have decided to use only documents in PDF format; PDF being the current state-of-the-art in this field. The main publishers either already supply us or will be supplying us PDF documents in the near future. Last, but certainly not least, the decision to use only PDF documents implies that the end-user will be faced with just one external application rather than with a distinct viewer for each document format.

The project succeeded in its goal to implement and integrate a system that is as open as possible, as generic as possible and as independent as possible from a particular technical environment. This is demonstrated by the fact that the same generic software, that was developed independent from the detailed technical knowledge of external systems and devices and adhering to the aforementioned standards, has been successfully implemented in three distinct technical environments. Examples of these differences between partners are to be found in the different bibliographic search engines that are used at the three sites (Trip at TU; Zebra at UAB and BRS/Search at LSE), the diversity of platforms and the different reporting tools (MS-Excel at LSE and UAB, MS-Access at TU) as well as the difference in the underlying rDBMS (Oracle at LSE, Ingres at both TU and UAB) of the reporting system. The latter was accomplished by the use of uniform standard SQL and reporting tools that use standard ODBC facilities to fetch data in a client-server environment. Even here a diversity in the implementation of the reporting software was due. The LSE was implementing the tool at a PC platform whereas TU and UAB both had accomplished the same on a DEC/Alpha platform while only the client software was running at a PC platform.

The project partners have established a main breakthrough in the relationship between libraries and publishers. The project succeeded in making a number of licence agreements with publishers in order to receive copyright material. Agreements have been reached with Elsevier Science and Kluwer Academic Publishers (both The Netherlands) and Academic Press (UK). Most licence agreements were of a bilateral type. It seemed that this was the only way publishers wanted to deal with libraries during the course of the project. One exception was made for the United Kingdom in which LSE, part of a consortium of libraries, enrolled into a consortium agreement with a consortium of British publishers, both established at national level. UAB also succeeded in interesting their own publishing house to deliver material to the Decomate project.

Although the partners only could engage into licence agreements with the main publishers, they also succeeded in setting up talks with other, smaller, publishers. Unfortunately these smaller publishers are not yet in a position to deliver electronic material, either caused by technical or by more strategic issues.

The user studies have revealed interesting data, but the project generally had to accept its short duration as its main drawback. Nonetheless, although the amount of data collected is limited, the idea that the end-user population consists of a variety of types, - early adopters, novices, experts and those who actually do not use electronic services at all-, gives the libraries more input to elaborate more specific promotional campaigns for those groups who are most eligible for these purposes.

Furthermore, the ease of generating management reports on the use of the system is a main step forward. Reports can be made almost on the fly and reflects a most up to date status. Nonetheless, a drawback is found in the fact that no distinction can be made between the viewing and the printing of documents in a WWW environment, which obviously show what a user is doing after downloading the electronic material.

The project furthermore succeeded in disseminating its results to the library society in Europe and even beyond. Already from the beginning of the project, emails from literally all over the world were received with requests for more information on the Decomate project. Furthermore, various occasions have been used to inform the audience about the Decomate project, through presentations in the field and through journal papers published in international journals. An international conference at the end of the project was announced through the important distribution channels (journals including electronic journals, newsgroups, homepages and personal mailings and emails) and resulted in a massive interest from European fellow professionals, but even from people from the USA.

3 Main observations and conclusions

Technical project work

The main deviation from the original plan, - system development in a WWW environment instead of improving and enhancing a dedicated MS windows oriented software package -, has proven to be a justified decision from both a systems and end-user point of view. End users seem to embrace the WWW interface to the catalogue as a major improvement compared to the more traditional ways of access. From a systems point of view, less or at least the same problems were encountered as were expected in a non WWW environment; problems that are closely related to the factors that in normal cases determine user acceptance and assesses the quality of the system: user interface issues, performance (including viewing and printing), reliability/ robustness and content.

The Decomate system itself can be characterised as a system that is a compromise between dream and reality. Compromises had to be made in order not to over challenge the objectives and to capture all aspects in a generic way. An example can be found at the input side of the system : the storage procedure of bibliographic data in a scenario with three different database systems as back ends, all of them customized to the local situation and policies, was found an impregnable barrier to make the system even more generic. On the other side, the Decomate system successfully communicates with the three different search engines to search the databases while the monitoring and reporting package of the Decomate system successfully communicates with every reporting tool that supports ODBC facilities, nowadays supported by almost every vendor of this type of reporting software. Obviously, the importance of good documentation in these highly complex system developments is obvious.

The Common Database Layer (CDL), a layer between Decomate server and search engine, was found an excellent solution to circumvent the main interfacing problems at a detailed level between a specific search engine backend and the decomate server as well as a way to deal with a variety of search engines that would not support Z39.50. This CDL consists of a set of common functions that are considered to be standard and supported by all main search engines. However, although this solution is working from a generic point of view, it still does mean that also interfaces can be made between Z39.50 origins (search engines) and Z39.50 target (decomate server) and therefore augmenting the generic character even more. UAB has successfully implemented their Z39.50 origin (ZEBRA) with the Z39.50 target of the Decomate server, and therefore circumventing the CDL. Obviously the advantage of using the CDL is that substitutions of search engines would take less effort by interfacing to the CDL rather than to make the detailed Z39.50 interfacing work.

The Decomate system manages to handle multiple document formats but from a users point of view multiple document formats introduce an undesirable side effect. During the project TIFF images were delivered by one publisher while another publisher was delivering (second year of the project) some 'true PDF' documents. The starting point in the beginning of the project was to take only those document format into consideration for which external viewers exist on the (commercial) market, but soon it was discovered that this is not an ideal situation for the end user. They would have been exposed to a diversity of viewer interfaces, unfortunately different for every document format. Other user surveys had revealed this aspect as one of the main drawbacks when users start using new software in which they got a feeling of „once again another new thing to learn", not in favour of the acceptance of „once again another new" system. With the eye on the world around us, in particular the developments that were taking place in the publisher scene, it was decided to use only one document format. Experiments with inline GIF formats (converting TIFF to GIF format) were unsuccessful due to bad readability on the screen and the problem of page oriented printing rather than full article printing. The solution was found in wrapping the TIFF images received from only one publisher into PDF. This solution indeed cuts both ways : the end user will only receive one type of document format, system maintenance is easier due to the lack of multiple document formats in the system and PDF is considered to become the leading document format. Fortunately, even when PDF will be overtaken by a new leading format in the future, the past proves that converters dealing with old formats will become available.

A good technical infrastructure is an important aspect and contributes to the acceptance of the system by the end users. Although no particular restrictions were set to any kind of equipment or network, - besides the obvious preferences of as „higher, faster and stronger" as possible - it became clear that at least from a printing point of view, high speed printers are necessary in order to serve the naturally borne impatience of end-users. And as a matter of fact, the same seems to be valid for performance issues. Waiting for a document to be displayed at the PC or workstation by more than 20 seconds, as an example, is almost unacceptable. Although from a project point of view, the Decomate system runs in virtually any technical environment, this should not be taken too literally. On the other hand it should be considered as a relief to know that the elements that form the infrastructure (equipment, network -ISDN as an example-) seem to improve over time.

Security of the material seems to be a main topic in the minds of the people but is properly taken by end users and adequately solved from a system's point of view. Implementing a system that handles copyright material needs protection. Classical ways of controlling access - personalized login based on existing principles of username/password schemes - are sufficient at the level of end user access, however something more need to be done from a system's point of view. Using PGP (pretty good privacy) and MD5 security (encryption techniques) software assist this protection as well as ordinary time-out mechanisms. Straight access to and retrieval of documents from a document server is rejected because of the lack of key information that is only provided by the decomate server. However this key information is generated upon request directed to the decomate server, that checks authorization at the front door.

User studies and reporting

The project did lack sufficient validation and demonstration time to allow users to customize, play around with the system and to provide relevant feedback at a deeper level on both the usage of the system and the perception of the system. With an up and running system in October 96, - even according to the project planning -, a certain time for customization by the end user towards the system was observed, yielding so called playing sessions based on curiosity rather than real useful information that would give genuine input to the interpretation of the perception of the system by the user.

Marketing your product was perceived essential to stimulate use. It seems no longer be the case that end users use a system that has been made available to them without a profound promotional campaign. In the present world end users can surf as easy to their neighbour library that may reside literally all over the world. Geographical borders are no longer in place which means that a library really needs to have contact with their customers in order to survive in the long term.

The project's monitoring approach demonstrated that local differences in standard software packages (spreadsheets) are of no importance in order to generate easy, fast and extensive reports, which are customized to the own wishes of the manager as long as standard communication facilities between client and server (like ODBC) are used. The biggest improvement is that the local software is used, with which much experience is expected to exist in the institute. The project team managers discovered that generating reports was more delayed by its customization rather than complex querying the database.

Publishers, relationship with publishers & licensing

The main learning curve during the course of the project was not imposed by technical aspects but by a main management aspect. To two of the three partners the negotiations stage with publishers was completely new in a time in which all parties seemed to search for their most optimal solution. This learning curve also had to include two different tracks simultaneously : that of the library and its 'opponent'. Mutual understanding and making compromises, sometimes against nature but in the spirit of the project, were „everyday's" practice. Nonetheless after these two years, an equilibrium seems to have established although it remains to be seen for how long given the fact that the aim to progress in the project influenced economic and political decision making on this topic during the course of the project. From the other side, all parties are presently (Feb 97) in the stage of renewing their original contracts with the publishers, which can be a sign of having reached a more stable equilibrium.

The main publishers seem to have prepared themselves better to the digital era than the smaller ones. This explains the observation that not too many more publishers could have been interested in delivering copyright material. The Decomate project was carried out in which can be said a transition time of all keyplayers in the field - both end users, facing new technologies at their own doorstep, libraries and publishers-, but not all of them respond as we would have thought they would do. End-users sometimes surprisingly shout for new developments and wonder why it is taking so long for publishers to produce real electronic material rather than deliver scanned material based on paper material while publishers can not answer them properly as they are faced with a main conversion process : not only from a technical point of view but also from a management point of view. New procedures need to be developed and new working methods adopted. Let alone the smaller publishers, who presently seem to be in the process of strategic decision making what to do in this digital era. Nonetheless, the project partners succeeded in establishing a relationship between libraries and publishers and can be considered as a main breakthrough.

Decomate's information dissemination

Information dissemination in this time of massive information distribution can be considered analogous to the main problem of most of the plants in their world : not enough daylight and not being attractive is equal to dying an early death or being forgotten. Nonetheless, only this is not a guarantee to survive because the content remains of vital importance too. Using regularly the main electronic channels - web sites, newsgroups, electronic journals- , added with efforts to get pointers at Web pages of related projects in the field as well as pages with project overviews, contributions to conferences, - submitted articles or invited talks -, and contributions to international journals in the field seem to serve sufficiently the international community. The Web is surely a perfect medium for an easy disseminating process, but can not be relied upon on itself. In a jungle in which URL's pass by in hundreds a day, one should behave like plants : the more colourful and the more it contains content, the more it attracts insects. Fortunately, Decomate has more than survived in this digital world, and is proud to have attracted attention from literally all over the world, finishing with its own dedicated conference with almost 100 delegates from all across Europe and even from the USA.

And finally, after the successful Decomate I project a new and follow up project is to start in 1998 with main topics in knowledge navigation (information brokerage), access to heterogeneous databases and to create a personalised library for every end-user, among others by providing them customized SDI's services.

4 Suggestions for further reading

Joost Dijkstra - Delivery of copyright material to end-users: new unit to the electronic document delivery chain, IN: Proceedings of the International Conference on Library Automation in Central and Eastern Europe. Budapest, Apr 1996.

Joost Dijkstra - From Online ordering to document viewing: electronic document delivery systems classified, IN: Information Europe, EBLIDA, June 1996.

Joost Dijkstra - A generic approach to the electronic access of scientific journals: the DECOMATE project, IN: Library Acquisitions: Theory and Practice, Vol 21, No3, Fall 1997, 393-402.

Hans Geleijnse - The Digital Library, ALearned Publishing, Vol. 9, No.4, Oct1996, pp 225-233.

Hans Geleijnse - Developing an Electronic Library: Strategic and management issues, IN: Proceedings of the 3rd International ELVIRA conference, Aslib. Lecture at 3rd International ELVIRA Conference. Milton Keynes, UK, May 1996.

Clare Jenkins -User studies: electronic journals and user response to new modes of information delivery, IN :Library Acquisitions: Theory and Practice, vol 21, no 3, Fall 1997, pp 355-364

Caroline Lloyd - Evaluating use of the Decomate system, IN: Proceedings of the 4th International ELVIRA Conference, Milton Keynes, UK, May 1997.

Thomas Place and Joost Dijkstra - Z39.50 vs WWW: Which way to go, IN: Proceedings of the 2nd International ELVIRA Conference, Milton Keynes, UK, May 1995, pp 40-53.

Author Index

Springer
and the
environment

At Springer we firmly believe that an international science publisher has a special obligation to the environment, and our corporate policies consistently reflect this conviction.

We also expect our business partners – paper mills, printers, packaging manufacturers, etc. – to commit themselves to using materials and production processes that do not harm the environment. The paper in this book is made from low- or no-chlorine pulp and is acid free, in conformance with international standards for paper permanency.

Lecture Notes in Computer Science

For information about Vols. 1–1332

please contact your bookseller or Springer-Verlag

Vol. 1368: Y. Masunaga, T. Katayama, M. Tsukamoto (Eds.), Worldwide Computing and Its Applications — WWCA'98. Proceedings, 1998. XIV, 473 pages. 1998.

Vol. 1370: N.A. Streitz, S. Konomi, H.-J. Burkhardt (Eds.), Cooperative Buildings. Proceedings, 1998. XI, 267 pages. 1998.

Vol. 1371: I. Wachsmuth, M. Fröhlich (Eds.), Gesture and Sign Language in Human-Computer Interaction. Proceedings, 1997. XI, 309 pages. 1998. (Subseries LNAI).

Vol. 1372: S. Vaudenay (Ed.), Fast Software Encryption. Proceedings, 1998. VIII, 297 pages. 1998.

Vol. 1373: M. Morvan, C. Meinel, D. Krob (Eds.), STACS 98. Proceedings, 1998. XV, 630 pages. 1998.

Vol. 1374: H. Bunt, R.-J. Beun, T. Borghuis (Eds.), Multimodal Human-Computer Communication. VIII, 345 pages. 1998. (Subseries LNAI).

Vol. 1375: R. D. Hersch, J. André, H. Brown (Eds.), Electronic Publishing, Artistic Imaging, and Digital Typography. Proceedings, 1998. XIII, 575 pages. 1998.

Vol. 1376: F. Parisi Presicce (Ed.), Recent Trends in Algebraic Development Techniques. Proceedings, 1997. VIII, 435 pages. 1998.

Vol. 1377: H.-J. Schek, F. Saltor, I. Ramos, G. Alonso (Eds.), Advances in Database Technology – EDBT'98. Proceedings, 1998. XII, 515 pages. 1998.

Vol. 1378: M. Nivat (Ed.), Foundations of Software Science and Computation Structures. Proceedings, 1998. X, 289 pages. 1998.

Vol. 1379: T. Nipkow (Ed.), Rewriting Techniques and Applications. Proceedings, 1998. X, 343 pages. 1998.

Vol. 1380: C.L. Lucchesi, A.V. Moura (Eds.), LATIN'98: Theoretical Informatics. Proceedings, 1998. XI, 391 pages. 1998.

Vol. 1381: C. Hankin (Ed.), Programming Languages and Systems. Proceedings, 1998. X, 283 pages. 1998.

Vol. 1382: E. Astesiano (Ed.), Fundamental Approaches to Software Engineering. Proceedings, 1998. XII, 331 pages. 1998.

Vol. 1383: K. Koskimies (Ed.), Compiler Construction. Proceedings, 1998. X, 309 pages. 1998.

Vol. 1384: B. Steffen (Ed.), Tools and Algorithms for the Construction and Analysis of Systems. Proceedings, 1998. XIII, 457 pages. 1998.

Vol. 1385: T. Margaria, B. Steffen, R. Rückert, J. Posegga (Eds.), Services and Visualization. Proceedings, 1997/1998. XII, 323 pages. 1998.

Vol. 1386: T.A. Henzinger, S. Sastry (Eds.), Hybrid Systems: Computation and Control. Proceedings, 1998. VIII, 417 pages. 1998.

Vol. 1387: C. Lee Giles, M. Gori (Eds.), Adaptive Processing of Sequences and Data Structures. Proceedings, 1997. XII, 434 pages. 1998. (Subseries LNAI).

Vol. 1388: J. Rolim (Ed.), Parallel and Distributed Processing. Proceedings, 1998. XVII, 1168 pages. 1998.

Vol. 1389: K. Tombre, A.K. Chhabra (Eds.), Graphics Recognition. Proceedings, 1997. XII, 421 pages. 1998.

Vol. 1390: C. Scheideler, Universal Routing Strategies for Interconnection Networks. XVII, 234 pages. 1998.

Vol. 1391: W. Banzhaf, R. Poli, M. Schoenauer, T.C. Fogarty (Eds.), Genetic Programming. Proceedings, 1998. X, 232 pages. 1998.

Vol. 1392: A. Barth, M. Breu, A. Endres, A. de Kemp (Eds.), Digital Libraries in Computer Science: The MeDoc Approach. VIII, 239 pages. 1998.

Vol. 1393: D. Bert (Ed.), B'98: Recent Advances in the Development and Use of the B Method. Proceedings, 1998. VIII, 313 pages. 1998.

Vol. 1394: X. Wu. R. Kotagiri, K.B. Korb (Eds.), Research and Development in Knowledge Discovery and Data Mining. Proceedings, 1998. XVI, 424 pages. 1998. (Subseries LNAI).

Vol. 1395: H. Kitano (Ed.), RoboCup-97: Robot Soccer World Cup I. XIV, 520 pages. 1998. (Subseries LNAI).

Vol. 1396: E. Okamoto, G. Davida, M. Mambo (Eds.), Information Security. Proceedings, 1997. XII, 357 pages. 1998.

Vol. 1397: H. de Swart (Ed.), Automated Reasoning with Analytic Tableaux and Related Methods. Proceedings, 1998. X, 325 pages. 1998. (Subseries LNAI).

Vol. 1398: C. Nédellec, C. Rouveirol (Eds.), Machine Learning: ECML-98. Proceedings, 1998. XII, 420 pages. 1998. (Subseries LNAI).

Vol. 1399: O. Etzion, S. Jajodia, S. Sripada (Eds.), Temporal Databases: Research and Practice. X, 429 pages. 1998.

Vol. 1400: M. Lenz, B. Bartsch-Spörl, H.-D. Burkhard, S. Wess (Eds.), Case-Based Reasoning Technology. XVIII, 405 pages. 1998. (Subseries LNAI).

Vol. 1401: P. Sloot, M. Bubak, B. Hertzberger (Eds.), High-Performance Computing and Networking. Proceedings, 1998. XX, 1309 pages. 1998.

Vol. 1402: W. Lamersdorf, M. Merz (Eds.), Trends in Distributed Systems for Electronic Commerce. Proceedings, 1998. XII, 255 pages. 1998.

Vol. 1403: K. Nyberg (Ed.), Advances in Cryptology – EUROCRYPT '98. Proceedings, 1998. X, 607 pages. 1998.

Vol. 1409: T. Schaub, The Automation of Reasoning with Incomplete Information. XI, 159 pages. 1998. (Subseries LNAI).

Vol. 1411: L. Asplund (Ed.), Reliable Software Technologies – Ada-Europe. Proceedings, 1998. XI, 297 pages. 1998.

Vol. 1413: B. Pernici, C. Thanos (Eds.), Advanced Information Systems Engineering. Proceedings, 1998. X, 423 pages. 1998.

Vol. 1414: M. Nielsen, W. Thomas (Eds.), Computer Science Logic. Proceedings, 1997. VIII, 511 pages. 1998.

Vol. 1415: A.P. del Pobil, J. Mira, M.Ali (Eds.), Industrial and Engineering Applications of Artificial Intelligence and Expert Systems. Vol. I. Proceedings, 1998. XXIV, 887 pages. 1998. (Subseries LNAI).

Vol. 1416: A.P. del Pobil, J. Mira, M.Ali (Eds.), Industrial and Engineering Applications of Artificial Intelligence and Expert Systems. Vol.I I. Proceedings, 1998. XXIII, 943 pages. 1998. (Subseries LNAI).

Vol. 1418: R. Mercer, E. Neufeldt (Eds.), Advances in Artificial Intelligence. Proceedings, 1998. XII, 467 pages. 1998. (Subseries LNAI).